MERGERS AND ACQUISITIONS

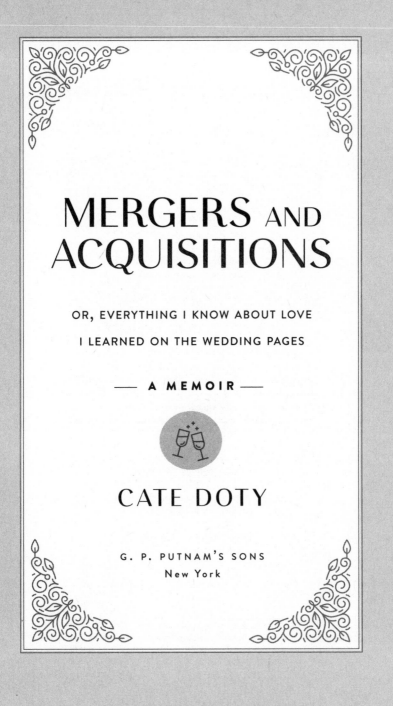

MERGERS AND ACQUISITIONS

OR, EVERYTHING I KNOW ABOUT LOVE

I LEARNED ON THE WEDDING PAGES

—— A MEMOIR ——

CATE DOTY

G. P. PUTNAM'S SONS
New York

PUTNAM
— EST. 1838 —

G. P. Putnam's Sons

Publishers Since 1838

An imprint of Penguin Random House LLC

penguinrandomhouse.com

Hardcover ISBN: 9780593190449
Ebook ISBN: 9780593190456

Printed in the United States of America
1st Printing

BOOK DESIGN BY KATY RIEGEL

For Flynn

Once you commit yourself, everything changes and the rest of your life seems to you like a dark forest on the property you have recently acquired. It is yours, but still you are afraid to enter it, wondering what you might find: a little chapel, a stand of birches, wolves, snakes, the worst you could imagine, or the best.

—LAURIE COLWIN, *THE LONE PILGRIM*

Author's Note

THIS BOOK REFLECTS real events and conversations I had with brides and grooms whose announcements and stories appeared in the *New York Times*. Names and identifying details have been changed to maintain their privacy, although you might be able to guess who a few of them are. Googling won't help you, though. I've also changed the names and some identifying details of my friends and families and those I worked with at the *Times*, although I wouldn't be surprised if a few recognized themselves. If they do, they should know: every word I wrote about my life at the *Times* was written in love and good faith.

MERGERS AND ACQUISITIONS

CHAPTER 1

Wishing and Hoping

THE MANILA FOLDER was slapped down on my desk with a flick of a large, hairy wrist, snapping me out of my daydream. My editor, Ira, stared down at me from above his mustache, standing with crossed arms as I scanned what he'd thrown down. I felt like Deep Throat was waiting for me in a parking deck somewhere.

"Think you can handle him?" he said, raising his eyebrows and looking down at the folder. "He's a pretty-well-known asshole. Not just your average politician jerk."

I was twenty-four, writing for the *New York Times*, and convinced of my invincibility. "Of course I can," I said, and snorted. "He's just a person."

"Yeah, but he doesn't believe that," Ira said. "You let me know if you need backup."

That was Monday. Then came Wednesday.

I was about two minutes into the call with the Pretty-Well-Known Asshole when he interrupted me, confirming his reputation. "How dare you ask me that?" he snapped. "My relationship with my future wife is none of your business."

"I'm sorry, sir," I said, as gently as I could, "but we ask these questions of everyone, even well-known people like yourself who need no introduction. It's part of the *Times*'s fact-checking process." I could have added, but I didn't, that he was making his relationship part of my business. This was a man who, after all, had called a press conference to trumpet his love for his last girlfriend, whom he also said he'd planned to marry, but she ended it before he had the chance.

Suzanne, his publicist, sighed. She was listening in on the conference line, of course—likely to protect me as much as the apoplectic man on the phone. The retired senior senator from the great state of New York was marrying a woman three decades his junior, a news item that had already been detailed breathlessly by the city's gossip columnists. His bride-to-be was a political operative and had spent a few years at City Hall, so she knew from assholes. I think that must have been her type. She and the senator had met at a Republican fund-raiser and soon afterward started showing up arm in arm at establishment restaurants, at more fund-raisers, and on Donald Trump's private plane. He even attended her intramural soccer matches out on Long Island and started calling himself a soccer dad, although there's no way he remembered his turn to bring snacks for the team. This went on for a couple of years and all seemed blissful—or if not blissful, then adequate enough to establish them as the city's newest political power couple. He finally asked her to marry him at her thirty-seventh birthday party, slapping a four-carat diamond ring on top of her cake, thereby making a celebration of her all about him. The affair was set for the first weekend in May. They booked a Catholic church on Long Island, registered at Tiffany's, and, presumably, wrote up one hell of a prenup. After the nuptials, Ms. Smooth Operative was to be known as Mrs. Senator.

"I don't have to answer these fucking questions from you or anyone fucking else," the senator railed down the line. "You should already know these things about me. Fuck you."

I heard the click of someone exiting the conference call.

His flack sighed again. "Cate," she said wearily, "could we answer your questions via email?"

I felt badly for this poor woman, who probably made three times what I did, but there was no way it could have been worth it. Spending seven days a week working the phones, protecting a craven, attention-hungry man from his nastiest impulses, drafting nonapology after nonapology, and fielding calls from reporters when he succumbed to them—and that was for political matters. But this, only his second time down the aisle, seemed to be as big of a brouhaha as any infrastructure bill he'd ever brought to the Senate floor.

"That's totally fine, Suzanne," I said. "Sorry about that."

"Don't apologize," she said. "This was her idea. It's such a mess."

We exchanged niceties and hung up, and I noted silently that she'd done the correct thing: protected her client and thrown someone else—even though that someone was her client's betrothed—under the bus. I turned to Ira, who'd been listening in across the desks. "How'd that go?" he said, grinning.

"Well, I think you heard the sum total," I said, and we both started to laugh. Ira shook his head. "I told you, he's a jerk. I can deal with it if you want."

"No, no. I want to do this. It's a test, right?"

Ira laughed again. "Well, you let me know."

I swiveled my rickety rolling chair back to my desk and looked again at the submission Ira had given me, which he'd marked through with his signature red ink, noting the alleged facts that needed checking. It wasn't like I'd never been hung up on before by powerful people. I'd worked in Washington during the Bush years, after all, when getting yelled at and hung up on was as routine as ordering Thai for dinner. But I'd never had a receiver slammed down over a matter as seemingly trivial as this: a wedding announcement, a public trumpeting of a couple's love and commitment. It wasn't a policy proposal. It was society news.

I stared at the dirty taupe wall for a minute. *I went to journalism school for this?*

And then I laughed. You *bet* I went to journalism school for this.

WHAT'S IN A wedding announcement? After all, weddings will (and do) happen without one. In fact, most American nuptials, successful or not, go unnoticed by news organizations and unannounced, except on social media and the occasional church bulletin. But the weddings we wrote about for the *Times*—they were different. They were, generally speaking, wildly expensive—far beyond the average American expenditure of $44,000. But they were more than the sum of their gilded parts. They were mergers of families and bank accounts, of aspirations and hubris. And these announcements were battle plans, and business plans, of class and warfare. They were incredibly difficult to obtain, which meant that they were worth far more than the soy ink they were made of. They were expected by a certain set. And they were, above all, *exclusive*. If your wedding announcement was in the paper of record, then your marriage counted—and, by proxy, so did you.

But I didn't know any of that when I pushed my way through the revolving doors at 229 West 43rd Street. Now, mind you, I *thought* I knew a lot, even though I didn't know much of anything. What I knew for certain was this: I was in the city I'd longed for since childhood, sleeping with an insanely hot guy who had both tormented and thrilled me for years, wearing the smallest jeans size I'd owned since middle school, and coming to work five days a week at the *New York Times*. I was relatively flush with cash and eating something interesting at least once a day. I'd made it out of double-A ball and was playing in The Show.

Here's how it happened. Most people, I think we all can say with confidence, don't land their dream job right out of college. The thing is, I didn't really have a dream job. I entered the job market in 2002, when journalism was about to take a major plunge into the abyss of shrinking revenues, layoffs, and outright closures. A dream journalism job in that economy was steady employment on a decent beat with the possibility of health insurance. My plan to avoid this personal realization of adulthood was to get the hell out of the country and as far away as I could, or at least until I ran out of funds. I had enough money in my bank account left over from scholarships—about two thousand dollars, more or less, plus graduation gifts—to spend the summer in Africa with an old roommate, Meghan, who'd gone into the Peace Corps in Zambia. My boyfriend's dad, a Muslim man whom I adored for his adventurous spirit and truly bonkers stories about his childhood in Turkey, got me a deal on a ticket to Dar es Salaam from one of his travel agent friends. "On KLM," he said, handing me the ticket in their kitchen one spring evening. "They're good. Get your shots."

At that point, I lived and breathed for his son, Adnan, and everyone knew it. We had started dating on Valentine's Day my junior year of college and had met because we both worked at the *Daily Tar Heel*, the student newspaper at the University of North Carolina, to which I basically devoted my entire college career. I'd wandered in there during freshman orientation and had found a home in the newsroom, like so many self-described misfits tend to do. Don't let any journalist fool you with their Brooks Brothers shirts, their devotion to the higher cause of telling the truth no matter the cost, and their world-weary outlook. Underneath it all, they—we—are all weird. Weird because of the personal cost and little glory of the profession, maybe; weird because we live for other people's stories. Weird because we don't blink an eye at working when the rest of the world stops to react; weird because we drive into storms instead of away from them. For whatever reason, as soon as I wrote a story for the *DTH* and spent the hours before deadline being edited, I knew this was exactly where I wanted to be and exactly what I wanted to do. My first story was about revolutionary new HIV drugs—the cocktail, they'd started to call it—being developed at the medical school, and it appeared under the byline *Catherine Doty*. I picked up ten copies the next day and decided that byline was pretentious. Cate I am, and Cate it was.

Adnan was a year ahead of me, and the moment I saw him working at a turquoise iMac on an information graphic, I fell hard. Haaarrrrrd. Hard enough to fast with him during Ramadan (I also lost seven pounds) and avoid pork. And hard enough to drive through a foot of snow just to spend the night at his house, leaving my Jetta on the side of the highway when I finally drifted out of the lanes. I'm telling you, *hard*.

He was tall and slender and moved with the grace of someone to whom nothing bad ever could stick, and his smile could power the football stadium. I daydreamed about his gentle, deep voice on my answering machine, wondering if I wanted to meet for coffee. We hooked up on Valentine's Day, after a few achingly sweet weeks of being inseparable, and we spent the rest of the semester under our own personal spell of romance, longing, and the imperfect joys of love in the spring, right as the tide of impending adulthood began to rise.

About that whole adulthood thing. Adnan had spent the year after his graduation at his parents' house doing freelance work, and we both knew it was time for him to strike out on his own. In my mind, we'd stay together and figure it out, no matter what, because we were in love and that was what you were supposed to do. I came from a culture and a family in which you met your partner in college, got married a couple years into your twenties, and just worked on working it out, no matter what. It sounds antiquated, and perhaps it was, and is. But the MRS degree was still a thing in 2002, no matter how we would have loved to deny it. It was not what my parents wanted for me, and it was not really what I wanted for myself. But as foolish as it sounds, I couldn't imagine much else for myself then.

Adnan wanted nothing to do with that. In his mind, he was going to move to New York, get work as a designer, and join the city's creative class, which he did that fall, right after the September 11 attacks. We were at his house that morning, with his younger brother and his mom, and we sat as stone creatures in front of their giant TV in the basement as the towers fell. Adnan and his brother went for a run around the lake; it was all they could think to do. Their mom, Jeanne, grabbed an old broom and swept the tile floor over and over, until I offered to help. "No," she said, and I saw that the blood had drained from her kind face, which had become the same color as the skunk stripe in her hair. She was white, but her beloved boys were brown-skinned Muslim men, who ate halal, or tried to, and worshipped separately from her and their sister at the mosque. She knew the score.

So Adnan moved to New York not long after that, and we broke up, more or less. Except that we really didn't. You're not really breaking up with someone if you call them nightly, visit them all the time, and tear their clothes off as soon as you see them. I had no idea what Adnan was doing in New York when we weren't together, and I frankly didn't care, as long as he called me.

Then came my own delayed launch into adulthood via a white-girl African odyssey. I got my shots, packed my red REI backpack, and said good-bye early one morning to my parents at a bus stop. I made my way to JFK and boarded a creaky 747 to Amsterdam, and then another to Dar es Salaam via Nairobi. My seatmate, a Kenyan bishop, was on his way back from Rome, where he and the other men in dresses had discussed what to do about the sexual predators in their organization—or, let's be honest, what *not* to do—suddenly being reported on by national news outlets around the country and the world. The pilot circled Mount Kilimanjaro for us as the sun rose, and I nearly wept with happiness and jet lag.

But I could not shake Adnan out of my head. I flew from Zanzibar to the mainland in a prop plane and stared down into the azure water where sunken spice-trading ships rested, and as the pilot picked his nose and asked me for a date, I wanted Adnan there. I got malaria in Dar es Salaam, and in my feverish haze, I wanted him to bring me some orange juice. I spent my birthday at Victoria Falls, and I wanted him to go bungee jumping with me over the Zambezi River. (I did that, and it was terrifying; *don't be dumb like me* is my advice to you.) It was the adventure of a lifetime, but I longed for home. One August morning in Lusaka, the Zambian capital, I drank some strong tea with Nido and ate an orange, and wandered out into the city by myself. I picked up a copy of the *International Herald Tribune*, bought some Cadbury, and traded a tube of Crest for a flat woven basket to bring back to my mom. Then I went back to the hostel and told my friends that it was time for me to go home, wherever that was. I needed to see what life held back there. I needed to see Adnan. It was time to grow up.

Back in New York, I took a cab from the airport straight to Adnan's apartment in Queens, where he'd left me a key and a note taped to the bathroom mirror: "Don't sleep! Makes the jet lag worse." I showered off the airplane funk and waited for him to get home from his job in the city as a photo assistant at a magazine. Later, naked and tangled on his mattress on the floor, we talked about what I was going to do.

"Go home, I guess," I said, wondering where home was.

"I'll just get a job. I can't stay here." But what I meant was, *Can I stay here?* He didn't say anything.

The next day, I took the train down to D.C., and my parents picked me up at Union Station. I hated Washington. There were just so many terrible pairs of pants, bad shoes, and uninteresting hair and faces, and so much pomposity and self-importance dripping down the marble walls of the buildings downtown. Washington in 2002 was a post-9/11 war-horny Republican town, full of bros in boat shoes masquerading as Serious People. Compassionate conservatism was being preached, if not practiced, while the drums of the second Iraq war had been beating for months. I hated being in the same square mileage as Dick Cheney. That night over dinner, I told my parents, "D.C. sucks. I'm never going to live here."

My dad laughed. "Well, where are you going to find a job?"

"I don't know, but not here," I said. "I'll never live here."

Ten days later, I packed a suitcase at my parents' house in the Shenandoah Valley, where I'd been sleeping on the floor upstairs, and boarded a Greyhound bus for Washington. Through sheer luck and a UNC connection, I'd gotten an interview in the Washington bureau of the *New York Times*. Joel Brinkley, David Brinkley's son and a UNC alumnus, had sent the job listing to one of the assistant deans at the journalism school, and she forwarded it to me, adding: *You need a job? Email him right now.* The phone interview was quick and charming, and that was that. I remain firmly convinced that the only reason they hired me is that I could start the next day.

I borrowed some money from my mom, bought some terrible black work pants at Ann Taylor, moved in with Erin, my best friend from college, and showed up at the Army-Navy Building at three p.m. on a steaming-hot Wednesday, as directed. I was officially an employee of the *New York Times.*

What came next was a year of pure entry-level grunt work, in the grand tradition of Big Media: answering phones, signing for packages, delivering the mail, and making coffee, as I was promised. My first official duty as a news clerk was to walk over to an optician on Connecticut Avenue and retrieve the bureau chief's glasses, and then stop on the way back for a case of champagne, because the bureau was running low. Budgets had been tightened, so I was directed not to purchase the Veuve Clicquot—we had to economize, you see.

These were the months before the second Iraq war officially began, and the world was tense. Administration officials called the bureau nightly, trying to find Judy Miller, and spent the first thirty seconds of each call screaming at the clerks. Late-night bureau dinners—sometimes pizza, sometimes filet mignon takeout from the Palm—

fed me. Bylines I'd read since middle school or before—Katharine Q. Seelye, Maureen Dowd, R. W. Apple Jr., Rachel L. Swarns—walked past me in human form, sometimes well dressed, sometimes stylishly rumpled. I helped Maureen's assistant stamp Christmas presents in the mailroom and took note of Michael Douglas's address on Central Park West. On Friday nights, when reporters wrote their weekend stories and pieces for the Week in Review, the bureau was a virtual open bar; the empties collected on Saturday morning by the housekeeping staff were plentiful.

In the middle of all this, I was dazzled. It was hard not to be. Sure, Washington sucked, but I had a front-row seat to history. I was also getting bylines, which was the point of being a clerk. The idea was that in your free time, you wrote and you wrote and you wrote, made connections, and then went off to cover City Hall at the *Charlotte Observer* or the *Dallas Morning News* or wherever, eventually making your way back to the *Times* as a seasoned journalist who already knew the ropes. Hopefully, you acquired a rabbi along the way who could ease your path forward, write recommendations when the time came, and make sure the door remained cracked open. The bureau was split between former clerks who'd climbed the ranks to become reporters, and people who had risen from small-town dailies to regional heavyweights to the big show in D.C. I loved all their stories. I loved the rumors about them, who'd slept with whom, who'd gotten shuffled off on "book leave" after their drinking started affecting their work, and who had crossed a Sulzberger. I loved it all. It was like being in the clubhouse of the most powerful team in baseball, except everyone remained fully clothed. For the most part.

But I still, *still* couldn't shake Adnan, even as I worked my way through some boring yet awful dating experiences in D.C. One guy had moved from Phoenix to join the State Department's training program, and he'd already hung DIPLO plates on his Mini Cooper. He corrected my grammar over sushi. That was one date. Another guy I'd met at the Boom Boom Room in Adams Morgan during a miserable night out with Erin and her horrible fundamentalist Republican boyfriend, Jeff, who had gotten shamed for sleeping with her by his religious officemates on Capitol Hill and had decided to revirginize himself without discussing it first. The Boom Boom Room guy was very sweet, but he insisted on wearing an Irish fisherman's sweater while we danced, sweating like a pig in a sleeping bag, and that was suspicious to me. What was he hiding under all that virgin wool? I didn't call him back. Yet another guy was a blind date named Lawrence, who had a head like a penis and decided that a street corner was the perfect place to shove his tongue down my throat, after two and a half hours of explaining to me his very important work at the

Labor Department. He smelled like my grandfather after church.

You should also understand that I did not think I was any sort of hot ticket in particular—although, looking back, maybe I should have. What's wrong with thinking you're hot shit when you're twenty-three, or when you're forty, for that matter? All women are hot shit, and I wonder often how things would have turned out if my mom and her sisters had been told that more often. Maybe we'd have a woman president by now.

Anyway, in my own *not*-hot-shit dating life, I'd already learned to avoid telling people where I worked; it was a calling card I didn't want to use. In a town like Washington, where secrets are currency and who you work for defines who you are, I preferred to hide the fact that I was employed by a newspaper that half the town believed was the god's truth and the other half thought was the work of the devil. Also, as a (very) junior member of the organization, I felt like an impostor even for offering up the *Times* as part of my identity; better, I mused, to keep it to myself, as a weird secret that people could discover only if they really wanted to know.

I still missed Adnan, and he missed me. We took the twelve-dollar bus rides and cheap off-peak trains back and forth occasionally, and we spent a snowy Valentine's Day holed up at a fancy D.C. hotel on the *Times*'s dime, for reasons I forget. After many months, it got old. We couldn't quit each other, but we couldn't stay on this ride, which had grown expensive, creaky, and fraught. We decided to stop calling each other except in case of emergency, although we had a hard time defining what that emergency was. I started to go to the gym a lot, trying to work my way down to a nine-minute mile, and dug into the stories in D.C. I wanted to know more about. That was one good thing about Washington: things were happening all the time, and there were never enough people to write about them. I learned more than I could imagine about the Bureau of Indian Affairs. I covered the Scripps-Howard National Spelling Bee, and on Saturdays, I wrote up four hundred words on the president's weekly radio address. I diverted the energy I'd been spending on Adnan to work, which felt very adult and satisfactory.

This may all sound boring to you. Where is the fabulousness, the glamour, the delicious whispers and secrets spilled of a Washington journalist's career? The secret is this: the takeout from the Palm and the Veuve Clicquot and the generous expense accounts helped make up for the incontrovertible fact that being a journalist is really fucking hard, and occasionally—especially if you're a very junior member of a Very Important Paper—it can be really fucking tedious. I'm not here to give you a lecture on why the First Amendment is important, and Indigenous land policies might feel a bit obscure. But I learned how to read a policy document. I learned how to develop sources, and I learned how this stuff made people's lives better or worse. Finally, I was there doing what I was supposed to be doing. I was learning to be a journalist.

As the months went on, I got pulled into election coverage. The 2004 presidential primary was in full swing, and the paper was getting ready for the Iowa caucuses. I was put in charge of the master candidate schedule, which, again, may sound boring to you, but you have to remember that I was in daily contact with the press shops for John Kerry and Al Sharpton, John Edwards and Wesley Clark. To a young journalist like me, this was what it was all about. But there was a problem. Up in New York, the powers that be had put a guy named Michael on the schedules, preferring to pull that work back to the main newsroom. I was pissed. Who was this guy, and why did he get to do this Very Important Work while I had to go back to covering spelling bees? I felt like my beat, such as it was, had been stomped upon for no particularly good reason, other than "New York knows best."

But then we started emailing. Each caucus year, a clerk was sent to Des Moines to do advance work for the politics team, setting up the makeshift bureau at the Des Moines Marriott, doing ground coverage and feeds for reporters, and generally doing everything that no one else wants to do. It was a plum assignment for a clerk, and Michael, whose dad was a reporter and who looked at *The Boys on the Bus* as a sort of bible, was salivating over the prospect of winter in Iowa. He had to run the candidates' schedules because soon enough, he'd be on the bus, or more likely in the van, with them, bouncing from a coffee klatch in Ottumwa to an American Legion post in Newton, the home of Maytag blue cheese.

OK, fine. He needed to do that work and I was acting like a baby. But then the emails got interesting. What began as something so mundane as tracking political schedules became about living in New York, the singular pain of an election cycle, his adoration of (and my total disdain for) musicals. Michael told me in veiled terms who the worst people in the newsroom were, and who he thought were the best. I told him about traveling in Africa, the books I hoped to write one day, and how I was aiming to be a foreign correspondent. Day by day, we began to know just a little bit about each other. And I started to know that when I logged in at three p.m. each day, I would have at least one friendly email waiting for me, with a joke, a tale of a subway passenger to be avoided, or, every now and then, an actual work request. I told him about Adnan too, and he didn't say much about that.

One day, Michael used the word *compunction* in an email about some stupid campaign operative. I fired back with cheeks tingling: *Compunction is an excellent word.*

Meanwhile, I planned a December trip to Paris with my friend Nicole. We'd found an unbeatable deal that no doubt would land us in a one-star motel in a neighborhood that would make our mothers freak out, but we were used to that. I took the train up to New York to fly out from JFK, and on the way up, I called Adnan, whom I hadn't talked to since early fall. He sounded surprised to hear my voice, and happy. My stomach did its old flippety-flop, which set off alarm bells in my head. I turned those off, though, and told him I'd be in town that afternoon if he wanted to grab a coffee or hang out. A few hours later, I hauled my backpack up to his fourth-floor walkup.

Adnan opened the door, wearing track pants and a red T-shirt, and my mouth watered. "Wow, Cate." He smiled, reaching to take my backpack. "You look . . . you look amazing."

I'd lost fifteen pounds since we last hung out, and the knowledge that he saw that both exhilarated me and broke my heart. But I smiled and said thank you, he pulled me inside, and it took less than an hour for our clothes to land on the floor, my mascara smudged, his guilt filtering through the air like smoke. We finally lay there on his mattress, wired and exhausted, the afternoon traffic noise from the Brooklyn-Queens Expressway straining through the dirty windows, and didn't say much. But I wanted to know: What the fuck are we doing? What was that? *Do you love me?* I didn't ask. And neither did he. We lay there silently, slowly untangling from each other, as Erykah Badu sang on from the living room speakers.

On the plane to Paris that evening, I ate the cold tofu vegetarian meal—I was not vegetarian—and thought. If I moved to New York, I thought, we could be together. Maybe that was the play. Maybe I just move, and we figure it out together. Maybe. I started plotting.

I found Nicole in our dingy motel on an unremarkable boulevard, and we took power naps before heading out for dinner. We had been good friends since sophomore year of boarding school and had discovered that we were perfect travel buddies. That was a hard thing to find, and we knew it. We had our routine down: We split entrées because we couldn't afford to buy separate meals, saving our food money for wine and dessert. We chose museums with the cheapest fees possible, never took cabs, and always knew when to splurge and when to retreat. We kept pace with each other.

We found a bistro and parked ourselves at a tiny table next to a giant glass window, lashed with a cold December rain. Over glasses of wine and a giant shared plate of frites, Nicole squinted at me. "What's going on with you?" she said. "You seem so sad."

She was totally right. I was sad. I missed Adnan, and I didn't know why. I was mad that I'd fallen into his bed yet again, and I was livid that I didn't know what the hell was going on. And in the back of my mind, a tiny, insistent voice chirped: *What about this other guy in New York?* I tried to quiet the voice, but my brain buzzed in confusion.

I burst into tears, and the Parisians around us looked startled. "So, I hooked up with Adnan before I went to the airport yesterday," I said, and stuffed a handful of frites into my mouth so I would stop bawling. It didn't work. Tears, hot grease, and salt streamed down my face.

Nicole stared at me. "Oh, bunny," she said finally, with complete sympathy. "I wondered if that was going to happen. You know this isn't going to work out, right?"

I shook my head and swallowed the rest of the frites. "No, it could. I could move to New York, maybe? I don't know. He's just . . . I don't know."

Nicole was wise. "Yeah, but you know this is just torturous for you," she said. "I like Adnan a lot and I know you think he's cute and all, but he always just seems to be walking away." She paused and ate a frite. "So how was it?"

I laughed and sobbed. "It was *so hot*," I wailed. "So fucking hot and I don't know what to do."

She handed me a napkin, and I wiped the tears and grease off my face.

"Well, I totally think you should move to New York because it's the best, obviously, and we could hang out all the time, but don't do it for Adnan," Nicole said. "Do it because you want to be there. And don't move in with him or something like that."

I stared out the windows to the street and watched dripping-wet pedestrians stream down the Metro stairs under an Art Nouveau arch. I loved Paris, but it was less its own particular Parisness than its hustle and juice. Everyone there looked interesting, like they had a book in their brains and a wry yet tender song in their hearts. I imagined New York was the same.

"It would save money if I moved in with him—"

"Cate, *no*," Nicole said. "Trust me; that is a bad, bad idea." Nicole had recently decamped back to her mother's apartment in Washington Heights after an unhappy year-long Upper East Side cohabitation with a doofus named Anthony, who was sweet, paid for everything, and didn't read books or care about much other than his banking job, the New York Jets, and saving for a five-bedroom house back on Long Island near his parents. After Nicole moved out, she sold all the silver Tiffany jewelry that his mom had given her on eBay and used some of the money to buy her ticket to Paris.

"I don't know what you should do, but don't think about him here," Nicole said. "Not here."

I worked hard at not thinking about him. We went to

the Rodin Museum, and I cried in front of *The Kiss*. We wandered the Left Bank and perused the shelves at Shakespeare and Co., and I tried not to think about a present to bring back to him. We walked from the Eiffel Tower to Montparnasse, and I considered buying French lingerie, just to see what would happen. But I spent half my paycheck at Fauchon instead.

But what about New York itself, my dream of all dreams? I mean, I did work for the *NEW YORK Times*. Adnan aside, I'd always wanted to live in New York, and but for an abortive semester at Barnard, I could have already been there. Surely the New York newsroom would have a spot for me. I'd pay my own expenses, and it wouldn't cost them a thing; ever deferential, I was worried about burdening a billion-dollar organization with a five-hundred-dollar moving bill. I sent the clerical supervisor an email from the airport: *Dear Jane*, I began. *I wonder if you might have room for me.*

A COUPLE OF months later, on a rainy Tuesday, I put on what I thought was my most interesting outfit: a sheer blue dress, fishnets, stompy knee-high boots, and a TripleFive-Soul combat jacket, bought with the understanding that my sedate life in Washington was about to get a lot more awesome. I was boarding yet another bus, but this one was headed north to New York. I was getting out of Washington to see what *the* city, *my* city, was all about. I'd also decided to see if we, Adnan and me, could make this thing work, whatever this thing was. I was bullish on me and New York. I was not bullish on me and Adnan. But I was super excited about my new job: I was going to write the wedding announcements, and that sounded just right to me. My true New York writing career was about to begin in a big, huge way.

This bus service was run by a bunch of Hasidic Jews, whom, you may be surprised to learn, I'd never before encountered, except in *Annie Hall*, which I'd rented from Blockbuster at least five times when I was in high school. I was fascinated by the young woman who took our tickets and wondered how she'd gotten her hair so perfect and shiny. I shoved my blue rolling duffel under the bus, gave her my twelve dollars, settled into a stinky seat, and popped in my earbuds, waving good-bye to my old boring life as the driver piloted the lumbering bus up North Capitol Street.

Five hours later, I stepped out of the bus into Midtown and was greeted by a wall of fetid air. It was hot for early spring, but it was exactly what I expected from my town. As I dragged my duffel through the crowds of 8th Avenue toward the subway, I tried to feel as fabulous as I knew I looked. I was *here*, where I was meant to be. If I'd been wearing a hat, I might have tossed it in the air. But I couldn't shake the sense that something was amiss. I could almost feel the hot air up my legs. I dropped my duffel on the sidewalk and felt around for my dress—but it wasn't there. Frantically, I swatted around my backside; as I was hauling my luggage a handful of blocks, the hem of my dress had surreptitiously crept up my sweaty legs and was now lodged between my combat jacket and my back. There was nothing between my bare ass and the Midtown crowds but some ratty cotton underwear and H&M fishnet. I was alone in a city I had longed for, walking toward someone I lusted after, and my ass was out for everyone to see.

My life in New York had begun.

"HI, THIS IS Cate Doty from the *Times*, calling about your wedding announcement," I said over the phone. I heard a gasp.

"Hello! So nice to talk to you!" The senator's bride-to-be, the Smooth Operative, was thrilled to hear from me. Over my brief tenure on the desk, I'd gotten accustomed to the enthusiasm that generally waited for me on the other end of the line. The weeks before their weddings, people are generally in one of two states: zen or bonkers. There is no in-between. It's when people show you who they are. If they're kind, they glow with generosity and love for the whole world. If they're not, the rot just shines right through. It's one of the most emotionally fraught times that anyone can live through, and with luck, it's wall-to-wall joy and wonder. Often, though, it's tempered with confusion, squabbling, expensive last-minute decisions that begin with "Are you serious?" and end with "Fuck it. I don't care." As far as hard times for the privileged go, it's not an easy couple of weeks.

Those are the weeks, though, when we talked to our brides and grooms, which meant those conversations were going to be fun and light, or just as fraught. This gave us fact-checkers a peek into these people's interior lives, and sometimes they offered up knowledge that they wouldn't even tell their priest or rabbi. The women often wanted to gush about their grooms; the men often wanted to gush about their titles at their current investment bank. I often wished they'd switch gender roles.

I started going down the questions: Your name is spelled S-M-O-O-T-H? Are you taking your husband's name? How old will you be the day after you get married? Have you been married before? All the usual stuff.

And then the Operative said, "I heard from Suzanne you had a run-in with him." She started laughing. "I'm so sorry about that. He has a bit of a temper."

"Oh, it was fine," I said breezily. "It happens a lot with people who aren't senators. This is a crazy time for you all, and we try to make this as painless as possible."

"Yeah, it does feel crazy," she said.

"Are you excited?" I always asked this.

She paused. "Oh yeah, I am. There's just a lot still to do." *She's overwhelmed*, I thought.

"But this is the fun stuff, right?" I asked. "All the details, the announcement?"

"Yes, and my last dress fitting, and the table assignments, and proofing the program," she said ruefully. "There's just a lot."

"Are you getting help with any of it?" I asked, and then thought that was maybe a step too far.

She was quiet. "Well, he's actually doing most of it."

That was surprising to me, because it was not generally the way it went. At this point, many, if not most, of the grooms were a bit checked out. They'd had their bachelor parties, they'd written the checks and made the payments on the ring and been fitted for their tuxes. "Makes it easier for you!" I said brightly.

"Yeah," she said. "It's weird how things turn out sometimes."

It was my turn to be quiet. "Yeah, it is," I said finally. "I guess you just never know, right? I mean, most people don't think they'll end up marrying a senator. Or *being* a senator, for that matter."

"He knew," the Operative said. "He always knew."

I thought about destiny and determination, and how the senator knew what he wanted, in life and in women. I wondered if the Operative knew. I wondered if this was what she wanted. I wondered if this was what *I* wanted.

Which, it turns out, was what I was about to find out.

CHAPTER 2

Forever and Ever, Amen

WHEN I WAS eight years old, I loved nothing more than going over to my grandparents' house and playing dress-up in my mom's homemade wedding dress. First of all, my grandmother didn't care what I did or watched as long as I didn't break anything or bother my grandfather, which meant that I watched my aunt's VHS copy of *Top Gun* early and often. Second, their house was full of relics of my mom's childhood, clues to who she was before marrying my dad, having two traumatic births, and worrying day and night about money. I loved finding bits and pieces of her as a girl, even if she had been forced to share many of those bits and pieces with her four sisters. Once, I was helping my mom and one of my aunts clean out the attic, and I opened up a cardboard box full of college detritus. On top was a *Playgirl* from 1972, and the centerfold, who resembled Burt Reynolds but who was not him, was my introduction to the existence of uncircumcised penises.

Anyway, this wedding dress, which my aunt Gail had had to share with my mom, hung in the guest room closet, wedged between some old coats that needed to be given away and a floor-length green velvet gown with a sweetheart neckline and white rabbit trim. That was what I played dress-up in when I didn't want to be married but wanted to be looked at and wanted, although I didn't know what that wanting was. When I wanted the full fairy tale, though, I pulled on the dress. It was the only wedding dress I'd ever gotten to touch: an ivory taffeta A-line thing with a lace bodice, cap sleeves, chiffon overlay, and matching lace hem, with unfinished inside seams and faded pencil marks where my grandmother had adjusted the dress pattern. It was completely of its era, but I'd still wear it today. My grandmother had made it for my aunt in 1976 when she, not quite graduated from college, married my uncle Mike. He wore a white tuxedo and exceptional sideburns, and my mom and her sisters wore seafoam polyester dresses that looked like something that a couple of Greek goddesses had donated to Goodwill. My aunt Alice looked like the Grim

Reaper in the photos that were taken in the church fellowship hall. But she always looks like the Grim Reaper in photos anyway.

My parents got married on April 9, 1977, at a small Presbyterian church in Leesburg, Virginia. They had no money, and no one else did either. So my mom wore her sister's wedding dress, and her two bridesmaids—more of my aunts—wore the green goddess nightmares, and they had tea sandwiches and sparkly punch and a huge chocolate marble cake that my mom had baked the day before and which her friend had decorated with yellow roses on top. She walked down the aisle to "Jesu, Joy of Man's Desiring," and she didn't get the bouquet she wanted because that spring had been particularly cold, and the blooming season was off. My parents were teachers then, so they were putting off their honeymoon until school got out, but they splurged on a night at a hotel and a fancy dinner at the Wayside Inn. (The menu included "slave kitchen stew"; don't Google it.) My dad had booked a room at the wrong Holiday Inn, the old run-down one that needed to be renovated, not the new one with the better beds, so they spent their first married night together in a snit. This remains unsurprising to me.

My mom's dress got shoved in a plastic bag by my grandmother, dragged back to North Carolina, and hung in the closet, where it stayed relatively untouched for a decade, until I got hold of it. At first, I was only allowed to play with the fingertip-length veil, a huge bouffy lace Juliet cap thing that felt like a diaper on my head. I pinned it to my hair and vamped in the old spotted mirror, not sure what was supposed to happen then, but I knew it was something good. But one day, with the door closed and out of sight from my grandmother, I pulled the dress out of its plastic bag and wrestled it on. My mom is only five feet, two inches and weighed ninety-eight pounds the day she got married, but that dress, already rotting at the seams, felt larger than life. I twisted my arms to zip it all the way up, and its weight on my shoulders felt like a whole story. I knew it, kind of: I'd already watched my parents' marriage go through the wash several times, and they were only on year eleven. Some days, I carried their moods and fights and worries in my bones, although I don't know if they ever knew it. But in that dress, that part of the story hadn't happened yet. It was only the joy and optimism of April 9, 1977, with no hopes for anything more than everything a life together could offer.

I HAVE LOVED weddings for as long as I can remember. I couldn't tell you why, exactly. Maybe it was ready access to a wedding dress that was a map to my homeland. But this love of weddings came before that. When I was a tiny thing, three or four, I had this bride doll whose big blue eyes closed when you laid her down, her long nylon eyelashes fluttering down to her blushed cheeks. She wore what had to be the most chaste wedding getup this side of the Reformation: a long-sleeve turtleneck lace bodice and ankle-length skirt, with three underskirts, a pair of bloomers, thick white tights that were a bitch to pull up over her rubber legs, and white plastic Mary Janes, which looked juvenile and out of place with her wedding attire. She was a doll, I should note again, and I of course made her do unspeakable things with my Ken dolls, after which I immediately felt ashamed. She also was twice their size, and that also made me uncomfortable. But I knew that the things I was forcing her to do with Ken were things you did when you were married and had had a wedding. The wedding cleansed the shame and made the coupling of two plastic dolls beautiful, or something.

So I don't know. My love of weddings didn't come from TV, which I wasn't allowed to watch as a small child save for *Sesame Street*, and I'm still disappointed that Bert and Ernie haven't tied the knot. But I was an early and prodigious reader, in part because I was at that point an only child and didn't have anyone to talk to during the day other than my mom, who maintains that I was reading full books by age three, and frankly I just don't see how that's possible.

But I ate up the *Little House* series when I was six, and read over and over the penultimate chapter in *These Happy Golden Years*, in which Laura and Almanzo—Manly, rather—stood before her friend Ida's father in his parlor and were married, the groom in his Sunday best and the bride in a black cashmere dress with a tight-fitting bodice and a high collar, and Ma's square gold brooch pinned at her throat. It sounded luxurious and full of hope to me, although I knew even then that Laura was poor and would stay poor for much of her life, until she pulled her family out of deep poverty by writing. I was bewitched by Laura's insistence that she would not say the word *obey* in her vows, while still denying that she wanted the right to vote. And I wanted to know what happened after the last lines of the book, when Laura and Manly went back inside their house after watching the twilight fade on the first night of their life together. I knew that the first four years were deathly difficult and ended in bankruptcy, a lost child, and crippling disease. But what were the interiors of that life together? I wanted to know what they talked about as they went to bed.

So maybe it wasn't just weddings. Maybe it was life itself I was curious about. But weddings were a way into that life, and I knew that entry could be beautiful. For years, my parents had a department-store gift box full of the relics of their wedding: bits of lace from my mom's dress, my dad's crumbly boutonniere, a yellowed program, and a copy of their wedding announcement from the *Fayetteville Observer-Times*, the paper from my grandparents' hometown. I read it over and over, and then I started reading the wedding announcements in the *Birmingham News* every Sunday. We lived in a tiny yellow house with a green stoop, and I spent Sunday mornings at the maple table my dad had made, reading the comics, the Mini Pages, and the wedding announcements.

And then, when I was five, I actually got to go to a wedding. My dad's father was remarrying in North Carolina, so we piled into our little blue Datsun and headed up I-20 to the wedding. He had been dating a tall, wispy-slender woman named Susan, who brought to their relationship four daughters whom I found fascinating. They had big hair, makeup, lots of nail polish, giant goofy 1980s sleeves, and *drama*: love affairs, breakups, college dropouts, car wrecks, you name it. Susan presided over it all, with kind blue eyes that sparkled with intelligence and sly humor. She specialized in understanding girls, and I loved her like a shot.

Anyway, Pa—that's what I called him, although most everyone else called him Monk—and Susan were getting married, and I was very excited. The day of the wedding, my mom dressed me in a smocked dress, ankle socks, and white Mary Janes, and herself in a red dress with a blue-and-white belt. We stood in the pews while my grandfather committed himself to Susan, and she to him, led down the bridal path by an Episcopal priest. She wore a sensible white column dress with an open collar and carried a small bouquet of pink roses and baby's breath wrapped in a white satin ribbon. And then, after the ceremony, she leaned over to me and said, "Would you hold my bouquet for me?"

Well. Would I? *Would* I? Yes, indeed I would. I paraded around the reception with that bouquet like it was my own wedding. I buried my face in the roses, breathing

in the scent of hothouse love, and the petals were cool to my face. I held on to the plastic stem of the bouquet with both hands at my waist, just like I'd seen Susan do, and walked up and down the yard, weaving in and out of the small crowd, showing off my flowers to Susan's daughters, my amused parents, and my dad's disinterested sister. When the cake had been eaten and the champagne had been finished, I gave the new unit of Pa and Susan a fierce five-year-old good-bye hug. Susan leaned down and whispered in my ear: "You can keep it." I told you, she understood girls. On the way back to our motel, I fell asleep in the back of the car clutching the bouquet, just like Ralphie on Christmas night with his Red Ryder BB gun. But my pride and joy was prettier.

WHEN I WAS twelve years old, I forgot to write my grandmother a thank-you note for my birthday money. This grandmother, my dad's mother, was, and remains, not gentle and funny. When I was six, she married a very wealthy man named Frank, and we were not invited to their wedding, another small Episcopal affair. I was oblivious to the politics surrounding that exclusion but later realized that she was somehow ashamed of my dad, for his left-leaning politics and refusal to chase a fat bank account, a stellar golf handicap, and white-supremacist propriety. My fiercely smart mom baffled her, and she didn't know what to do with me, a precocious child who considered myself one of the adults. Instead of affection, she gave us money. To me, the mercenary nature of our relationship was fine. I had a lot of grandparents, aunts and uncles, and cousins, and frankly I didn't need another person telling me what to do. I came to expect a check on my birthday in July and then another under the Christmas tree, to be unwrapped slowly after our torturous annual holiday luncheon, like one of Willy Wonka's golden tickets, but with less suspense. This all continued apace until the summer I turned twelve, when I went away to camp, got my grandmother's card at mail call, and in between swimming and craft time and taps, forgot to write her a thank-you note.

Christmas rolled around, and so did the holiday luncheon. After a catered lunch in the dining room, complete with three kinds of stemware and seven polished silver utensils each, we adjourned to their new sunroom, where a small pile of presents reflected the white lights on the tree. (Stop me if you've heard this WASP tale before.) I looked for an envelope with my name on it, but all I saw was the outline of a book in expensive wrapping paper. My grandmother distributed the presents, and I felt my mom's eyes on me, curious, and suspicious of her.

I peeled back the paper to reveal a thick yellow tome:

The Amy Vanderbilt Complete Book of Etiquette: A Guide to Contemporary Living, revised and expanded by Letitia Baldrige, who had served in the White House as Jacqueline Kennedy's social secretary. *There are new entertaining concerns*, the flyleaf warned. *How do you serve a sit-down dinner without a maid? How does a couple entertain successfully in a one-room apartment? Or how does one address an invitation to a couple when the woman has retained her maiden name after marriage?* I was confused as to how these particular questions applied to me, and I looked to my mom for help. Her face was red, which was also confusing.

My grandmother leaned over and guided my hand to the stationery section, and the book fell open to page 517. There, wedged next to the section called "The Age to Begin Note Writing," was a stamped Crane envelope, addressed to her, with a note card inside. "I always appreciate thank-you notes," my grandmother said with sweet venom, and turned away to watch my four-year-old brother open his Brio train set.

I was still confused. I flipped to the frontispiece, where she'd written in her precise script: "As you travel your earthly round/May Grace precede you in abound. We pray this book may help." Signed, herself, her husband, and my aunt Gina, who hadn't gotten me a present and had just signed on to this one. My mom took it out of my hands, read the inscription, and shook her head at me. "We'll talk about this later," she hissed.

Everyone was quiet on the ride home, except for my brother, who was banging pieces of his train set together like drumsticks. My mom finally whipped around to me from the front seat and demanded, "Did you write her a thank-you note for your birthday present?" She'd been stewing since we pulled out of the driveway.

"I . . . I don't remember," I stammered. "I was at camp."

"I know," my mom said.

I thought about it. "I probably didn't. But I just forgot."

"I know," she said again. "This is what happens when you don't send thank-you notes. She'll do it again too. When we get home, I want you to sit down and write that dang thank-you note and go put it in the mailbox so we don't have to hear about it anymore." That *dang*, impressively strong language from her, carried a dozen years of vitriol as well as a fresh fury at my grandmother for humiliating me and attempting a life lesson in such an underhanded, sniveling way.

I never heard another word about thank-you notes from that woman. But here's the thing about that etiquette book: it became one of my favorite things to read. I have it still, and while I have yet to test my knowledge of the codes of conduct when visiting a naval vessel, never mind the tricks to truly enjoying an audience with the pope, I know etiquette. Did you know, for example, that when corresponding with an Italian baroness, you should sign your letters with "sincerely yours," but when writing to the Spanish foreign affairs minister, please, for the love of God, change your tone to "respectfully yours"?[*] Or that a picnic table may be enhanced by a paper tablecloth; however, the hostess should remember the wind factor and secure it with four pretty rocks in the corners? Or that four-in-hand ties are more slenderizing, and should always be worn by men who are not, in fact, slim, or who suffer from rounder visages?[†] Did you also know, pray, that female wedding guests look more appropriate, in fact *finished*, if they wear gloves to and from the ceremony and reception? And that if you *must* invite a woman who is separated from her male spouse to your wedding, you must address her as Mrs. George Hart, as if she were still tethered to the person or, in a perhaps sadder turn of events, widowed?[‡]

I should pause here to note that I do not, in my daily life, exhibit particularly good manners. I slouch, I still forget to write thank-you notes, I talk over people and interrupt, I almost never remember birthdays, and I am not particularly nice, although I do always say please and thank you

---

[*] Page 627.

[†] Page 671.

[‡] Page 136.

and, generally speaking, keep my elbows off the table. It's also worth noting that, just as Ms. Baldrige worked to bring the Vanderbilt guidance up to 1991 standards, these rules of etiquette—which, let's be clear, were created and maintained by white people—have continued to change with the times, such that, in our blessedly advanced era, we are not required to address a separated woman by her husband's name. Thank goodness for that.

But the spirit, and often the letter, of the myriad guidelines offered by Ms. Vanderbilt and Ms. Baldrige live in my bones. I know that shit backward and forward. I read it, over and over, when I was bored in the afternoons and when I was out of library books. I read it curled up on the couch with the cat, and on the screened-in back porch, with an orange and a dish towel to put the peel in. It was a good education in grace, just as my grandmother had hoped, and it held hints of a world of which I knew almost nothing, but which fascinated me nonetheless.

I was particularly into the section starting with chapter 11: "Wedding Invitations and Wedding Announcements." My favorite piece of advice from this chapter was that if your wedding was being given in a country where English was not spoken, under no circumstance should the bridegroom expect to receive a separate set of invitations in English to send to his friends and family. This blatant lack of forbearance, with a whiff of "you break it, you buy it,"

was delicious to me. Ms. Baldrige brooked no special treat-
ment for a man who just wanted to tell his poor non-
Hungarian-speaking guests where to book their hotel
rooms in Budapest. (I can tell you conclusively that the bar
snacks at the Four Seasons there are exceptional.)

There's no good reason for me to have known this stuff,
except that I was curious and had time on my hands. I spent
the afternoons poring over the line drawings that laid out
processionals for double Christian ceremonies, secular
ceremonies, and Orthodox Jewish ceremonies; in that one,
all the line-drawn women wear long sleeves and high necks.
I questioned Ms. Baldrige's choices for a modern trousseau
and wondered how, when I came to be married, my monogram would look on my silver service of choice, and what
that monogram would be.

About the silver: months after the Amy Vanderbilt inci-
dent, I visited my aunt Jean (I told you I had a lot of aunts)
and uncle Lu in Birmingham. We'd moved to North Carolina, and every summer I spent a week or so with my aunt
and uncle, who had no children and treated their nieces
and nephews like their own. My cousin Greer (who, years
later, had a *fabulous* wedding) and I spent hours floating on
inner tubes in the murky waters at their lake house out in
Shelby County. Lu taught us how to shoot, how to clean a
rifle, and how to drive a manual transmission. Jean taught
us how to fiddle on her grand piano, how to play spoons

and hearts, and how to treat people with grace. I had a big time with them each summer, even though they also made me go to Vacation Bible School at Briarwood Presbyterian Church, where I led my class and yet still retained virtually nothing of those teachings.

One day, Jean and I were kicking around Mountain Brook Village, which was the closest shopping area to their house, near the botanical gardens. Mountain Brook, as you may know, is an old-money enclave, and its residents enjoy leafy winding streets, long tennis matches and drinks at the club, and fresh hot baguettes from the Continental Bakery. I should not give the impression that I disavow some of these things. I love leafy winding streets and warm baguettes, and I love my family who still live on those streets. But I never felt entirely comfortable in that world. When my parents and I lived in Birmingham, our neighborhood, the South Side, was literally on the other side of the mountain, and the tracks. We did not employ an underpaid class of Black maids and gardeners, and we did not belong to private steakhouses that required a code to enter. I had no hopes of being presented at the winter debutante ball, a sheath of long pale roses cradled in my gloved arms. My artist parents had grown up on the edges of that milieu and, years later, kept it at arm's length. As a child, I had only a dim understanding of the white supremacy that underpinned the lives of many people in Mountain Brook, and those who cleaned up after them and kept their children and lives running on schedule. But I loved swimming at the club and knowing to sit up straight without being told while eating lunch afterward. I was terrified of my aunt's maid, but I still loved playing in the laundry room while she did the ironing. I did not know that the same people with whom my aunt and uncle socialized and played golf and vacationed likely supported Bull Connor's fire-hose tactics, and I have little doubt that my uncle did, even though he might have hid behind his fundamentalist faith. I did not know that four little Black girls, who lived on the same side of the mountain as I did, were blown apart by a bomb that may well have been silently applauded by these selfsame country club goers. I was there for the grilled cheese sandwiches, the pool, and the ice cream bars. The politics came later—but not that much later.

Anyway, Jean and I were bopping around Mountain Brook Village, running errands and looking at all the treasures to be had at Smith's Variety Toy and Gift Shoppe, still truly the greatest store in existence. Jean had to pick up a repair at Bromberg's, a jeweler across the street, so we popped across Petticoat Lane and headed inside. Now, when I was a child, Bromberg's was like the Tiffany's of Birmingham. A certain class's engagement and wedding rings came from there; they registered for china and crystal there, just like their mamas and grandmothers did; there, men bought their wives apology presents, which the wives picked out ahead of time and told a discreet salesperson how to direct their erring spouses, who came in later. The striped awning held entry to a world of sparkle—some subdued and tasteful, some completely over the top—and tradition. It was the tradition that my aunt was interested in.

She picked up her repair, and we wandered around the store. I gawked at the engagement rings, the shell-pink cameo pins, the diamond anniversary bands that, it seemed, every long-married woman in Mountain Brook expected and wore like a Purple Heart. We drifted back to the china and crystal, which held less interest for me. I recognized my mother's china pattern, Wild Strawberry by Wedgwood, and I kept my hands to myself when we came upon all the sweet little hand-painted porcelain figurines.

Then we got to the silver patterns. Forks, knives, spoons, and serving pieces of various sizes and usage were fanned out across the wall like cards to be dealt. Next to the pieces were the names of their patterns: the scalloped Strasbourg by Gorham, and Buttercup, with its pretty edging of a trio of flowers. Grande Baroque, a dramatic pattern by Wallace, reminded me of a violin gone wrong. I passed over Wallace's Rose Point and Acorn by Georg Jensen, finding their intricate patterns harsh. My eyes wandered up to the intensely designed Repousse by Kirk Stieff, one of the oldest silver patterns still in production. The late

Marilyn Schwartz, who wrote *A Southern Belle Primer, or Why Princess Margaret Will Never Be a Kappa Kappa Gamma*, noted in her silver pattern zodiac that girls who chose Repousse often had mothers and grandmothers who had Repousse. One girl marrying into a Repousse family didn't even have a pattern, so her future mother-in-law insisted that she choose something. The hapless bride-to-be passed over Repousse, calling it too fussy, and that was how the mother-in-law knew that this marriage wouldn't last. It didn't.

"Which one do you like?" Jean asked, as I surveyed it all. She pointed out her own, a relatively obscure pattern whose name I forget, and others chosen by the women of our family. I recognized my mom's, Greenbrier by Gorham, chosen with the understanding that after her mother died, she would inherit half of that fine woman's chest of Greenbrier, so her table settings would match.

"Oh, I don't know," I said. I recognized other patterns that had appeared on our table. My mom's silver chest held pieces from several wings of the family, and we ate with it all, preferring to use it rather than let it tarnish in the pantry. "I don't think I have to choose right now."

Jean smiled gently; everything that lady did was gentle, even when she criticized. "Oh, goodness, no. But every girl should have a silver pattern. You don't have to wait until you get married. You do want to get married, don't you?" She looked at me curiously. At thirteen, I was a bit of a mess. I had the beginnings of acne, and the Alabama humidity had done no favors for my thick shock of wavy dark hair, which my uncle had told me to brush more often, since boys didn't enjoy girls who don't groom. In Umbros, a tucked-in Banana Republic T-shirt, and dirty Keds, I was not exactly one of the girls Jean was used to seeing, the slender, tanned blond girls who populated Mountain Brook's swimming pools and debutante balls, went to the University of Alabama, and ended up registering at Bromberg's. Whatever I was going to turn out to be, it was likely not that.

"Um, yes?" It was all I could say. I mean sure? I guess? It was a crazy question for a thirteen-year-old to hear, much less answer. I thought of this boy named Charlie, on whom I had a major crush. We were—are still—adoring friends, and I vacillated between wanting to be his friend and then, you know, *be his friend*. We're both far better off where we are. But in 1992, I totally wanted him to kiss me.

"I like that one," I said, pointing to a knife on the wall. Jean peered up. "Wild Rose. I believe that was your grandmother's pattern," she said. Still raw from the etiquette book debacle, I made a mental note not to ever purchase, or register for, Wild Rose silver. (Years later, my grandmother gave me a shoebox full of her silver, and I turned around and sold it so I could afford to go to someone else's wedding.)

So it all added up to—what? A weird teenager who knew how to set the table for a state dinner, dreamed of fingertip veils, and had decided opinions on silver patterns? Pretty much just exactly that. When Martha Stewart debuted her weddings magazine in 1994, I jumped on it. By that time, I was working under the table for my mom's friend Helen, who ran a restaurant and catering business in Fayetteville and had known me since I was a baby. All the fancy people catered with Helen, who knew their ways and spoke their language and really was one of them herself. I spent a lot of time in custom-built kitchens, old slave quarters on plantations that had been converted to event spaces, and maid's pantries, polishing silver trays and arranging canapés on them.

Under Helen's tutelage, I learned how to make rumaki, carve flowers out of mangos and kiwi, roll salmon roulettes, and pour champagne without spilling a drop. I came home each night stinking of old food and sticky with cake frosting and punch, and I loved it. The weddings we did ranged from grilled chicken buffet package deals, duchesse potatoes optional, to $250-a-head fully plated dinners, with thousands of glasses, monogrammed napkins, and a twelve-piece big band. The waitstaff was a curious bunch: military

wives who needed extra income; a toweringly tall gay guidance counselor named Nick, who was our unofficial captain; Carolyn, a singer who worked to save money for her
son's dance education; and me, whose mom had called in a
favor to get her a summer job. We prepared for these weddings as if we were going into battle. In the days before the
big ones, we stocked our brown dish trays with everything
we'd need for any contingency. Over time, I learned exactly
what to pack for a carving station, how many cake plates
and serving tools for a four-tier cake, and that a first-aid kit
was always a good idea.

One blistering day in August, Carolyn's son, Jones, and
I were hiding behind the azalea bushes near the catering
van. We were on hour six of this outdoor Greek wedding,
and everyone and everything had wilted. The bride had insisted on a massive cheese table, which we finally decided
to tear down before anyone got sick. The brie had melted,
the hard cheeses had sweated into oblivion, and the specter
of food poisoning loomed like a question above the table.
Jones and I stood at the trash cans, scraping away hundreds
of dollars' worth of cheese off giant mirrored trays. In an
act of rebellion, I had unhooked my black bow tie and
unbuttoned the top two buttons of my shirt. We were hot
and miserable, and the only saving grace was watching the
guests dissolve into their drinks as the day went on. Jones
and I worked silently, gagging at the smell of the cheese

tumbling into the garbage cans, and all I wanted was a shower.

The azalea bushes rustled, and we heard drunken laughs. I wrestled my bow tie back on, and we darted behind the van, peeking around the corner. Through the bushes burst two people: a woman in a tight pink sleeveless sheath and a man who had misplaced his sport coat. The only thing that was keeping this woman vertical was the man's arms, encased in a sweat-stained blue button-down. She was so drunk that her eyes were looking at two different hemispheres. The man wasn't much better, but he was able to stand up straight, more or less.

Jones and I looked at each other and giggled. We'd seen this scene play out many times before. Drunk wedding guests were par for the course, and I didn't judge them at all, especially since I'd sometimes sneak a little champagne myself. If weddings were a stage, these people were the comic relief: they were the Dogberrys of the event, those who spewed forth such malapropisms as to make the most jaded catering staff laugh. So we watched.

The pair started mauling each other, sucking on each other's faces and tearing at clothes, although they were so drunk that there was no way they could have dealt with zippers. They had a hard time finding their mouths; it was like watching farm animals. We heard the woman choke, and her body convulsed. And then, to exactly no one's surprise, she threw up all over her paramour's face. In his mouth, down his shirt, down his pleated khakis, onto his shoes. He reeled away and spun her around to face the azaleas, where she deposited the rest of her wedding lunch, probably several gin and tonics, some champagne, a bit of cake and fondant, and, most likely, a lot of sweaty cheese.

Jones and I watched from behind the van in horrified fascination. He whispered to the air, "It's like *The Exorcist*." I nodded. Nick, who had been sorting dirty glasses in the van, jumped out onto the gravel. "What do we do?" I asked him, pointing. Nick clucked quietly and shook his head. "Leave them alone," he said, turning us away. "We don't want to embarrass them."

I couldn't see how a waiter helping them would be any more embarrassing than stumbling out of the azalea bushes, covered in vomit, and attempting to find help among the guests. But Nick usually knew best, so Jones and I watched them navigate the shrubbery and wobble to the man's BMW, which was parked near us by a brick wall. Thankfully, they didn't drive away, although I doubt the man could have even found his keys. We watched them slump on the hood, attempting to clean each other off, and then we turned back to other matters, grateful that the sun was setting and the end of this wedding was near.

IT ISN'T LOGICAL to love weddings, I know. The statistics aren't on our side. And even without the numbers, we see what was supposed to be long-term love falter all the time. What comes after the wedding is marriage, and, well, marriage is hard. But a wedding is hope. It is tradition, decorum, a door into life itself. A large portion of the American economy depends on weddings, which means that they're also pragmatic, even necessary, for a capitalist society to survive. We don't need weddings to propagate the species, but we do need them as a pause, a reminder of possibility, a rejoinder of joy, and a catalyst for economic growth. Sometimes joy and capitalism *can* go hand in hand.

But I never thought about them as mergers of joy and capitalism. Truly, I just loved the pomp and ceremony. I loved the gleaming eyes of a bride after the ceremony was over, relaxed and happy to sink into the reception she'd been planning for months, perhaps years. I loved the traditions and history behind a single silver knife that told the story of the women in my family. It was the future, yes, but it also held captive the past in ways that my family treasured, for better and for worse.

The season of weddings for me opened the summer after I started working at the *Times*, when my friend Jamie got married in a field outside Little Rock. It was the first wedding of a close college friend, and we were all excited about it. I bought a vampy red-and-white silk dress and matching red lipstick, and during the ceremony, I read a poem about my friends that Jamie had asked me months before to write. Ever the journalist on deadline, I wrote it in the motel bathroom the morning of the wedding, still a little drunk from the bachelorette party the night before.

At the reception, I started talking to one of the groom's friends, an aid worker who had flown in from Kabul for the wedding. I was immediately besotted. Greg had moved around the Middle East and South Asia for an international nonprofit, and he was helping expand its Afghan mission, which was reeling from the first years of the war. We exchanged information, danced slowly to "At Last," and said good-bye early the next morning at the Little Rock airport. Over the next few months, he sent me trinkets of lapis lazuli and called me from the bazaar, the sounds of Kabul lighting up my imagination. I fantasized about leaving my post at the *Times* and joining up with an aid organization, disregarding the fact that I really didn't care to work for an aid organization, nor was I remotely qualified to do so.

We finally met again on my trip to Paris with Nicole. I'd planned to stay a few days longer after she left to see him, not expecting that I'd still be reeling from an unplanned hookup with Adnan. I met Greg at a hotel on the

Left Bank; we had tepid sex and two awkward days together; and, when we left each other at Charles de Gaulle, neither of us looked back. I was already planning my move to New York, and Greg was a bothersome afterthought. I'd already moved on to my life in New York with Adnan. I started thinking: what if we actually did stay together, after all this? We'd be in the same city, and we were both finally adults, living on our own. We'd play the long game. That was what commitment was, right? I started to plot the board.

CHAPTER 3

Society and News

THREE MONTHS LATER, I swiped my ID badge at the turnstile and crowded my way onto the cranky old elevators at 229 West 43rd Street. For my first day at the mother ship, the Gothic Revival building that housed the main operations of the *New York Times*, I wore a gray windowpane plaid suit, a pink cashmere sweater, spiky boots, and tousled hair that I'd had streaked with blood red at a salon on Bedford Avenue. I thought I looked professional, but not stuffy; adult, but flexible. It was, I thought, the perfect ensemble for someone about to conquer the world. I flew out of Adnan's apartment at seven thirty and hoofed it the ten blocks to the L train, eager to join the creative hordes on the Manhattan-bound side of the platform. Today was the day I'd been waiting for since—I kind of figured my whole life, I'd been waiting for this day.

The first thing I noticed was that no other woman on the train was wearing a suit. As a recent émigré from Washington, the land of the polyester work pant, I was not used to this. I took off my jacket and stuffed it in my sturdy black work bag, which was making me self-conscious, since I also noticed that the few women on the train were not carrying sturdy black work bags. It was already too hot to wear a suit anyway, and pit stains were imminent. The other thing I noticed was that the subway car was half empty. When did people go to work here? I was used to the jammed Metro cars of up-and-at-'em-early D.C., with calls scheduled early and crowded trains at seven a.m., guys melting in their Men's Wearhouse suits, someone else's *Washington Post* shoved in my face. This train car held none of those things; it was just me and maybe ten other early risers, none carrying a newspaper or wearing a midgrade suit. It was a relief. I took an empty seat by the window and wished I'd stopped for coffee, and my ears popped as the train lumbered and then tore its way under the East River.

I changed at 14th Street to the uptown A and emerged into Times Square as far away as I could be from the *Times* building. Adnan had warned me about pre-walking, figuring out which end of the train would put me closest to the right exit, but I'd never taken the A train to Times Square and I figured it was all the same, and anyway, I was already hot from hauling ass ten blocks in a wool suit and cashmere sweater, so I neglected his advice and got spat out with the hordes four blocks away from the office. Four blocks may not seem like a lot, and in fact four blocks is just a nice little jaunt, but for perhaps the first time in my life, I loathed everyone else on the crowded sidewalk. Day one, a city stripe earned.

Do you know how thrilling it is for me to order a bagel in New York? I should note here that I grew up on the plastic bags of Lender's that my mom got out of the freezer aisle, which were less an actual bagel and more just a puffed wheel of Wonder bread with a hole in the middle. I realized as I darted through the crowd that I could get a bagel for breakfast, and every day if I wanted to, and a good bagel too. I ducked into the Lucky Star Café across the street from the *Times* building and ordered an everything bagel with cream cheese, not toasted, and a large coffee, light. I listened to the street while I waited: cabs honking, the iron sides of a delivery truck clattering as it lumbered past. I took my aluminum-wrapped breakfast and a deep breath and crossed the street to 229. It was time to get down to business.

EARLY SPRING WAS the cusp of the busy time for wedding announcements, which was why they brought me on in the first place. I joined a crew of stalwarts, and the captain of the ship, one of the most sought men in New York journalism, was a tall, quiet man named Ira Goetz. He certainly wasn't a figurehead of the *Times*. Almost no one asked him to join public events or write guest columns, appear on CNN, or speak at the Aspen Institute, which had been the bread and butter of so many people I worked with in Washington. He didn't appear regularly in society photos, or really ever. But he occupied a position that, for a certain time in people's lives, held tremendous power, and he could confer immense joy. He was the society editor.

But I should back up. When the clerical supervisor told me what I'd be doing for the spring and summer, I didn't really understand what a great gig it was. I thought I'd be answering the phones on a news desk, sorting mail, delivering morning papers to news editors, that sort of thing. With luck, I thought, maybe I'd pick up some reporting assignments. The *Times* wedding announcements had only entered my brain as something to read when I flipped through the Sunday Styles on Sundays. Occasionally I saw someone I thought I recognized from boarding school, and every so often I read a name like du Pont or Vanderbilt, or a double-barreled last name that sounded like something out of an Evelyn Waugh novel. They weren't the wedding announcements I was used to. The *Times* has a strict formula that they've stuck to for decades: names, ages, occupations, educational background, parents, parents' occupations, and, only if it's relevant, the bride's or groom's prominent ancestors, like a president or the first chairman of Standard Oil. Every so often, and I mean like once a summer, I'd read about someone's great-grandmother's veil that she decided to wear for her own wedding at the chapel where her great-grandmother first wore that same veil. Each of these bits of data is a signifier, and research bears it out: for example, a woman who indicates that she'll keep her last name is far more likely to be better educated, and far more likely to be a feminist.

Of course, it wasn't always like this. The first piece of content that can be identified as a wedding announcement appeared in the *New-York Daily Times* on September 18, 1851: "In Trinity Church, Fredonia, on the 15th, inst., by Rev. T.P. Tyler, JOHN M. GRANT, Esq., of Jamestown, to SARAH, daughter of Hon. JAMES MULLETT of Fredonia." In that same edition, the governor of Pennsylvania empowered his fellow citizens to help capture enslaved Black people who had crossed the border into Maryland and who had, in the course of protecting dozens of other fugitives who had holed up in a barn, shot and killed two of the enslavers in pursuit, who went by the name of Gorsuch. The paper also declared that George P.

Putnam would soon be publishing *The Book of Home Beauty* by Mrs. Kirkland, complete with "twelve elegantly engraved Female Portraits," and that "A Bloomer Costume," otherwise known as a woman wearing pants, had made an appearance on 6th Avenue two days before, but had encountered a group of self-described Conservatives, who had manifested their hostility toward such a progressive movement. This was where Sarah Mullett and John M. Grant, Esq., pledged their troth: a young America with the manners of a preschooler and the morals of a pawnbroker, where enslaved people faced charges of treason for just trying to get free, and where anyone who was not a white man faced diminution and disregard.

By 1865, as many as twenty couples an issue submitted their matrimonial announcements to the *Times*, which, as with the notice for the Grants, gave only the barest of details. These were the plebeians, however—those who did not live on Washington Square. For at least twenty-five years, newspapers had already been in the practice of reporting and writing about society and royal weddings, the details of which set trends for years and decades to come. Take, for example, Queen Victoria's 1840 wedding to Prince Albert of Saxe-Coburg and Gotha. British newspapers breathlessly reported the details of their sumptuous wedding, including a three-hundred-pound wedding cake, and more important, her cream satin dress embellished with

Honiton lace and orange blossoms. Before then, most women chose colored wedding dresses, and those who wore white at all were known to have the money and wherewithal to keep their white clothing clean. Through the power and reach of the press, Victoria changed all that, influencing women across the decades and centuries to choose white or cream for their wedding dress, and it had nothing to do with bridal purity.

Over the nineteenth century, reports of weddings, parties, and social affairs became more entrenched in what newspapers were expected to provide their readers. By the 1880s, society journalism was well established, and society reporters thronged every major bridal event in New York. While old-line society families may have feigned horror at the infiltration of the dirty masses into their well-protected enclaves, they wanted that publicity to keep power. The write-ups of society weddings were, on their surface, details of wedding parties, veils, trousseaus from Paris, and wedding tours to the Riviera. But what they really signaled was a family merger: a connection made legal in the eyes of the church, and state, that consolidated social, political, and academic power between families.

Consider, for example, the 1880 wedding of Miss Mary Virginia Smith, known as Jennie, to Fernando Yznaga. Miss Smith's sister, the former Alva Erskine Smith, was married to William Kissam Vanderbilt, a grandson of

WELL-KNOWN PEOPLE MARRIED.

MISS MARY V. SMITH WEDDED TO FERNANDO YZNAGA AT W. K. VANDERBILT'S

A very quiet but elegant wedding attracted a handful of representatives of New-York society to Oakdale, Long Island, yesterday. The bride was Miss Mary Virginia Smith, sister of Mrs. William K. Vanderbilt, and the groom Mr. Fernando Yznaga, son of Fernando A. Yznaga, the Broad-street broker, and brother of the beautiful Miss Yznaga, whose marriage to Lord Mandeville, not long ago, will be remembered. It was intended that the affair should be very private, and the number of invitations issued was, consequently, very limited. They were distributed mostly among the immediate friends and relatives in this City, for whose accommodation a special train containing two drawing-room cars left Hunter's Point at 11 o'clock A. M., arriving at Oakdale just in time to witness the ceremony, which took place at 12:30. A delightful drive through the woods for a mile or more, past cozy farm-houses, brought the guests into a broad park of some hundreds of acres, lying upon the margin of a broad river curving lazily in and out on its way to the sea. In the midst of this ground, bordered with clumps of oak, pine, and willow trees, gnarled and picturesque, and dotted here and there with clumps of flower-bearing shrubs, stands a many-gabled and gayly-painted country house—one of the largest on Long Island. The southern margin of the lawn is defined by a high tower rising out of the thick Autumn leafage and by long lines of low greenhouses and pretty cottages of workmen and other employes. The mansion fronts upon the river, on which lies a small steamer, the Mosquito, the only symbol of busy civilization that disturbs the quiet landscape of "Idle Hour."

A few stages, impressed into service from the Summer hotels for miles around, waited at the depot to take the guests to "Idle Hour," whose interior was, in the meantime, being decorated with floral emblems from the adjacent greeneries. A large bell of white roses and camellias depended from the carved oak ceiling, and clumps of exotic ferns and palms leaned against the oaken wainscoting of the broad hall and parlors on the first floor, which are so arranged that they can all be thrown together on festal occasions. The landing of the broad staircase, from which one looks out through painted window-panes upon the southern landscape, was set round with ferns and flowers, half concealing the stained glass that formed the background. On either hand of the main entrance stood sentinel clumps of tall, broad-leaved ferns, and the steps to the broad veranda were picketed with Oriental palms, whose fleshy boles were tipped with heavy, drooping blades of verdure.

The ceremony was performed by the Rev. Reuben Riley, of St. Mark's Chapel, Islip, according to the usual ritual. The bride wore a brilliant toilet of white satin, and the bridesmaids— Miss Mimi Smith, the sister of the bride, and Miss Emily Yznaga, the younger sister of the groom—were in simple toilets of white muslin, with white veils. The gentlemen present were in simple morning dress, with or without gloves, according to their fancy, and the host himself was in a simple costume of the same description. The granduncle of the host, the old Commodore's brother, Mr. Jerome, Mr. Webb, son of James Watson Webb, of this City, Mr. Morton, and a few others, with the younger friends, relatives, and associates of the parties, composed the circle. The formal reception was not long, however; the collation was soon served, and after that the music of the band stationed behind a screen of ferns in the rear of the drawing-room got into the feet of the younger members of the party, and they danced and waltzed until 4:30 P. M., when all went to the train and returned home. The groom and bride had already taken their departure on the 4:17 P. M. train for this City, handfuls of rice being thrown after them as they drove away in the carriage. Mr. Neilson, of the Four-in-Hand Club, was there, and drove into the lawn just as the ceremony was beginning.

The New York Times
Published: September 23, 1880
Copyright © The New York Times

Commodore Cornelius Vanderbilt, whose father, William Henry Vanderbilt, in 1877, became the richest American after he took over the Commodore's fortune. (At this point, the Vanderbilts were still considered interlopers by New York's upper crust, although they were fast on their way to being as rich as Croesus and as powerful as any Astor. In fact, when Caroline Schermerhorn Astor died, Alva, who by that point had dropped the Vanderbilt and married a Belmont, took her place as one of the leaders of the Four Hundred, Ward McAllister's list of the people in New York society who really mattered.) Fernando Yznaga, quite the man about town, was a Cuban sugar heir who knew what he was doing. Right after he married Miss Smith, he was awarded a seat on the New York Stock Exchange and a big job with a big banking firm—"Presto!" noted the *Times*. And even after they divorced six years later, he stayed close enough with Vanderbilt to be considered part of the "Three Vanderbilt Musketeers," a fact that was mentioned with no small amount of pride in his obituary in 1901, after he died of diphtheria. Anyway, the Smith women knew what they were doing too. Upon the occasion of Jennie's second marriage, to a cousin of Louis Comfort Tiffany, the *Times* had this to say: "It is understood that Mr. Yznaga settled a handsome income on the bride of yesterday, but she will not need this, as Mr. Tiffany is an exceedingly wealthy man."

Is that news? Not really. Is it gossip? Absolutely. For decades and centuries, people—women, really—have established, gained, and consolidated power through marriage, and wedding announcements bear that out. Edith Wharton knew that gossip was and is power, and those who hold the most knowledge hold the strings of power. Understanding bank balances and legal this-and-that is important, to be sure—but families are made and destroyed by the stories we tell, and wedding announcements are no different. Which brings me to my other point: even though New York society families may have eschewed these write-ups in private, they used them to publicly signal where their money was going and what their priorities were. In *The Age of Innocence*, May Welland's mother might have been horrified to know that reporters would be gathered just outside the church awning, to report on May's Parisian bridal gown and who among the blue bloods was in attendance. But those selfsame blue bloods were rapidly, furtively using the press—behind drawing room doors and in public—to further their own interests.

Of course, times are different now. But they aren't *that* different. The *Times* wedding announcements are signalers not just of social class but of intellectual and economic achievement. The du Ponts and Rockefellers still pop up occasionally, but for the most part, the pages are filled with a new guard of American society: still pretty white, but way more Jewish and far less straight than they used to be.

David Brooks wrote a lot about this in his book *Bobos in Paradise*: since the Gilded Age, the pages, and the announcements, have traced the evolution of America's ruling class from a consolidation among a hundred or so ruling families, to an ambitious establishment created by those who have gained entry on merit.

Well, sort of. Merit is as merit does. The announcements largely feature white upper-middle-class people, which means, of course, that they were born with at least one leg up. I will tell you that I can count on one hand the number of Black couples that I wrote about during my tenure on the desk, despite Ira's attempts to reach out to Black churches and community groups. This was a historical failing and not one that had improved much with time. The *Times* did manage to cover the nuptials of Ida B. Wells, the anti-lynching journalist who the newspaper's editorial writers, seeking to justify lynching just the year before, had called "a slanderous and nasty-minded mulatress." Her wedding in Chicago to Ferdinand L. Barnett, "a local colored attorney of prominence," warranted a notice on the front page of the edition of June 28, 1895. It was a remarkable development for a Black woman born into enslavement and who was herself, as Nikole Hannah-Jones later noted in the *Times*, "by definition, remarkable." The nine-line item abutted another bit of society news: the second wife of Fernando Yznaga, the former Mabel Elizabeth Wright, was holed up with her artist father in Yankton, South Dakota, and seeking a divorce.

Ira was certainly not blind to the lily-whiteness of his pages, but, as he repeatedly pointed out, he couldn't run announcements that weren't submitted. But that's also not entirely true; for the occasional high-profile wedding that could be considered legitimate news, Ira would concoct an announcement that drew on details that were known in the press already, and he would then play cat-and-mouse with the couple's publicity team, who of course knew that all press—especially wedding press—is good press.

Until I started reading the *Times*'s announcements, I only paid attention to the ones I read in the papers I grew up reading. I loved the details. Every so often, I pulled out my mom's wedding announcement that my grandmother had clipped from the *Fayetteville Observer-Times* on April 10, 1977: "Escorted by her father, the bride wore a traditional candlelight chiffon over taffeta enhanced with French lace. Her veil of candlelight illusion was held by a Juliet cap. She carried a nosegay of spring flowers." I already knew that the candlelight chiffon dress was rotting in my grandparents' guest room, and the nosegay was full of flowers that my mom didn't want. Their engagement announcement from the *Birmingham News* that March was more informative, to my mind: "Of much interest here was the engagement announced Sunday of Nancy Ann Riggs of

Fayetteville, N.C. and Mark McConnico Doty of Raleigh, N.C." Let's pause here to question that whole "of much interest" thing, but fine. "The groom, son of Mr. and Mrs. Mercer M. Doty, also graduated at North Carolina State. His father grew up in Birmingham and his grandmother, Mrs. Luther Doty, whom friends call Bill, still lives here." That's all true, although Bill, whose given name was Willie, was at that point knocking at death's door.

But my favorite family announcement was that of my great-grandmother Virginia Burke, who married Albert Burchett on May 31, 1927, in Chattanooga, Tennessee. The *Chattanooga News* reported that the bride wore blue and her mother wore white, and the new Mr. and Mrs. Burchett were to spend their honeymoon on a tour of the Deep South, stopping in Biloxi, New Orleans, and Gulfport, before making their home at 1968 Vinton Avenue in Memphis. For traveling, the *News* noted, "Mrs. Burchett wore an ailleur of blue and white combined. Her close fitting hat of navy blue ribbon was ornamented with a cluster of rich red cherries. All accessories were of tan."

Again, not one tiny detail of this whole thing even remotely approaches news the way I was taught. But society news was women's news, and when women were shut out of public affairs and public life, then they had to effect change in subtler ways: fashion, for example, or cooking. They held parties to raise money for charities and garden clubs, and those parties were covered in the society news sections. The connections made in these pages reflected the priorities of women in the towns that these papers covered. And the details of these announcements signified something else important: it announced to the world that this woman had gained legitimacy on the arm of a man. She had made it through her teen years more or less unsullied, and any dirt left on her record had been washed away by the cleansing waters of a wedding. She had arrived, no matter the path.

One more thing about this: while white women were relegated to the women's pages, Black people in the South were relegated to the Negro news pages in white-owned and -operated newspapers, if they deigned to include it at all. Until the mid-1960s, the news of Black people, even prominent business leaders, was often printed only in pages or sections segregated from the rest of the paper. That included wedding announcements, church doings, and social events that, had they been held by white people, were regularly reported on in the main pages. These pages were often only distributed to Black businesses in Black neighborhoods, with the tacit acknowledgment that their weddings and marriages, lives and deaths, were unimportant to the white community at large. In 1969, a Black couple sued the

Montgomery Advertiser for refusing to print their announcement in the paper's Sunday society news section. The paper claimed that the announcement would appear in its Thursday "Negro News" section, and the plaintiffs said that its refusal to include their notice among the white announcements was a violation of their First and Fourteenth Amendment rights. The court ruled against the plaintiffs, but the newspaper changed its policy anyway.

The changes on the society pages often filtered to the rest of the paper. In the 1960s, Vivian Castleberry, the women's page editor at the *Dallas Morning Herald*, said she looked at society with a small *s* instead of a capital *S*, understanding that the real stories didn't usually happen at the Dallas Country Club. She fought against the paper's policy to exclude photos of Black brides, writing memo after memo to the publisher to extinguish the practice. She finally got it changed in 1968, and photos of Black people began to appear in other sections of the paper, and not just for alleged crimes, which was the main way white editors saw fit to include them.

Whether or not Ira thought about the history of the announcements, he knew that what he did was a chronicle of the times in which we lived. They show us how we are, and sometimes they show us how we could—or should—be. In 2002, nowhere in the United States was gay marriage legally recognized, and same-sex couples were stuck joining themselves together for life via civil unions. *Obergefell v. Hodges* wouldn't reach the Supreme Court until 2015, and Massachusetts, the first state to recognize same-sex marriages, didn't open the marriage bureau doors to gay people until May 2004, a month after I started writing the announcements.

The *Times* sees itself as an agent of truth, not necessarily an agent of change. But in this instance, the brass knew it had to harness the change that was coming. The first same-sex wedding announcement in the *Times* appeared on September 1, 2002: Daniel Gross and Steven Goldstein, who had been together for ten years, affirmed their partnership in two ceremonies, one in Montreal and the other just over the U.S. border, on an island in Vermont. They had waited for Reform Judaism to support rabbis who performed same-sex unions, and for Vermont to give legal recognition to civil unions. (They split in 2015 after twenty-three years together; as David Dunlap pointed out in the *Times*, they're only human.)

The *Times* wasn't necessarily holding on to a homophobic practice for the sake of being homophobic. One of the basic rules that we lived by on the desk was that the wedding announcement had to appear on the same weekend, or at least in the same basic time frame, as the marriage was declared legal by the state, and that rule kept gay unions off the pages for a long time. The rule was a bummer for many of the straight brides and grooms we wrote about. A lot of them got married in the Caribbean, and while resorts that operate as wedding factories will help them in the licensing process, it's a whole lot easier to do the legal thing at City Hall before getting on that plane to Montego Bay and hold what a lot of people consider the real binding ceremony, religious or not, when you get down there. But that was the thing that Ira said I should ask first, before anything else, not even before spell-checking the names: "Is this your *only* legal wedding with this person?" If there was a pause on the line, then you knew what was about to happen.

Here's the way it went: each week, Ira would sift through the announcement submissions that had been printed out by the desk's faithful secretary, April, a blond woman from Long Island who arrived on the 8:17 from Syosset and left on the 5:14. She had two kids and a husband, and a nose for bargains; she used to take a long lunch hour to hit up Fortunoff for ornaments during its after-Christmas sale. She was the one who held the keys to the submissions inbox as well as to the mail, although few people by that point submitted their announcements via the postal service. Anyway, she printed them all out and stapled them together with hard copies of their engagement photos and passed them on to Ira for his perusal. In the high season, the stack could include up to two hundred submissions, and the print paper could only accommodate forty to forty-five, max, and fewer when printed ad sales started dipping. And that leads me to the question that I know you bought this book to answer: how does someone get their announcement into the *New York Times*?

Sometimes it was just as easy as submitting it, being honest, and answering all the questions. Really. Especially during the low season, when the volume is lower, it was easier to get Ira's attention. But when the corn was high and weddings were plentiful, Ira had a lot to choose from. I asked him over and over how he chose, and he always shrugged and said, "I just look for people who have done things."

But it was more complicated than that. Ira had the New York Social Register in his head and could pick out the names that Meant Something, and not just the names that landed in the tabloids. We all knew the Astors, the Kennedys, the Bloomberg girls, the Vanderbilts. But Ira knew Newport and Palm Beach society; he knew who was friends with or could get a personal message to the publisher, and he knew who a Sulzberger was likely to run into at a party on the Upper East Side or in the Hamptons. Not long after

I joined the desk, I opened my week's stack to find a purple engraved notecard with two addresses, one on Fifth Avenue and one on Bellevue Avenue in Newport. It was addressed to Bill Cunningham, that wonderful, wondrous photographer who was also in the business of cataloging society with a lowercase *s* but moved easily among the rich and powerful. *Dear Mr. Cunningham*, it began in an old lady's crabbed script. *I am enclosing a notice of my granddaughter's coming marriage on June 5th for release on Sunday, June 6th, in the Social section of The New York Times. Always Very Sincerely, The Heiress.*

"Who is this?" I waved the card at Ira.

"Ah," he said. "Your entrée into high society."

The Heiress, whose real name I had never in my life heard, was a socialite and Republican fund-raiser who occupied both a penthouse apartment that overlooked Central Park and a mansion on Bellevue Avenue—"the *ocean* end of Bellevue Avenue," Ira assured me—with twelve bedrooms, a forbidding iron gate, and stern portraits of America's white founders in every room. (I found a real estate listing for it once, and no, I am not going to give you the address, but it is a place in which women didn't walk across the inlaid marble floors; they glided.) One of her many granddaughters was getting married in Newport, and while the Heiress's poor health was keeping her away from most of the festivities, ensuring that the Junior Heiress's wedding announcement would be in the paper was the least she could do.

"But it's late," I said, looking at the date. The wedding was scheduled for that weekend, which was bumping up against deadline, according to the guidelines that had been presented to me as law. Ira preferred—and the rules stated—that submissions land at least a month before the actual wedding.

"Yes, but we should do this one," Ira said.

"It's not like this woman is a senator or something," I said.

Ira looked at me. "No, she's more important than that."

I went down the Google hole and realized that the Heiress was a cross between Louisa van der Luyden and Mrs. Manson Mingott. She was a widow, fabulously wealthy, and moved in glamorous circles. But she used her homes in Palm Beach and Newport as enclaves of decision making, for New York high society and for Republican circles, which share space. She was truly one of the last grandes dames, one of the few women who actually looked good in Lilly Pulitzer, and she commanded respect and the ears of both the White House and the Astors, with whom she had been connected her entire life.

The bride herself was a lovely, unassuming woman who had done a master's at the Courtauld Institute in London. I was soon to understand that names like Courtauld and Winterthur, the du Ponts' place in Delaware, would pop up with frequency in wedding announcements for the old guard, no matter how descended they might be. Anyway, she was marrying a nice Frenchman who likely made gobs of money, not that that really mattered because she didn't really need more money, but if the Heiress's family fell on hard times, the bride would be taken care of. Thank God.

The Heiress wasn't the only person to send a kind but straightforward note essentially demanding placement in the *Times*. Ira and April got boxes of candy, handwritten notes from the publisher, calls from senators' offices, calls from the White House. Ira faced a lot of internal pressure too. Newsroom brass would come up to the fifth floor—a windowless, airless, beige room that smelled weird on Monday mornings—and rap on Ira's desk. It was fun to watch. He would spin around from his computer to see who had come knocking, and it was almost always someone pleading a friend's case, because no one just happened to wander up to the fifth floor without an express purpose in mind. Sometimes he said yes, and sometimes he said no. It was a way of flexing his power. For a mild family man from New Jersey, saying no to Important People just because he could was as venomous as Ira ever let himself get.

Anyway, that explains the rich people: money plus

power equals announcement above the fold with photo. But what about the people who didn't frequent the Newport clubs, or summer in Maine and winter in Mustique? Ira had been well trained by his predecessors, who looked for proximity to New York, the schools they went to, the firms they worked at, the public service they'd done (we were suckers for anyone who had served in the military), the books they'd written, the mountains they'd scaled, and the people they'd been descended from. Often it wasn't the bride or groom who was of interest; it was one or two or all of the in-laws. I wrote announcements for people who were, let's say, auditors, but their mother had written books on tantric sex. Often it tracks that people who do interesting things have children who do interesting things; I assume they hope that's the case, because who wants to believe their child is boring? Heaven forfend that those who considered themselves worthy of a *Times* wedding announcement were actually boring.

And I think that's what it ultimately boiled down to: a little bit of luck, and a little bit of hubris. After all, most of us don't go about our daily lives figuring out how to get into the *Times*. Ninety-nine percent of the time, who cares? But the *Times*'s wedding announcements chronicle American power as it has shifted over time, and who wouldn't want to be identified in some way with that power?

Well, not me, or so I thought. I mean, we were talking

about weddings. They might have been one of my most favorite subjects, but I just didn't see the news value. But as I started talking to these couples, one thing became clear: this was one of the best, most entertaining jobs in the whole building, and by some sheer force of luck, I was sitting in the hot seat. And so even as my own romance was already in a little bit of trouble, I thought, *Oh what the hell. Might as well have some fun this summer.*

CHAPTER 4

The First Season

YOUR NAME IS spelled M-E-L—" I began, but the bride cut me off. "Yes, but I'm known as Mitzi," she said.

"Mitzi? Can you please spell that for me?"

Mitzi, otherwise known as Melanie but whatever, sighed. "You don't know how to spell Mitzi?"

I ignored her tone. "I need to know how *you* spell Mitzi. We check every single name, even the most commonly used names."

"Why can't you just look at my submission?" Mitzi was getting irritated. "I don't have much time for this call."

This was not the most common reaction to this fact-checking call, but after just a few weeks on the desk, I came to expect pretty much anything. Some brides were beyond elated to take my call, and I could practically hear them settling in on their slipcovered sofas with a glass of pinot grigio, ready to gab. Others got nervous and clammed up at the questions, even though they were excited and willing to answer. And a few, like Mitzi of zip code 10021, née Melanie, were irritated by these queries. *How dare you*, her tone proclaimed, *question anything about my existence, when I've already provided that for you on paper?* I should pause to note here that she was a rich white woman, but then, you likely already knew that.

One thing I learned very quickly on the desk: people lie. I knew that, of course, but some people—I should stress not all—who submitted their announcements to the *Times* thought extremely highly of themselves and saw no problem with blowing a little smoke around their accomplishments. A vice president at an investment bank was soon up for his review, and they'd likely make him a director then, so we really should just go ahead and call him a director— in fact, it was sure to happen by the time the thing ran, the very same week he was getting married. Or a woman felt she was owed the *magna* next to the *cum laude* on her college diploma, but it wasn't awarded, and no reason we shouldn't include it; after all, she had been a *very* good student and to her mind had earned it, even if the university believed differently. Sometimes, although very rarely, you caught people in outright lies: they didn't work for Harvard anymore, or they neglected to mention that their dad, a lawyer by profession, had been disbarred and was no longer a partner in the firm. Once, a weddings reporter—not me—discovered that not only was a bride not licensed to practice therapy in the state of New York, or anywhere else for that matter, she had fabricated her academic credentials out of whole cloth. That didn't discourage her from seeing dozens of patients over the years, until she submitted her wedding announcement and got called on her illegal dealings.

For the most part, though, you had people like Mitzi, who was a very valued assistant vice president at her dad's boutique real estate company, which she joined not long after graduation. There's nothing wrong with joining the family business, but Mitzi's printable accomplishments perhaps paled in comparison to those of other couples I was writing about that week. One bride, at twenty-nine a year younger than Mitzi, was a deputy chief of staff in the White House. Another actually was a managing director at Lehman Brothers (I checked it with human resources) and likely handled billions in assets, and she still found time to serve on a few nonprofit boards. Mitzi gave penthouse tours a few times a week and spoke fluently of private elevators, oak-paneled libraries, and butler's pantries. I find no fault with being a real estate agent; I have enlisted the services of many and, on balance, found them to be mostly delightful. Also, one day I too would like to enjoy unfettered river views from my living room and a rainfall shower in my marble bathroom. But this woman's effrontery raised my hackles, and my own snobbery that had been bolstered by the past weeks of weddings work. I wondered how on earth Mitzi and her fiancé, Trey, had made the cut this week.

Mitzi sighed. "*M, I, T*—did you get that—*Z, I*," she said, simply exhausted by the effort it took to talk to me. I imagined her doing this call in her manicurist's chair while a masked Korean woman scrubbed at her gel polish and spoke unsparingly of Mitzi to the other manicurists.

"Thank you so much!" I said. We moved on to other details: her age, her relatively short academic career, her title at the real estate office ("I am an assistant vice president!" "Yes, and you have that title because you work as a real estate agent?" Silence. "Yes. But my card says assistant vice president"). I ticked off the facts that needed checking on the paper scrawled over with Ira's red felt pen. *FAMOUS IN SOME FASHION?* he'd scrawled next to a few names on the submission. *DIRECT DESCENDANT? WHAT PROOF CAN HE PROVIDE????* Adding multiple questions marks on a keyboard is one thing, but to actually write them out takes commitment to the craft.

The thing that had gotten Mitzi and Trey into the pages that week was not who they were, but who their people were. The original submission included five lines about the bride herself, and fifteen about her parents and ancestors.

Same thing with the groom, who was a first-year associate with a fancy law firm that showed up in the news pages frequently. (It also included an engagement photo in which the pair were wearing matching camel-hair coats with a single Burberry scarf wrapped around their necks, for what Scottish cashmere has joined together, let no man put asunder.) Mitzi's family were minor stalwarts of the Upper East Side and the lower reaches of Connecticut, and their family names, including Mitzi's first and second middle names, were spackled all over public buildings and road signs in Greenwich and Westport. Trey was descended on his mother's side from one of the men who founded Connecticut and, on his father's, from the postmaster general under President John Quincy Adams. I wasn't sure why I should care about a postal service worker who lived two centuries ago, and I was directed to find out from Trey if this person was of any significance other than, presumably, having been in the same room at least once with John Quincy Adams, the lesser of the Adams men. According to the information provided, the bride was a great-great-niece of someone who was present when General Lee surrendered to General Grant at Appomattox. This whole thing was a nice history lesson, but it wasn't necessarily one for the Wedding pages.

I found these lineages fascinating, especially when Ira decided they were important enough to be included in the pages. The basic rule for inclusion was direct lineage that could be proven, no matter what: no uncles and aunts, no cousins twice removed, even if they were George Washington himself. By *proven*, Ira meant membership in the Mayflower Society, family Bibles, something on a legitimate piece of paper that established the applicant's bloodline straight back to the person in question. Beyond the instantly recognizable names in American history, it got a little fuzzy and subject to Ira's whims. Granddaughter of a president of the New York Stock Exchange? Sure. Great-great-granddaughter of a Marx brother? Obviously. Descendant of one of the brothers who invented Mountain Dew? Maybe, but only if there's room on the page.

You will of course note that most of these great ancestors were white men, often Protestant, generally mustachioed, some bald, and all eventually very rich. Great female ancestors were rarely mentioned, unless they were New York or Newport society doyennes, and they were included in the submissions with their married names, their actual selves obscured by the *Mrs.* It was the rich white men who got name-checked in these things, and for one reason: while the women of the Gilded Age were perhaps the ones who decided who was in and who was out in society, the men's names were still chiseled on granite across the city. So for our purposes, the men mattered more. Mrs. Manson Mingott, after all, was still Mrs. Manson Mingott. Also, let's be real: if these women weren't fairly recognized for their achievements when they were alive, no way in hell were they going to appear as a minor character in the Wedding pages.

The lineages, and the last names, were clues to the true transactions that took place in these state-sanctioned events of the heart. A story: a few years ago, some friends of mine who got lucky in the tech industry bought a $2 million house from a couple whose occupations were somewhat inscrutable. They had moved into the house a couple years before and done a deep renovation that included hand-tiled everything and a stove that cost more than a Subaru. Not long after, they decided to move elsewhere and sold the house at a modest profit. One of the sellers was a part-time writing teacher, which didn't explain the six-burner custom La Cornue that my friends gleefully acquired in the purchase. Fine, you never know about people's incomes and bank accounts. But I got curious. It turns out that this part-time writing teacher was descended through her mother from the founder of a major multinational pharmaceutical maker, so of course she could parse sentences by day and make vegan omelets on her Subaru stove at night. She was fully funded, and so was her partner and their children, by the world's self-perpetuating ill health.

This lineage, should you care to trace it yourself (just kidding, I'm not telling you who these people are), is all revealed in a few decades of *Times* wedding announcements. The writing teacher's mother's announcement had been in the *Times*, as had her grandmother's, and both of these unions merged families of Northeastern wealth and power. The pharma person wasn't the only remarkable character in the writing teacher's lineage. There was a high-ranking government official during the Kennedy years, a high-powered Democratic fund-raiser and socialite, and a few artists of middling achievement and quality who, it's probably safe to assume, were well funded by the pharma guy's work. None of this is revelatory, of course. Inherited wealth is a pillar of the white capitalistic world as we know it, and certainly the mode of financial solvency for many of the couples I wrote about. Never mind their political affiliations, the coast they lived on, or where they taught: if they didn't have to do anything for money, then someone else's money was working for them.

Consider, for example, the case of the bride who couldn't quite tell me what she did for a living. One week, my assignments included the announcement for the daughter of a man, a billionaire real estate investor, whose name is chiseled onto at least two buildings in Boston. Now, one of my main charges, when speaking with these brides and grooms, was to ascertain what their jobs were. "We need to know what they do every day for money," Ira would say, which led me into the weeds on many occasions. "I assign

CUSIP numbers," one bride told me, not a little proudly, when I asked what she did at a major trading firm. In case you don't know what that is, and there's not much reason you should, a CUSIP number is a nine-character label that serves to identify financial instruments that— Oh, never mind. Anyway, the point is, we had to know what the work was behind the title.

Ira's eyebrows always shot up when one of the people in question called themselves a freelance writer, and that was all they did. Unless you're a superstar and Anna Wintour holds a cover line for you on each month's *Vogue* cover, it's awfully hard to make ends meet on a dollar a word, especially in a city where the rent is too damn high. So when I had a freelance writer on the phone, I always probed a little further, which sometimes felt dirty; after all, as a private citizen, how and where they got their money was no business of mine. But they had opened themselves up to the *Times*, and so I had to earn my money by finding out where they got theirs.

This freelance writer in question was, and is, a lovely person. But even the nicest of people can get a little testy when questioned about their choices, and Ira made me call the bride back after our first interview to figure out what she did for money. The thing is, he already knew: her dad made more money in a year than she could spend in a lifetime, so why should she toil in a cubicle job in an airless office building, assigning nine-character codes to bank transactions made by and for other people? She wrote a freelance piece here and there for a magazine that chronicled doings on Martha's Vineyard, and other than that, she decorated her townhouse in Beacon Hill, planned her wedding, and enjoyed being generous with what she had. And that was a lot. But I still had to call.

"Mary Elizabeth," I said, "I'm really sorry, but I just need a little more information about what you do."

"What I do for what?" she said pleasantly.

"Well . . . what you do for money."

There was a cold pause, of ire and disbelief. "I told you, I'm a freelance writer. I write for *The Vine* and a few other places."

"Yes, but do you make a living off that?" I cringed as I asked the question, because I knew the answer too. This was miserable.

"I mean," she said, and stopped. "Cate, you know who my dad is."

Thank God she said that. "I do, of course. But we just have to tell people what it is that you do with your days."

Mary Elizabeth snorted. "I guess you can't write that I play tennis and do volunteer work."

"We can include your volunteer work, and it's impressive." It was; the woman served on every under-thirty board in New England. "But editors here always need to make sure that we're representing the whole person, and that means your profession."

More silence. "I get that. I do. It's just—"

I was putting this woman in an impossible situation. If she told me on the record that, well, she just didn't have to or want to work full-time, then that would have been an admission of weakness. And if she lied to me, it would have been worse. This interrogation was somehow belittling her as a human. It's true that she could have divested herself of all her dad's earnings, moved to the middle of nowhere, and explored the meaning of life from the inside of a yurt, but that sounds miserable and, in the long run, would likely contribute less to society than her giant yearly donations to the Boston Public Garden. I knew she felt demeaned and small—and all this, four days before she was to be married. I mean, the woman was a Harvard graduate, was raised with every single advantage on earth and had literally billions at her disposal, and, despite all that, radiated humility and honest generosity.

"You know what, I shouldn't have asked," I said. "I have everything I need. You go get married, and I am so happy for you, Mary Elizabeth. I hope everything goes wonderfully."

"Are you sure? I can send you some of my clips," she said, in complete earnest. "I have a piece in *The Vine* next month."

"No, no, it's fine," I said. "I've seen your work. Please, forget this phone call happened."

We hung up, and I walked over to Ira's desk. "Mary Elizabeth Magliozzi is a freelance magazine writer," I said. He raised an eyebrow at me and wiggled his mustache.

"Yes, but that's how she makes money?" he asked.

"I mean, she makes some money doing that," I said. "But you and I both know that she has more cash in a cereal box hidden in the kitchen than I make in a year. She doesn't need to work."

"I know that, but how does she spend her days?" Ira was on a tear about this particular Mary Elizabeth Magliozzi. He did this from time to time; he was king of bees in the bonnet.

"Honestly? She plays tennis, serves on boards"—I pointed to her lengthy submission on his desk—"and right now is planning her wedding. She has a piece coming out next month in a magazine. Maybe she'll have a few kids soon. I don't know. I mean, she's fucking rich. What would you do if you were a billionaire's daughter?"

Ira laughed out loud and held up his hands. "Fine, fine," he said. "If you think that's good enough."

"I do," I said. "But maybe don't include the tennis part."

I grabbed my wallet and headed to the elevator bank for some air and a coffee. On the ride down, I chewed over what had just transpired: a very nice, very rich woman had been baffled when I asked her what she did for money, and that conversation had made us both feel a little icky. She loved her fiancé, and she had a good time in her life. Who was I—who was the *Times*—to question how she spent her days?

Ira would say that these announcements were part of the public record, so we had to be clear and accurate—and the couples also opened themselves up to it. After all, these people, even the nicest among them, were signaling to the world via their announcements that they were in love, they were about to join the married elite, and, above all, they belonged in society. They meant something to someone, and to the world.

I hurried through the lobby and out the revolving door, and bumped straight into Michael, the guy who I'd been emailing with before moving, the one who used *compunction* correctly. I'd only seen him a few times outside the building, but he always had his face in a book, even walking down the street. These were the days before iPhones, before white plastic cords sprouted from every pair of ears on the sidewalk. He clapped the pages of his Stephen King novel together and waved when he saw me. "Hi!" he said, shoving his book into his shoulder bag. We moved away from the door to get out of the way. "Where are you headed?"

"Going to get an iced coffee," I said. "I just had a not-great interview and thought I needed some air. And it's nice out." It *was* nice out. I looked up to the blue sky peeking between the buildings and thought: *New York does a nice spring.*

Michael fidgeted with his bag. I noticed he'd put gel in his hair, which struck me as not quite right, and he smelled like the entrance to the Macy's cologne counter. "Well, I'm about to be late," he said. "But I was wondering—I have to work in Washington in a couple of weeks, and I was hoping I could pick your brain about the bureau. Who the jerks are and all that. Lunch, maybe?"

"Sure. Tuesday or Wednesday?"

"Great. Have you been to the Westway?" I shook my head, and Michael lit up. "Oh, man. We have to go there. It's where Jerry Seinfeld and Larry David came up with the idea for the show." I could tell he was very proud of this piece of knowledge, and thrilled that he could flex his New York trivia to a recent arrival.

"That would be great. Just let me know when. Want me to bring you a coffee?"

"Gross, no," he said. "I mean, no, thank you."

I shrugged. "Suit yourself. Don't be late!" I skipped down the street to the bodega, and I knew he watched me go before rushing upstairs. Michael had the potential of a good friend, I thought. He was generous and funny, and I liked how he was always reading, but not in a pretentious way. I have my own opinions about Stephen King, but the man wasn't signaling with Foucault or, heaven help me, Jonathan fucking Franzen. I grabbed my iced coffee, watched the clouds between the buildings, and wondered what I'd do if I were Mary Elizabeth Magliozzi.

AS I DELVED into the love stories of Mitzi and Trey, and Mary Elizabeth and what turned out to be her first husband, my own love story, already in peril, shattered like a plate on the kitchen floor. It started off with a slow roll, and then we realized that we didn't want to keep the dish from its inevitable demise as gravity caught hold. The crash was loud, sharp, and irreversible.

You know when you're comfortable enough with someone not to have to talk, and you revel in that comfort, understanding that what you have is rare and deserving of respect and preservation? Adnan and I had that, sort of. We certainly spent a lot of meals in the quiet, unless of course someone else was around. We lit up together when someone was there to distract us from the faint whiff of misery that blew when we were alone in each other's company. But we had kind of run out of things to talk about, and so instead we talked at length about how delicious whatever we were eating was. I once waxed rhapsodic about pierogi at a Polish joint in Greenpoint just to have something to discuss; the pierogi were fine, but not necessarily worth the airtime. We'd also started to just kind of dislike each other. The dislike was an interesting thing to watch grow. It blossomed like weeds on the side of the road. It made my brain fuzzy and my chest heavy, just like the ragweed it resembled.

You may be wondering at this point what we were still doing with each other. It remains a good question. But you have to understand two things: one, we remembered how enamored we had been with each other at one point, and that still held us captive. My last months of college were Valhalla-like because we spent so much time lolling about together, lingering over coffee and our last studies before opening the door to the rest of our lives. My household full of journalism students got the Sunday *Times* for free, and Adnan and I would bring the paper into bed and linger over the Arts section and the magazine, reading the cover stories to each other before we put our feet on the floor. We were two old souls with young, ardent desires, for each other's bodies and brains, and for our own futures, which we both wanted to devour like street food.

But that was then. Once we made it to the future, to the city that we loved and longed for, where we could eat street meat whenever we wanted, the shine had been replaced by a tarnish that deepened all the time. So to my second point: it's possible we may have just been too nice to fail. We didn't want to hurt each other, and we loved each other in a way, even though our rough edges grated. So we kept on being nice, like two old married people refusing to jump ship because of the kids.

That spring was a cool one, cooler than usual. One night we went with Adnan's sister, Noor, and another friend to a hip-hop show at Irving Plaza, and the lineup was insane. The crowd was restless; it was scorching hot in the hall, and a bunch of drunk English soccer lads were linking their arms and ramming other groups up front by the stage. We moved back toward the exits, but the waves of people kept getting pushed harder and harder by these morons, most of whom had stripped down to their sweaty pale chests. I could see the people in the boxes upstairs leaning over, waiting for the eventual fight to break out. And then one of those drunken assholes pushed Noor down, and all hell broke loose.

I bent down to grab her and felt a sharp kick to my legs. We scrambled back to our feet to see Adnan and our friend Will pushing back against the Brits, who seemed to have decided to go after us. I heard Adnan yell, "Stay the fuck away from my sister!" Somehow his shirt and Will's got ripped off in the struggle. The music stopped, and all Noor and I could do was yell at these guys to get away, step back.

Security guards finally pulled the drunks off Adnan and Will, who had someone else's blood on him, and we all staggered to the back, to find something to stop Will's bleeding and to get out of sight of these creeps, who, just like in the movies, were threatening us from over the burly guards' shoulders. The guy on the mic yelled at them: "Are you gonna dance now?" Everyone turned back to the stage.

I looked at Adnan. After three years together, I'd never seen him like this. His entire body was drenched in sweat and pulsed with rage and disbelief. "Should we leave?" Noor asked. Will shook his head. "They might be waiting for us. I want to finish the show anyway. What do you think?" He directed this to Adnan, who'd found a cool spot by the door and was leaning into it for air. "Let's stay," he said quietly, and he wiped his face. "Fuck those guys."

We hung back at the wall and finished out the show, which, minus the fight, is still one of the best concerts I've ever been to. My leg throbbed where I'd been kicked and my foot was on fire, but I ignored it until we gathered our bags at the coat check. "I think you're bleeding," Noor said, pointing down at my foot. We slipped out with the crowd as best we could, and when we got out under the streetlights, I saw that I'd left half my big toenail inside somewhere, and also that someone had stolen my red polka-dot umbrella from my bag.

We hobbled back to the Union Square subway and waited what felt like hours for a Brooklyn-bound train. Adnan had found his shirt, but Will's had been shredded in the fight. The dried blood on his chest caught the eye of several people on the platform, and they moved away from us. We kept looking over our shoulders, waiting to hear the voices of those shitfaced louts, and didn't feel safe until we were back in our apartment. I tried to shower off the sadness, wrapped my toe with gauze and tape, and lay on the bed under the ceiling fan, aching for the calmer hours before the concert. Adnan and Will sat up in the dark living room until the wee hours, stoic and mute in their fury. Right before dawn, Adnan came into the bedroom we shared, and we had silent, mournful sex as the sun rose.

Something had been taken from us that night; maybe it was an illusion of safety, although Adnan, being Muslim and of this country, perhaps never had much of that at all. A sour feeling had permeated everything, and the room felt crowded with anger, but still empty all the same. That evening, we met for dinner at Dojo, a cheap Japanese place in the West Village that had reliably good tempura. I plowed through my salad with the world's best carrot-ginger dressing, and Adnan was still quiet.

"I think I want to travel," he said finally.

"Where do you want to go?" I said calmly, still eating.

He took a breath. "I thought I might want to move abroad,

actually. I'm not sure what I'm doing here, and I think it's time to keep moving."

I put my fork down. "Move abroad for how long?"

He shrugged. "I've been thinking about an English teaching program. Maybe Bolivia, maybe China. But—I think it's time for me to go."

It was my turn to be quiet for a moment. "So you're really talking about leaving New York for good. Like, gone. For good."

"Yeah. Last night, I mean—I don't know. This just isn't my town."

And I am not yours, I thought. *And you are not mine. Crystal clear, this is.*

I picked up a tempura-fried green bean and put it back down; I wasn't in the mood to eat anymore. "How long have you been thinking about this?"

"A couple weeks," he said. "But I thought about it more last night. And today at work, I was just like, *Dude, what am I doing? Why am I even here?*" The money at his magazine job was OK, but it was pretty silly otherwise, although he did have a lot of good celebrity stories.

"When do you want to be gone?" I asked.

"Maybe the fall? Seems like a good time to make a break for it," he said, and I considered what, exactly, he was really making the break from.

"Well, OK," I said. What else was there to say? He was basically telling me that we were done sometime that fall.

"Cate," he said, leaning forward. "You know this needs to happen."

I nodded. "Yes, but I would have liked it to be more on my terms, rather than just being told that this person I love is leaving the country to go elsewhere, and by the way, obviously I can't come, nor would I want to, but still. Yes, this needs to happen. Absolutely."

I decided that I was going to eat because, fuck him, I wasn't wasting my dinner, and I picked up my hijiki burger.

"You know this is suffocating for both of us," he said slowly. "We shouldn't be living like this. You know that."

Stop telling me what I know, I thought. But he was right. Neither of us had been able to breathe in a while, and I knew that the toll it was taking wasn't worth— I didn't even know what it was worth. And I realized something right then: the last evening's fight had been a violent moment of clarity for both of us. He was living a life that was smaller than he needed, and I was holding on to something that needed to be taken off life support. The solution was crystal clear. I reached for his lovely long fingers, and we tangled ours together.

"So what's next?" I said.

We tossed around ideas: the Peace Corps, teaching programs, semester-abroad-type stuff. *I can't believe I'm sounding rational*, I thought. On the train home, we leaned against each other in quiet solace. For three years, I had loved how I was just tall enough to fit in the cavity where his chest met his arm, and I rested there for the ride, knowing I couldn't stay much longer. That night, he stayed up late again, looking online at teaching programs, while I sat behind him on the couch, scanning Craigslist for roommate-needed listings. We were doing what we needed to do.

A month later, I set off on the subway to my new three-bedroom share in Park Slope, yanking my giant blue duffel onto the lumbering G train and regretting that I didn't go to the bathroom before I left. I emerged an hour and a half later at 7th Avenue and 9th Street, right by an old pizza place and a jeweler. I dragged my stuff down to 5th Street, my new block by the old high school, and buzzed the door at 537.

"You're here!" a voice chirped from the brass speaker, and I hauled my stuff up three dank flights of stairs to the top floor, where my new roommates, Rebecca and Layla, were waiting for me. "Pete!" Rebecca yelled over her shoulder to her boyfriend, who made the seven-hour drive from Pittsburgh nearly every weekend. "Come help Cate with her stuff!"

They all helped me in, shoving my bags and me through the front door and into my new bedroom, which over-looked the ginkgo trees and the high school basketball court across the street. The windows were open, and the beginning of summer had brought with it warmer breezes and clearer skies.

"You want a glass of wine?" Rebecca said. "Let's go up-stairs."

She and Layla retrieved an old quilt and four Solo cups, and Pete grabbed a bottle of cheap red wine from the kitchen counter. I used the bathroom, finally, and remem-bered from my first tour of the place the claw-foot tub, the clutter of products, and the mess of towels hanging on the back of the door. I realized that I had missed that deeply while shacking up with Adnan: the mess and camaraderie of women who were totally at ease with each other, and the kindred spirit that it all meant. We went around the land-ing and up one more flight of steps even narrower and creakier than the ones below, and emerged through a banged-up door to the tar-papered rooftop.

"Whoa," I said, and I stopped to take it all in. There in front of me was Brooklyn and all its rooftops and water towers, and beyond, like guardians, rose the Brooklyn and Manhattan Bridges above the East River. The city twinkled at me as it does for everyone, framed by the purply glow of a summer sunset. I heard music playing from a building be-hind us on 4th Street, which, I had been told, was where some pretty famous people lived.

Rebecca handed me a red plastic cup of wine. "So, tell us everything," she said. She and Layla knew a little, but not everything, so we ordered falafel, and Pete got more wine, and I told them about Adnan, my couples, everything. And as we refilled our cups and ran out of pita, and we held our pee until we just couldn't take it because we didn't want to stop talking, I thought: *Here is where I am, just where I should be.* In that moment, even with grief on my skin, all was well. And I knew, as the night breeze filled my lungs with new air, there was more to come.

Chapter 5

There You Are

"M EG IS THROWING up in the bathroom." The whisper shot down the pew.

"What?" I leaned over to my friend Jess, while an old church lady poked out a pre-show tune on a grand piano nearby. We were in a Catholic sanctuary in North Carolina, waiting for our friend Charlie—the same Charlie on whom I had a major crush in 1992—to marry his college love, Anna, who carried God in her soul and Charlie in her hands. They were silly for each other and had been since the first week of freshman year, when they were paired up in orientation. I watched my old friend and his groomsmen milling about up front, pretending to look busy before the ceremony began, all the while sweating in their rented tuxedos. My heart swelled with love and pride for him; the crush had long since subsided, of course, and what was left was a mutual understanding and respect that bridged pretty much every difference you could think of. And God bless Anna for taking him on.

It's not the most complimentary way of thinking about a human, or marriage, but there's a lot of truth in it. We're all messes and fixer-uppers, of course, but deep love demands deep understanding—and if not understanding, then the most profound tolerance and deafness in one ear. You could say that those about to commit their lives to someone else are willing to overlook a whole lot of bullshit to get that ring and that title. I knew a lot about Charlie's bullshit. I didn't know Anna's, but I assumed she was getting the rawer end of the deal.

What you don't know at twenty-four is a lot. Or at least, what I didn't know. I didn't know what home felt like with another person, which is what Charlie and Anna had found with each other. I didn't know that silence actually could be comfortable and didn't need to be filled with non sequiturs about pierogi and tacos. Over the past few months, I'd written about a lot of couples. I'd interviewed brides and grooms, mothers and stepmothers, priests and rabbis and HR workers perplexed as to why a writer for the *Times* wanted to know about someone's exact job title. And because I am nosy, I'd started to ask these brides and grooms about the relationships themselves. How did they get to the point at which marriage was the next right thing?

Which brings me to Meg throwing up in the bathroom of the Catholic church. She was another college friend, and she was deeply in love with Shawn, her boyfriend of less than a year. He'd already given her a ring that she wore on her right hand—a starter ring, they'd called it. Meg was a bit of a mess, and Shawn helped her get her money square, apply to graduate school on time, and just get her feet on the ground. She in turn fit into him like a puzzle piece. There's no such thing as "made for each other," but they were cut from the same stone. Naturally, marriage could be considered the next right thing, and that scared the unholy hell out of Meg. So as she entered the sanctuary and smiled at our very nervous friend waiting up front for his bride, she felt a wave of nausea come over her and hightailed it to the bathroom.

"Is she OK?" I asked Jess. She shrugged. Shawn was sitting at the end of our pew, his neck craned backward, watching for the door to open. Our friend Maggie leaned back from the next pew up and said, "Should I go help her?" She'd started to dig in her clutch for some tissues.

Shawn shook his head. "She said to leave her alone," he said. I could see his own nerves aflame as he waited for the person he adored to come back from vomiting over the idea of lifelong commitment with him. We were all so young—so *young!*—and our little group of college friends, all writers and journalists, had gone from doing shots at our favorite bar to raising our glasses at each other's weddings, and then following up with shots at the bar. Danny and Juliet, ninth-grade sweethearts, were getting married two months later, and her mother had made a huge donation to the parish so she could walk down the aisle to the *Rocky* theme song. Maggie was up next, with a Baptist double-aisle ceremony, soon to be followed by Josie, with a lovely affair at a Victorian inn. Matt and Jess were still hanging on to a senior-year romance that had gone long distance, and he had picked Charlie's brain about buying a ring, even though we all knew that relationship was doomed. Our friend Mike had already officiated enough weddings via his Internet ordination that he'd considered hanging out his shingle and calling himself *Reverend*. He was Jewish, so no way he'd call himself a rabbi. But anyone, especially a Jew, could be a reverend.

Adnan had left the country the week before for Laos, where he'd secured a two-year gig with a Peace Corps–like organization, digging clean-water wells for small villages. The day he left, I watched the clock on my computer until the moment his flight was supposed to leave the gate. Then I went into the dark bathroom near the society desk and cried great, giant gulping sobs. They bounced around the bathroom like coyote yelps in a canyon. They were raw, grating, and probably too dramatic for a cry in the work bathroom. I slumped on the old couch in the lounge to catch my breath and rubbed at my face with my hands to stop crying.

The door creaked open, and in stepped Tracy Ann Walker, a longtime copy editor whose transition had pushed the *Times*—if only just a little—to accept that the times, they were changing, and so were people. Tracy Ann had come out as a woman several years before, and after some protracted brow furrowing, the *Times* gave her a key to a private bathroom on the eleventh floor; for reference, Tracy Ann worked on the fourth floor, so anytime she needed to pee, or adjust her clothing, or take a moment to her own damn self, she had to hike up seven floors. After she had her gender-confirmation surgery, though, she started using the women's bathroom, and if anyone blinked an eye, it would have behooved them to keep it to themselves. Tracy Ann was tall, with close-cropped gray hair, and wore a lot of wool skirts and low square heels, rather like Queen Elizabeth with an old sports injury. Even with hormone therapy, her voice had maintained a bit of brittle bass. I loved seeing her around the floor; her courage to be who she truly was took self-love and commitment, I thought, and I also enjoyed her sweater sets. I wondered if they were Pringle of Scotland, like the queen's.

Tracy Ann looked a bit startled to see me howling on the couch and hustled herself into the stall. I splashed my face with cold water in the sink and looked at my splotchy red cheeks in the mirror, even splotchier and redder than usual. Tracy Ann tottered on her square leather heels out to the sink, washed her manicured hands and dried them, and handed me a tissue from the box on the wall. "Here," she said, not unkindly. "You can't go out there looking like that."

Of all people, Tracy Ann knew what she was talking about. She patted my shoulder with heavy grace and walked out. She was right. I had to get a grip. I sat in the bathroom until the heat drained from my face a little, and thought about what to do next. I knew exactly what to do next.

BUT YOU'RE HERE to read about the wedding announcements, not me crying in the bathroom. I used to work with a woman who cried once a month in the bathroom near the executive editor's office, not because of some gendered bullshit like her period but because monthly budget meetings—this was during the Great Recession of 2008—were so awful and dispiriting that she had to go cry in the bathroom after. I sometimes wished she would have those cries in the middle of the newsroom so we could all join her.

Anyway, it was getting hotter in New York, and my assignment stack had grown. The height of the wedding season had once hovered between May and June, tapering off
in July to accommodate for the hellish August heat and to
allow the roving band of merry wedding attendees to de-
camp for the Hamptons. But no longer. Competition was
fierce across the summer, and into the fall months, for the
tri-state area's most coveted priests, rabbis, and reception
spaces. After a few months on the desk, I had figured out
the signalers: A ceremony at the Church of the Heavenly
Rest meant a good WASP couple, Episcopal by breeding
and by their very natures, with a ceremony at the Yale Club
or, if they were feeling naughty, a loft space in Williamsburg, with town car service arranged for the guests. A do at
the Angel Orensanz Foundation, a super hip, super expensive former synagogue on the Lower East Side, meant cre-
atives who had arrived: magazine editors with rich parents,
artists marrying lawyers, journalists marrying journalists.
A Roman Catholic church in Merrick meant a classic Long
Island Italian or Irish party, with lots of booze. And a musty
church in Greenwich Village meant a Famous Music Producer for a Very Famous Band.

One thing about Ira: he gave me good stuff to write
about. Nearly every week, I had one couple who he thought
I might enjoy. It wasn't all investment bankers and market-
ing managers, which, no offense, they do help the world go

round. But he'd try to toss me a stand-up comedian, or a semifamous writer, or just a truly odd couple. That week, I leafed through my stack and found one that made me get up out of my seat.

"Wait," I yelled over the desks to Ira. "This guy is actually U2's producer. Like, he did *Achtung Baby*. He's *that* guy?" What seemed like years before, Adnan and I used to drive around in the evenings, with nothing to do but pick up milkshakes and listen to *Achtung Baby* over and over, loudly, singing out the windows and sunroof into the dark with the insistence of youth and love.

"You'll have to find out, but I guess so," Ira said wryly, obviously chuffed that he had given me something fun to do. His shoulders were bent with years of brides and grooms and their parents yelling at him, and the work could wear on a person; the same fights with the couples, the same fights with people dying to get their announcements in, the sameness of soy-ink romance week after week. He knew he was likely in that seat until he decided to retire, and although he relished the relative power, the day-to-day of it ground on him. It showed in his shoulders and passive-aggressive all-caps emails that we received on a weekly basis. *IS IT TRUE THAT YOU HAVE NOT YET SPOKEN TO THIS BRIDE?* He wrote me once about a woman who, rather than returning my calls, sent him an email, demanding to know why she had not been contacted for her wedding.

My hand shook a bit as I dialed the number listed for Mr. Big Shot. After a few rings, I heard a click, and some chatter. "Hello?" A pleasantly clipped British voice rang through the noise. "Mr. Big Shot? This is Cate Doty from the *New York Times*," I said.

"Yes, hello, I've been expecting to hear from you! Hold on a minute. Hush, lads, it's the *Times*," he said, and I could hear his companions laugh and quiet down a bit. *Oh my God, that's U2*, I thought.

"I'm so sorry to disturb you." I definitely was not sorry to disturb him if he was actually in the same room with Bono.

"No worries at all," he said. "We're just wrapping up a piece—hold on—yes, that's better. Quieter in here. We were making a bit of noise, that's all."

I laughed. "Well, I have to say, I'm a huge fan of that noise, so I'm excited to talk to you." Obviously that violated every rule of ethics I'd ever learned in journalism school, but it's not like I was writing about U2's new album, and anyway, it was *fucking U2*.

We ran through the usual list of questions, and I could hear the band members going in and out of the room. I pictured a smoke-filled studio somewhere downtown, Bono in a leather jacket, Adam Clayton probably wearing another leather jacket—I still don't really know what rock stars wear when they aren't onstage, but I'm guessing leather, ripped things, and bandannas? Why have two wardrobes for the same music? Surely Bono does not wear cargo shorts and an old T-shirt while recording.

"And you were previously married, yes?" I said.

"Yes, we divorced, but she passed away some years ago as well," he said.

"I'm so sorry," I said, and immediately made a note to Google *Mr. Big Shot wife*. "And you've been together how many years now?"

"Ten," he said. "Two kids too. We figured now was as good a time as any. I have to be in New York for this album, and the kids are off school, so why not?"

Why not was good, I thought, and filed that away. We wrapped up with him promising to track down the details of his dead parents' employment, which, frankly, *who cared*, U2 was in the room, and to have his assistant fax over a copy of his diploma from the University of Nottingham, which, I mean, again, who cared.

Before we hung up, he said, "I assume you'll be talking to my other half about all this?" I heard him open and close a door, and there was that lovely noise again.

"Yes, I'll be calling her next thing," I said.

"Great. Cheers," he said. "Oh, the Edge says hi."

I swear I heard him grin through the phone. Before I could say anything more than a "WHAT?" he hung up.

I put down the phone and turned around to look at Ira, who had been watching me this whole time. "So that was definitely U2's producer," I said.

"Guess it was," Ira said. He grinned at me and turned back to his filthy keyboard.

I immediately wished I could have called Adnan or sent him an email. *You'll never believe who I just talked to* would be the subject line. But we had agreed to cut off contact after he arrived in Vientiane, unless there was some sort of emergency, and it was hard to imagine what that would have been. It was just too hard, and what would have been the point? He was literally on the other side of the world, and I had a new life that I was learning to swim in, crazy conversations with brides and grooms to decipher, and a city that I already loved so much to learn. As if you could ever learn New York. But I was trying.

I rang up Mr. Big Shot's fiancée, and the background noise on this call was quite different. "Sorry it might be a bit loud, I've just got the kids at the playground," she said, and I could hear little voices fade in and out behind her. I wondered if those kids got Christmas presents from Bono. I decided that they did: little leather jackets with their names embroidered in the collars so they wouldn't lose them, and a donation to amfAR in their names.

We ran through the usual questions—age, name, et cetera, "Yes, I did graduate from Yale with honors, I'll have my assistant send over a picture of my diploma"—and then I asked a question that had been bugging me since talking to Mr. Big Shot. "So you've been together ten years already," I said, and she chuckled a bit.

"You want to know why we're bothering now," she said.

"Well—yes, actually."

"My parents asked me the same thing—hold on a sec, so sorry—Jack, stop hitting her!—and he had to be back here for the summer to wrap this new album, so we decided to go ahead and do it. My family is too big for them all to fly over to London, so we thought a wedding here would work better. And he wanted to get married. You know his first wife died," she said.

"Yes, he mentioned that. But they had divorced before she died, yes?"

"They had, but they were still close. Their kids saw the accident happen, and he wants to do everything he can to make new good memories for them, so we thought this would be a way for us all to start over together. It'll be fun to have all four of them together while we get married."

"It sounds like you're pretty much already married," I said.

The Taste Maker laughed again. "Almost," she agreed.

"Sometimes it feels like much longer than ten years. But you know, we want to be married. We did all the other stuff, the fun and the mortgage and the kids, and now it's just time. And we wanted to get married in a church, with a priest. I think the kids need to see that, and I need it too. And I don't know—I've never been a bride before. I'm excited about it."

"Are you having a big ceremony?"

"No, a pretty small one, just my immediate family and his siblings. But we're having a big party on Saturday night."

I desperately wanted to know if Bono would be there, but I decided that would be far too gauche to ask. And also, chances were high that we'd written about other weddings where he had been a guest. Sometimes I forgot I worked at the world's biggest newspaper and did not, in fact, just roll in off the pumpkin truck, which was how I felt most of the time.

"How's everything coming together?" I said.

"I have one more dress fitting this afternoon," she said. "It's hard to buy a wedding dress when you're not on the same side of the ocean."

"I bet. What is it?" I loved these details and always wanted to know: Where's the dress from? What about your veil? Do you have an open bar or cash bar? (I never asked that, but you bet I'd judge if a couple in these pages made their guests pay for drinks.)

"It's a Vera Wang," she said. "And it's white."

I loved that. The Taste Maker was close to forty, and she had two kids in various stages of meltdowns on a playground in the West Village. She had been with the same man for ten years, and she had herself worked to shape the musical tastes of a generation; really, the musical tastes of my generation. And fuck the rules, she was going to wear a long white dress on her wedding day, in a musty old Catholic church downtown, with her two—really, four—children by her side.

"I love it."

We hung up, and I had one more task to complete on this: I Googled *Mr. Big Shot wife.* My stomach dropped when I read the Wikipedia page: Penny Vicks, formerly of London and several bands, was killed by a wealthy man on a Jet-Ski while on vacation in Bermuda. She was swimming with her two children, whom she'd pushed out of the Jet-Ski's path before it ran her over, killing her instantly. And now her two children, who had witnessed the accident and borne the unbearable, were perhaps getting something new, yet familiar: a rebuilt, renewed family, joined together before God and a big Irish clan who drove in from Pennsylvania, and by two grown-ups who had long ago found a home in each other's arms. The dress and the party, and this announcement, were deeply beside the point.

I RETURNED TO my desk from the bathroom, having dumped about a gallon of cold water on my face, and a wedding reporter named Tony eyed me. "You all right, kiddo?" he said.

"Fine, fine!" I breezed past him to my desk. It was Thursday, which meant we were proofing the pages. The page proofs were a deeply important but mind-numbingly dull part of the process: it was where problems were solved and errors were caught, and without proofing, we'd likely have a lot more pissed-off couples on Monday morning. (Everyone had one or two irate brides or grooms in their voice mail on Monday morning, arguing over the veracity of some piddly detail in their announcement; I always loved reminding the couples that they were the ones who shared these details with us in the first place.) We sent the pages to press on Friday afternoon, meaning that our drafts needed to be put into the page design system by Thursday. The proofs started rolling off the oversized printer on Thursday afternoon, and I often took mine up to the cafeteria on the thirteenth floor, where I'd eat a chocolate chip muffin baked by union employees and mark up my pages with a bright red pen. We looked for everything from possibly misspelled names to overshot margins to stray commas. This was my chance to catch up on the couples whose announcements I hadn't written, and I sometimes got a little jealous over the ones I didn't get to write, even though Ira made sure I got a fair share of the interesting ones. The daughter of the Speaker of the House, for example, or a high-ranking official in the White House. I never caught everything I should have on the proofs either; I got distracted by the skyline just outside the windows, and the honking from the streets. I folded up my pages and grabbed my wallet, ready to head upstairs to the cafeteria, when I saw Michael rounding the corner by the file cabinets.

We'd had a nice long lunch at the Westway, where we tried to figure out where exactly Larry David and Jerry Seinfeld had sat and created the idea for *Seinfeld*. I liked him. I was happy to have what felt like a real friend in this building, which I was still nervous about entering each morning. No matter how long I worked there, or how used I got to seeing the columnists and random famous people strolling through the newsroom, I didn't feel completely of that place. I think most clerks had that feeling. Being lowest in the pecking order will do that to you, especially in a place that runs on rank and titles and every promotion is wanted by ten people, and then questioned by a hundred when it's given out. The *Times* is a weird, fractured family that's hard to feel comfortable in, and the holidays are a real bitch. So I was glad to have a friend, especially one who seemed so pleased to see me all the time.

He stopped by another desk occupied by a clerk named Carla, who was tall and blond and stood with a loucheness that showcased her skinny arms and huge tits. She floated around the newsroom doing different jobs and was preoccupied with reporting for the gossip column, which allowed her entry to movie premieres, parties where she was cornered in the stairwell by TV stars, and events where she could drink a little champagne, cozy up to famous people, and try to get them to say revealing things, or dumb things, and sometimes both. She was very, very good at it.

I saw him drop something on her desk, to which she smiled and nodded, and then he walked over to me. The thing he'd left on Carla's desk was the same thing that floated down to mine: a postcard flyer for a play. His friend Mark, an aspiring magician and playwright, had gotten a piece into the Fringe Festival, and Michael was the money man and the off-lead. He played a young man with developmental disabilities who lived in the Louisiana bayou with his brother. The play was about family, and love, and getting out of the place that made you who you were. I knew about that.

"Please come," Michael said. "We could go get drinks after." He seemed a bit nervous, and he had gel in his hair again. I picked up the postcard and looked at the artwork that depicted Cane, the character that the play was named after.

"Who did this?" I asked. "I like it."

"Mark's friend Luther," he said. "He works with him in the stockroom at Williams-Sonoma."

Michael and I, I had figured out, had caught the brass ring young. So many of our friends were in New York to do the thing they loved to do: acting, or magic, or fashion design. To make ends meet, Mark worked in the stockroom at the 59th Street Williams-Sonoma with Luther, an artist who was working to pay off his loans from Pratt. Mark's girlfriend, Jessica, was a saleswoman at Anthropologie down on West Broadway and loathed it; she desperately wanted to break into window styling, but she was stuck toting $150 blouses back to the changing rooms and scribbling women's names on the doors. All these people, and all this talent, were being supported by chain retail jobs and the occasional under-the-table gig. But Mark and Jessica and Luther knew it was just a matter of time before the brass ring came along for them, even if they had to forge it themselves.

"So will you come?" he asked again, shyly.

I raised an eyebrow at him. "Is Carla going to come too?"

He blushed. "She didn't seem very interested," he said,

and then quickly added, "I don't care. I would really like you to come, though."

I looked at the date. It was right after I was supposed to get back from North Carolina. I'd decided to stay a day or two longer to visit my maternal grandmother, who had started to exhibit definite signs of dementia, and I never wanted to leave after seeing her. "If I can get back in time, I think I can," I said. "But I'll let you know."

I'll let you know can mean many things, but I think Michael decided to take it as a good sign. "Great. What are you up to after work tonight?"

I started to head for the elevator and the cafeteria. "I have plans." He walked me to the elevator bank, and I pushed the up button and opened my mouth to ask if he wanted to come along and grab a coffee. But he headed for the stairs. "Enjoy your plans!" he said as he pushed through the door, and it felt like I'd somehow hurt his feelings.

At six o'clock, I turned off my monitor and headed out to the subway. It was a gorgeous summer evening. A storm had rolled through overnight and lifted the humidity that blanketed the city, and the streets felt almost clean. I decided against the subway, grabbed a cold seltzer, and headed north toward Central Park, against the tide of commuters hustling toward the train and home.

As I walked the long blocks to 58th Street, I thought about where over the world Adnan's plane might be. I knew he was supposed to transfer in Tokyo, and then again in Bangkok. I decided he was over Alaska somewhere. He had probably finished one book already and taken a long nap. That dude could sleep anywhere, I swear. Once in college I found him curled up in a ball the size of a small laundry basket—and he was over six feet tall—and wedged underneath an old school desk. Sleeping on a plane, even a flight that was taking him to a new life, was not going to be a problem for him.

I was lost in thought, but I knew exactly where I was going. At the corner of 58th and 5th, I stopped and tossed my seltzer into a trash can. I figured I shouldn't take an open drink into Bergdorf Goodman.

If you have never perused the shoe department at Bergdorf's, well, I just don't know what to tell you. It is luxurious, wildly priced, and epic. Some people prefer Saks, and others prefer—or preferred—Barneys. I enjoyed those departments, but I came to prefer Bergdorf's for two reasons: the service felt more democratic than Barneys and more courtly than Saks, and every time I bought a pair of shoes, I got a thank-you note from the salesman, always an old man who'd probably slung leather-soled pumps there since I was in grade school. I still get a thrill thinking of it. I should pause here to note that, barring one completely reckless full-price purchase of Louboutin heels, over the course of fifteen years I only ever bought off the clearance rack, which almost brought the three- and four-figure sticker shock of Chanel and Chloé down to bargain-basement tolerance. I also enjoyed using the restroom there; the hand soap smelled of lilies of the valley, and the ladies' lounge was cinematic.

This was what I'd decided to do while icing my face in the bathroom at work. I had this new life, I was newly single, and all of a sudden, I was making more money than my dad. I was also paying more than twice my parents' mortgage in rent, but I disregarded that. My longtime love had left for a different hemisphere; I was writing about other people's love and romance; and I was so lonely in a city that didn't know, or care, who I was. I wasn't sure who that was either. So, shoes: fancy, lovely, Italian-sewn shoes sold to me in the velvety hushed department of a place I'd read about since I first picked up *Vogue* at age nine. Shoes it was, and shoes it had to be. I justified it to myself (as if I needed to do that, and my advice to you is fuck that ten times and buy the goddamn shoes) by remembering that I had a friend's wedding in two days, and I was wearing a borrowed dress and a necklace I'd bought off a folding table on Canal Street, so I could splash out on the shoes. I was fully aware that I was sliding into a loathsome stereotype, that of the young female arriviste to New York who spends an entire paycheck on a pair of shoes. I did not drink cosmos and had watched exactly two episodes of the Show

That Shall Not Be Named, but I still knew from Manolos, although I'd yet to experience a bad date or a bizarre sex-capade worth writing about.

But still, shoes. I rifled through the clearance rack, picking through scuffed-up ballet flats and Ferragamos for women with impossibly narrow feet. (My aunt Jean always wore Ferragamos, size 7 AAA, and even when I was ten they were too narrow for my feet.) I tried on some two-tone Chanel Mary Janes, but they weren't right. I kept looking, and moved down the aisle to the seven and a halfs. And there they were: green printed silk pumps in a Prada box, size 37, a full size and a half smaller than I would normally find comfortable, and 70 percent off. Their toes were as sharp as glass, their heels were high but not trampily so, and they were exactly right. I forced my feet into them and decided that they'd fit just fine, and that my feet were swollen anyway from the heat and my long walk uptown, and I didn't care either way. They were coming home with me, to Brooklyn and to North Carolina. It is patently silly to admit this, but when I handed over my card to the kind man helping me, I felt a tiny bit of grief melt away. My old boyfriend was in the atmosphere somewhere over Alaska, and I was alone in a giant city, but these green lovelies were mine. The man spirited himself back from around the corner—the Bergdorf's shoe salespeople would never let you see them do anything so plebeian as print out a receipt—with my new shoes in a lavender carrier bag, and I thanked him three times. Prada pumps shouldn't make anyone feel better. They don't really cure what ails you. But sometimes they can help.

I WORE THOSE shoes to Charlie's wedding two days later and got what remain the worst blisters of my life. I also dumped a whole glass of cheap red wine into the right shoe, and while I was too drunk to care then, I lost my shit the next morning when I saw the stains. Juliet asked me where I'd gotten them, and I told her, to which she rolled her eyes and asked me how many *a*'s were in Prada. Friends like that are rare and needed, like a tetanus shot against assholery.

Anyway, I left my desk at two on a Wednesday and went downtown. Michael's show was in a small black-box theater near the Brooklyn Bridge, and as I took my seat next to our clerical boss, Brett, who had helped direct the play, I thought: *What am I doing here?* I didn't know until I walked out the door that I had really decided to go. I wasn't sure why I was so hesitant. Michael was a friend, and these are the things you do for friends, right?

And then the lights came up. Michael as his character, Cane, ran out onto the stage. He'd told me the general outline of the story, and I knew that Cane ran wild in the bayou and his brother, his sole caretaker, was run ragged all the time trying to contain him.

However: I did not know Michael was going to be completely naked. Naked and splattered with mud.

My jaw dropped. I had some recollection he'd casually cautioned that the play was R-rated at times, but I really didn't think that meant balls-out, undressed R-rated. The lighting was artfully done so that you couldn't see everything, but I saw nearly everything. My face burned like lava. It trickled down my neck and my body, and I thought, *Well then*. Even with the scattered lighting, I could see his lean torso and muscular shoulders. Then he left the stage, returned clothed, and the play continued on. Luther came onstage later, then Mark and Jessica, and their other roommate Stanley, and I realized that I was being introduced to Michael's whole world through this play, as well as to his nether regions.

The lights finally came up, and Michael, dressed in his street clothes, came out into the audience and gave me a hug. "What did you think?" he asked. I noticed that his sandy hair didn't have gel in it, and it was much better that way. But all I could think of was his naked body, and that I'd see him in the newsroom, day after day, and we were supposed to be friends and Adnan was in Laos, and what just happened, and I had to get back to work. We stood in front of the elevator, and I hit the button repeatedly and smiled like a crazy person. I wanted to get the hell out of there. Mark and Jessica walked up behind us, and they clearly knew who I was.

"I loved it! You were so great!" I said brightly. "Gotta get back! Ira will wonder where I am!"

Michael's face fell. "We were all going to go for drinks down the street," he said. "Can you skip out and come with us? Just for one."

"No, no, I need to go," I babbled. I gave him another awkward hug and immediately thought of what was under his T-shirt and jeans. "Gotta go!"

I forgot about the elevator and ran down the stairs out into the molten air. *What the hell was that?* I thought, as I booked it to the subway. But as I stood at the corner, waiting for the light to change, I started to laugh. *That*, I thought, *is the guy.* I almost turned back around to find him. But I stopped myself and turned toward the Fulton Street station. I still had work to do.

CHAPTER 6

The Fairy Tale

To MY MIND, Hugh Grant has delivered two completely perfect performances in his career: that of Phoenix Buchanan, the washed-up actor turned bad 'un in *Paddington 2*, and of Charles, the hapless never-groom in *Four Weddings and a Funeral*. Yes, he's hot and chiseled in *Bridget Jones's Diary*, and he romances Emma Thompson splendidly in *Sense and Sensibility*. But the purest Hugh Grant, the Hugh Grant with the stammering and eyelid fluttering that spawned a million imitations and contributed to my romantic and sexual awakenings, the Hugh Grant surrounded by stacks of books that shaped my type—that's the one who's never on time for weddings or anything else, looks extra dashing in a waistcoat, and seems to be pained just to be alive on a warm Saturday morning in London.

Don't talk to me about Divine Brown or the execrable *Love Actually* or that time he threw a tub of baked beans at a paparazzo. As it is for so many of my age group, the Hugh Grant of 1994 is the one who lives in my heart always.

Four Weddings holds up, although every time I watch it, I do wonder why they chose to make one of the exactly two characters of color a £4,000 black "pygmy warrior" statue that Andie MacDowell and her wealthy Scottish fiancé, Hamish, put on their registry at a very fancy shop. It looms large in the scene where Charles, out of his league financially, goes to purchase a wedding gift for his one true love. "Just get me an ashtray," Carrie says, laughing off the fact that he can't afford a pygmy warrior statue, and that she and her fiancé saw fit to register for a pygmy warrior statue in the first place, which reminds me of Princess Michael of Kent's insistence on wearing a blackamoor brooch to Meghan Markle's first Christmas luncheon with the queen, but never mind that. Of course you know that many of the weddings we're talking about here—in the *Times* and in *Four Weddings*—were likely paid for by wealth built upon the backs of the people enslaved, colonized, and portrayed in unfailingly racist ways by people like Princess Michael, and the artist, shall we say, who carved the pygmy warrior statue. A different time, my white ass.

At any rate, not long after, Charles, stammering in a bad button-down, uses the words and wisdom of David Cassidy to express his love for Carrie, a chic former fashion editor who, for reasons that remain unclear, is determined to marry her pompous politician fiancé twice her age. She says she loves him, but no one in the movie believes it, least of all herself. It all goes poorly from there, especially when Charles's friend Gareth dies from a massive heart attack at Carrie and Hamish's very Scottish, very aristocratic wedding, which leads to John Hannah's reading of "Funeral Blues" that spawned a thousand purchases of W. H. Auden anthologies.

But fear not: Carrie and Hamish lose interest in each other, and she and Charles pledge their troth on a sodden sidewalk after he runs away from his bride at his own very English, very posh wedding. The twist, of course, is that these two, who after all seem allergic to marriage, decide to stay "not married" for the rest of their lives. The filmmakers seemed to consider that the more responsible, not to say romantic, choice for a woman whose marriage died after six months and a man whose path to the altar ended when his begloved meringue of a bride decked him after learning he loved someone else with his whole heart, as the movie likes to say.

Four Weddings likes to say a lot of things, *fuck* and *bugger* being the least of them. One thing it reiterates, throughout the four weddings and the funeral, is that you should love someone with your whole heart before deciding to marry or otherwise partner up with them. The other thing it says, again and again, is to expect thunderbolts, not just a light rain shower, when you meet the person with whom you're going to live your life. It also intimates that attending weddings is not for the weak of heart; long-term partnership is vastly more joyful and rewarding than singledom; and yet, with all the requirements and hurdles we must face before walking down the aisle, marriage can still be as easily thrown away as a container of sesame chicken that's languished at the back of the fridge. (Apropos of nothing, I once knew a woman who nannied for Andie MacDowell, and a friend who visited her said it was like going into a house occupied by someone insane who was obsessed with Andie Mac-Dowell.)

The 1990s were a golden age of wedding movies, which aided and cemented my own obsession with weddings. *Four Weddings* is top of mind, of course, followed quickly by *My Best Friend's Wedding, Father of the Bride, The Wedding Singer, Runaway Bride,* and others. In each of these, a white woman falls in love with a white man and in some way subsumes her desires and powers to be with him, to win the title of wife and a wedding ring. Julia Roberts's character in *Runaway Bride* is the least believable of these, because (a) who could ever believe Julia Roberts would ever really put a man's wants before her own, and (b) has there ever been a woman in modern history who has changed her egg order to match her fiancé's? I know the patriarchy is strong, especially for women in the dating world, but there's not a man on earth who could make me eat a soft-boiled egg to maintain his affections.

Anyway, watching these movies as a teenager—on a Saturday afternoon at Mr. Shamdasani's discount movie theater, a dollar box of popcorn in hand—always left me with a nagging sense of confusion. On one hand, these floofy dresses were beautiful, and the men were conventionally handsome, and the women seemed to love them, more or less. But the happy endings always felt unfulfilling. In *Father of the Bride*, what happens after Annie and Brian get home from their Hawaiian honeymoon? Would he actually leave her the fuck alone so she could develop her architecture career, or would he start expecting a daily breakfast smoothie made in the retro blender that he gave her, as she'd feared? Drew Barrymore's character in *The Wedding Singer* had already done backflips to please her cheating asshole of a fiancé; even though Adam Sandler's character was far sweeter than the awful Glenn, and comes out of the movie with a wife and a sweet recording deal with Billy Idol, what would Julia do to keep his affections? Niceness and a good singing voice can mask a whole host of flaws, especially when we're talking about a man-child.

I'm not arguing against the existence of these movies, and they filled a great number of my Saturday afternoons, not to mention daydreams while walking home from school. What I am lamenting, though, is their deep, bedrock existence in a whole lot of women's psyches, like mine. Because what these movies did, generally speaking, was erase the women's interiors. What did Carrie get out of not-marrying Charles, besides a baby? Did she keep her glamorous wardrobe and jet-setting life, or did she move into his slobbish flat, kick out his roommate, hire a housekeeper to take care of it all, and settle into domesticity without a care in the world?

Julia Roberts's character in *My Best Friend's Wedding* gets the best deal, I think, even though Julianne ends up alone, not getting to marry the man she thought she was in love with. But, you know, she knew his bullshit, and I firmly believe there was some truth to her speech to Cameron Diaz about putting up with Dermot Mulroney's mess for the rest of her life. Julianne knew the score, and I have to believe that sometimes the devil you don't know is better than the devil you do. She returned to her glamorous life as a food critic, making chefs quake when she appeared in their dining rooms, while Cameron Diaz got to follow her baseball writer husband around the country during the regular season, making a home on the road in any number of Holiday Inns. Which really, who doesn't dream of that; at least she had housekeeping service. I challenge you to find a single romantic comedy made before, I don't know,

2010 that puts the woman's whole desires at the center of the movie, and don't even start with *What Women Want* because Mel Gibson still gets away with shit to the very end of the movie. His attentiveness to women's true desires happens on his timeline, not on Helen Hunt's. The hell with that.

Oddly enough, the rom-coms of the 1980s were slightly, *slightly* more progressive. I'm thinking of *Some Kind of Wonderful*, in which the pretty girl learns to stand on her own and Watts, the tomboy, gets the boy and the diamond earrings, which John Hughes made as a sort of atonement for the wretched ending of *Pretty in Pink*. Sally Albright had a career and opinions, and knew how to come (and fake it too) before she and Harry went to bed in *When Harry Met Sally*. And in *Say Anything . . .*, John Cusack follows the very brainy Ione Skye to England for her fellowship, thereby transferring complete responsibility for their financial health to her, because I am pretty sure Lloyd Dobler did not apply for a work visa before their plane took off. In an odd way, the women in '80s movies—some of them, anyway—somehow had more autonomy than the women of the 1990s, who got stuck in a bunch of tropes and stayed there for about twenty years.

I'm not even talking about the whole "having it all" idea. I'm talking about remembering that life goes on after the credits roll, and while the male characters' existences were never in doubt—things would generally go just fine—the women's were, and are. And this is the deal we strike with ourselves when on the hunt for a mate. We trade an unknown future alone—that belongs to us completely, totally, without reservation—for something that, oddly, feels more certain: a partnership built on love, that most binding yet most ephemeral of things. A domesticity built on the signaling that marks our lives and tells the world who we think we are: the houses we buy, the cars we drive, the problems that we choose to wrestle with. We think we're controlling for the X factor, the partner themselves, but in fact we're adding a wild card to the hand we've already been dealt.

I don't mean to sound cynical, but it's annoying that there's been a whole industry and culture bent on guiding us—and I mean women—to a decision that often has not felt like entirely ours to make. Not that we don't get to choose the partner, but that a partnership and the social and economic status it provides is worth all the trade-offs. Women who trade it all for love, so many of these movies say, end up living happier lives.

I know it's 2021, I know, I know, and these tropes feel stale, old-fashioned, completely out of sync with the way modern women and men live their lives. But consider this:

in 2018 in the United States, 2,132,853 couples got married, or 6.5 people per 100,000. That rate has slowly ticked down since 2000 because of population growth, but the actual number of people getting married has remained more or less steady. By contrast, the number of divorces has dropped from 944,000 in 2000 to 782,038 in 2018. How many of those marriages would have taken place if we didn't remain so fascinated and entranced by weddings, and the fairy tale, themselves? For her 2002 book, *The Starter Marriage and the Future of Matrimony*, the journalist Pamela Paul (now an editor at the *Times*) interviewed sixty white, middle-class couples who were divorced five years after they married. What she found was that these people were focused on their weddings to take their minds off their unsteady relationships, and that they looked upon their wedding day as the one consistently happy day of their marriage. Their one day of a fairy tale trumped years of marriage. So you tell me: why did they get married at all?

For women, marriage is no longer the economic imperative it once was. If anything, long-term relationships in which the partners maintain their economic independence from each other are more beneficial than combining their finances via marriage. (But if they do combine them, they'd better divorce quickly or stay married; when American women divorce after age fifty, their standard of living drops 45 percent.) We marry for tradition, of course, and for maintaining or improving our social status. We marry because we all have the right to now, finally, and we marry for the legal status that affords us employee-sponsored healthcare and next-of-kin status. We marry because our parents did it, and their parents did it, and we want the KitchenAid stand mixer. But all that still doesn't explain to me why 4,265,706 people got married in this country in 2018. The supremacy of the wedding and the fairy tale still exist, even if we're on the fourth wave of feminism. After all, we don't *have* to get married for love. We just have to love.

To get back to the point at hand, even now, wedding announcements play a huge role in this fairy tale. In a 2020 report by WeddingWire that studied newlyweds, more than 90 percent of the respondents announced their engagement on social media with a #justsaidyes hashtag. Although the *Times*'s wedding announcements are coveted for their status and reach, social media announcements get their own hashtags, countdowns to the big day, floral displays, and art-directed sunset photo shoots with glow filters. Social media has of course democratized the wedding announcement, which was until the Internet the realm of a certain economic and social class. Wedding announce-

ments in newspapers across the country used to detail floral arrangements, bridal parties, point d'esprit veils, the
number of pre-wedding parties given in honor of the bride
and groom, and all the rest of it. The *Times*'s announcements now avoid those details, unless it's a veil of historical
importance; Ira liked to focus more on what the brides
and grooms did and where they went to school, rather
than on the bride's bouquet of lilies of the valley (very expensive out of season). While *Times* announcements help
cement social status, social media announcements, hashtags included, pick up the mantle that old wedding announcements left off, and they in turn reinforce the fairy
tale.

There's a singular crucial way in which the *Times* up-
holds the fairy tale, though: through the Vows column. You
know what I'm talking about. Even more important than
the announcements at the top of the page, the Vows column has served as the anchor of the pages since 1992,
when Lois Smith Brady started writing about love and
weddings for the *Times*. (She's since abdicated the weekly
byline to a roster of freelancers and, every now and again,
a *Times* staffer.) When she first began the column, she
looked for artful ways to describe the wedding's details:
the dress, the cake, the first dance. But after a few columns,
she said, she realized that people were far more interested
in the love story behind the details. And in a way, she be-

came a sought-after expert on love itself, even though she politely protested that she was as mystified by it as anyone else.

"Love will find you," she assures readers of her 1999 book, *Love Lessons: Twelve Real-Life Love Stories*, and details how it found her: in a stationery store in East Hampton, New York, where she was searching for a typewriter ribbon and her husband-to-be was scouting out Filofaxes. Their first date lasted nine hours, and they had an odd thing in common: they both believed a heads-up penny meant good luck, and yet were both afraid to pick them up. (If that isn't a metaphor for love, I don't know what is.) Anyway, Lois's own dating experience, and ensuing disastrous wedding, is a blueprint for the classic Vows column: indicative of class and breeding, signals of intellectualism and status, and persevering through even the most challenging of nuptial situations, like a minister who decided the wedding homily was the perfect time to discuss the distresses of menopause.

An optimist could point to the nonwhite, non-upper-middle-class couples profiled in the column. A realist, and that's me, could point to their very small percentage compared to the luminaries, private and public intellectuals, and members of the upper economic echelon that dominate the announcements and the Vows column. For reference, the people profiled in the column during my first season included a vows renewal for Kirk and Anne Douglas, who had managed to look past Mr. Douglas's infamous womanizing. The column also recorded the marriage of the socialite Hilary Geary to the industrialist Wilbur Ross, Donald Trump's octogenarian commerce secretary who slept through cabinet meetings; and Salman Rushdie's union with Padma Lakshmi, who, in her memoir years later, said he called her a "poor investment." Shortly after they divorced, three years after their Vows column ran, he told *Elle* magazine that he didn't think marriage was necessary, even though he'd been married four times. "Girls like it, especially if they've never been married before—it's the dress. Girls want a wedding, they don't want a marriage. If only you could have weddings without marriages." The column also profiled the grown son of a *New Yorker* cartoonist who, as the lede claimed, "likes food from Ethiopia and Vietnam, which he prefers to call international, rather than ethnic." That was in the *lede*.

Here's the other thing about *Four Weddings*: Carrie and Hamish's announcement would have been a slam-dunk candidate for the Vows column. A young glamorous American, former *Vogue* girl, marries a very much older conservative politician in a stone church in the heathered hills of Scotland. Opposites on first glance, yes, but like draws to like:

ambitious, well traveled, moneyed, attractive, and robustly healthy. Hamish might be used to the rough-and-tumble of conservative British politics, but we all need love, after all, and he recognizes the comfort that his American bride can provide. She too isn't quite what she seems: her Southern roots lend grace and softness to the edge of her big-city life, and she's also got legs for days, perfect for tramping through the Scottish countryside as well as standing by her man when he's under political fire. It's *Brigadoon* meets *Steel Magnolias*, culminating in a chic cream silk column dress with a beaded bolero, traditional vows said by candlelight flickering over red roses, and the most energizing of receptions at an actual castle. I mean, the thing practically writes itself:

When Sir Hamish Banks, 69, a firebrand conservative politician, first locked eyes with the glamorous American Judith Caroline Hartnell at a fashionable soiree in Knightsbridge, he thought he'd finally found the perfect love match, not to mention a sparring partner. But Ms. Hartnell, 29, a former editor at British *Vogue* who is known as Carrie, had other things on her mind, and she was in no mood to joust, romantically or otherwise, with a man twice her age and on the wrong side of politics. But true love brooks no boundaries, and before the end of the evening, not only had

Mr. Banks convinced the raven-haired Ms. Hartnell to have a drink with him at his club in Mayfair, she'd persuaded him to donate $1,000 to the Save the Whales fund, one of her many causes. It didn't matter that she was supposed to board a plane bound for New York in two days. For what is an ocean when true love is to be had?

Even for all the scrutiny it endures each week, the Vows columns were always entertaining, and Ira knew it. He took special care with editing them, twisting and turning each phrase and thought until it fit the mold that Lois had created in 1992. Ira and Lois had more or less developed the column together, and he felt particularly proud and protective of it; he understood in his bones its prominence and its reach, and knew that of all the announcements he would edit each week, even with the big names and the tiny details that could go awry, Vows was the most important. He didn't trust writing them to just anyone either. So when I found a story that was primed, I tell you, just absolutely primed for Vows, I felt like I needed a stiff drink before I opened my mouth to tell him about it.

"I've got one for you, Ira," I said one Monday morning not long after I'd been introduced to Michael's penis. "This could be a Vows."

My stomach quaked a little as I said it. This was swinging for the fences. Because if getting your wedding announcement into the *Times* is akin to getting into Harvard, then being chosen for the Vows column is like winning the race for class president, or beating the Yankees for the World Series, or whatever impossible simile you want. The point is, many, many people think their love story is worthy of a Vows column, and many reporters think they've found a story to fit the mold, and some of them might even be right. But for Ira, only one per week fit.

I looked at the submission in front of me, splattered with Ira's fact-checking handiwork. He loved including wedding announcements for journalists, and he had a soft spot for service members. That was something he'd inherited from his predecessors, including Charlotte Curtis, the former "women's pages" editor who placed a premium on public service as entry to the pages. This one was perfect on both counts: a high-profile journalist who had come to Iraq for the second Gulf War, and a Marine with the perfect pedigree: the Naval Academy, Ivy League, Wall Street, Jewish, and built like the Humvee he rode in while marshaling his troops to battle. The bride was the chief producer for a Very Famous TV Personality, and she had seen it all: wars, shootings, presidential campaigns, protests, and political pandering. She was weathered like an old boot and yet still optimistic enough to find love in wartime. For his part, the Marine was gentlemanly and looked good in his field uniform. They were getting married in Washington on a crisp fall day. The leaves would be popping, the ceremony would be peppered with personalities, and I would be there, notebook in hand, to document love in its fullest feathered glory.

"You sure you want to write this? I can find a freelancer down there," Ira said, after he'd agreed that it was Vows-worthy. My neck prickled.

"No, I've already talked to them. I want to do it. I can stay for free at my old roommate's." I was not going to give up this opportunity to some freelance features writer in D.C. This was *my* story.

"OK," Ira said. "Make sure to talk to as many people as you can. You've got to be able to show what makes these people tick, not just that they have a good story. There are lots of good stories."

What Ira meant was, we needed to understand how these people loved each other. The setup was cis-het per-fect: boy meets girl, guns go off, boy proposes to girl, yada yada. But what was the punch line? What was the thing that made them thrill to each other each dawn in the kitchen, unkempt with morning breath, or drew them back to center after a knock-down, drag-out fight that made the neighbors worried? That was the meat of a Vows column. And the longer I worked on the Weddings desk, the more I began to realize: that was the whole damn point.

A few days later, I left work a little early to catch the

Acela to D.C., which I was splurging on because I could expense it. On the way down, I ran into Helene, a tall fake blond who had entered the building as a clerk and whose ambitions were known to everyone in the building, from the publisher on down. Clerks with ambition—like ourselves—were seen as amusing by the upper brass, who had worked hard to narrow paths upward for those of us who toiled at the lower levels. Years before, clerks had been allowed to advance slowly through a reporter trainee plan known as the 8i program, 8i being the union pay band for those positions. But in the decade before I arrived, that program had been largely shuttered; the clerical supervisor had decided it wasn't worth the time or the trouble to train clerks as journalists, and a member of the masthead, whose power and authority over the newsroom was probably as strong as the publisher's, agreed with her. As far as we could tell, they reasoned that reporting and editing jobs at the *Times* were at a premium and needed to go to people who had worked their entire careers with a singular purpose, which was to see their byline in those hallowed pages. How dare a young, green clerk think they had the talent to join the editorial staff as anything other than a gopher or phone jockey?

That, of course, didn't stop the *Times* from using eager clerks to do freelance reporting, often called "legs," without any hope or expectation of credit for their work. With the exception of two articles, every single thing I wrote for the *Times* until I wrote this first Vows column appeared under the byline *By The New York Times*, giving the credit for my work to the entire institution. My first byline was granted me by a kind sports editor who had commissioned me to write about a Maryland–Florida State football game, which was my first and last experience with a men's locker room, and the second was given to me by the loveliest man, a bespectacled editor with a walrusian mustache, for a piece I helped assemble in the now-defunct Week in Review section. It was a lesson in humility, I suppose, but what it really did was breed rage among the clerks, all of whom loved the newsroom and the mission with the heat of true believers. We were the least jaded and the most hungry.

The really fun part about this whole thing was that once in a very blue moon, when a reporting trainee slot opened up, one clerk was sometimes pitted against another for the job. This happened far more with women than men, by the way, especially when they loosened the rules and decided to rejuvenate the 8i program. I watched many male clerks shirk their actual jobs as clerks—leaving their deskmates to pick up the slack—and instead use their time to schmooze and slide into reporting gigs. Many talented female journalists in my group of clerks left the newsroom for other places, and I still very much enjoy seeing their bylines in vaunted positions. And if you were a person of color, forget it. I can think of exactly one Black female clerk who was seen as worthy of being elevated to higher editorial rank while I was there, and she eventually left for a masthead position and a giant payday elsewhere.

Helene was one of the clerks being pitted against another for a reporting slot. She was a few years older and had toiled in the trenches longer; none of this, however, relieved my jealousy that she was finally getting a shot at the bigs. If Helene won out, she'd receive a reporting gig on Metro—nothing glamorous like City Hall or Albany, probably more like the cop shop, but there's no better place to learn reporting. Helene's carriage, cascading blond curls, and cashmere sweaters indicated that she'd probably prefer a slot on Style or Real Estate, but you had to start somewhere.

I waved at her in the lobby, and we walked out the door together. "Where are you headed?" I asked, noting the tiny edge of fall creeping into the wind blowing down 43rd Street.

"Uptown, Washington Heights," she said. "I'm going to do a Neediest."

Each year, starting in the fall, the *Times* runs a campaign of stories for the Neediest Cases Fund, profiling people and families that their charitable fund has helped over the past year. The *Times* generally assigned these stories out to clerks hungry for bylines, and the stories were always good. They were light-years from the people I wrote about; no $100,000 Asscher-cut diamond rings for them. The stories were rife with the markers of poverty and loss in New York City: bedbugs, lost homes, lost spouses, lost lives. The story could be about a young man with developmental disabilities who just needed a new pair of nonslip shoes for his new job as a dishwasher, or it could pay the rent for a young mother whose multiple sclerosis kept her at home, in pain and without relief. The assignments were good, and the stories gave you a little room to write.

"How did you get to do that?" I asked.

"Eh, just ask," she said. "They'll kind of give them to anybody." She eyed me and my overnight bag. "Where are you off to?"

"Oh," I said casually, "just to D.C. for a Vows column." I almost said *No big deal* but didn't.

She arched her well-drawn eyebrows. "So, not a Neediest."

I laughed and shook my head, while noting that she'd chosen to wear for this reporting assignment some designer jeans and a black cashmere sweater and topped it off with a baseball cap. It was a curious nod to the reduced circumstances of whoever she was about to interview—her own way of slumming it, I suppose. The baseball cap was the thing that made me wonder what she was thinking. I didn't look to see if she'd left her giant Louis Vuitton tote at work.

I headed down to Penn Station, bought a coffee and boarded my train, and settled in to the quiet car. It all felt so luxurious. You have to remember that I arrived in New York on a twelve-dollar bus likely operated on an expired license and had that morning eaten for breakfast a one-dollar sticky bun from the coffee cart by the subway. I always felt wildly unsophisticated walking into the building each day, but I could feel my confidence grow by centimeters. It helped that I was headed back to a city I hated to write about something I was learning to love: love.

The next afternoon, I walked over to the wedding venue from my old apartment on Constitution Avenue, where I'd spent the evening eating takeout and drinking with my best friend from college, Erin. The fall air had blown into Washington overnight and cleared its swampiness. The sky was as brilliant as I'd ever seen it, and a cold snap tossed my hair as I walked down 8th Street. I thought about the cheese people and the fishmonger in Eastern Market, and the Ethiopian restaurant we were going to after the wedding, and I felt lucky to be alive on this day, in this place, doing exactly this. I didn't love D.C. at all, but I did love my old neighborhood and was glad to be back in it to write what I'd already decided was going to be the best Vows column since Lois Smith Brady filed her first story.

I walked into the venue and introduced myself to someone who looked important, while keeping an eye out for the photographer assigned to the story. "You must be Cate!" It was the groom himself, standing tall and freshly buzzed in his dress blues. "We're doing shots. Come join us."

"Um—better not, but I'll follow you wherever you'd like me to be," I said, giving what I thought was my most courteous and professional half smile. The groom ducked through a curtain into an anteroom, where the bride, resplendent in a sleek white satin dress, was splashing Johnnie Walker Black into a few highball glasses clearly borrowed from the caterers. "Babe, this is the woman from the *Times*," the groom said, pointing in my direction.

She waved me over. "Cate, come have a drink! We're almost ready to go," she said, teetering on her heels. *She's super drunk*, I thought. This was going to be amusing, at the very least.

I shook my head at the glass and said, "You know the rules," trying to appeal to her journalistic code of ethics. The Very Famous TV Personality, who was standing next to her, laughed at me. "Oh, come on, Cate, it's a wedding."

I was a bit taken aback, not only by his celebrity glow, but his quick familiarity with me. I knew the tactic, though; I'd used it myself on reporting assignments. "Thanks, Peter, thanks," I said, and shook my head again. "So, tell me, how's it going?"

The bride and groom were by this point at the end of their Johnnie Walker Black, and I didn't have the heart to ask them how many they'd had already. "Time to sign the ketubah!" Peter said cheerfully, and pulled out a Montblanc from his suit pocket, waving it first at the bride. She took it and scrawled something that approximated her name on the line where the rabbi had placed his pointer finger, and then waved the pen to the groom, who had poured himself another. The room had started to reek a little of peat.

"Babe, here!" the bride said impatiently. "We have to go soon." The groom took the pen and scribbled his name, and then threw back the rest of his scotch.

"Ready?" The rabbi smiled at them. He'd obviously seen this before. Peter deposited his Montblanc back into his jacket, adjusted his tie, and offered his arm to the bride. I saw the rapport between them immediately; it had been forged in war zones, late nights in the newsroom with bad coffee, quiet meetings with sources, and screaming matches over what to keep and what to cut. I understood that relationship far better than the one she shared with the groom, who, in our pre-wedding interview, had gushed about her toughness and fairness and was ebullient about the idea of having children with her. But everything he said was just kind of stock. And the bride, for all her journalism skills, couldn't find much more to say about him than repeating his résumé. "We have fun together," she said. Well, OK.

The ceremony was as cut-and-dried as you'd imagine anything crafted by a Marine and a journalist, and the reception was as drunken as the ketubah signing. After the speeches, I cornered Peter the TV Personality to find out what made this couple tick. We huddled in the back of the white tent, and I finally accepted a glass of champagne. "It's a good question," Peter said thoughtfully, and turned to his wife, who was very nipped and tucked and very, very tan. "What makes them a good couple, Betsey?"

Betsey smiled, tightly, and shrugged. "Well, they seem to have a good time together."

I laughed. "That's what she told me—they have a lot of fun."

"Sometimes that's all you can ask for," Peter said. "Look, they're both tough and seasoned, and they need to be with someone who understands their lives and their jobs. She's the job, just like I am. And they found each other at war. I mean, that's the story right there. You couldn't make it up."

Peter the TV Personality was right about that. You couldn't make it up. I threw back the rest of my champagne and decided I'd had enough. I ducked out the side of the tent, preferring not to say my good-byes to the bride and groom, who were shoulders-deep in love and liquor. I was there to observe, not to distract. I called Erin for directions to the Ethiopian restaurant and stumbled on my high-heeled boots down the inoperable escalator at the Eastern Market metro. I was ready to go back to New York.

MICHAEL HAD INVITED me to lunch to deconstruct my thoughts about the play. "You didn't tell me you were going to be completely naked," I said over my turkey cheese-burger at the Westway.

He looked startled, and then angry. "Yes, I did," he said, prickly. "I wouldn't have not told you that."

"I don't remember you saying, 'Hey, Cate, watch out for my penis.'"

His face turned red, with either embarrassment or anger, I couldn't tell. "Obviously, I wouldn't say that," he said. "But I would never, ever not warn you about that. That would be shitty. A shitty fucking smarmy move."

We ate our burgers in silence. "But what did you think?" he pressed.

"About your penis or about the play?"

"Fine. Either. Both."

I chewed and thought. The truth was, the play, and his nudity, had left far less an impression on me than our awkward five minutes together afterward. I had turned it over and over in my head. What kind of drink was he asking me for, and what did his friends think about me? I noticed that he didn't have gel in his hair, and he was wearing this

Salvation Army T-shirt with a ratty neck, which was entirely inappropriate for most workplaces. But ratty-neck T-shirts were sort of par for the course at the *Times*, along with scuffed shoes, coffee stains, and handfuls of ibuprofen eaten for a midday snack.

"I liked it," I said. "I'm sorry I couldn't join you guys for a drink. I really did have to get back to work. I lied and told Ira I had a doctor's appointment."

Michael smiled ruefully. "We just went over to Toad Hall," he said. "We go there a lot. Have you been?"

I rolled my eyes. "I've only lived here for like three months. I haven't been anywhere. Well, I've been to Dojo and a bunch of places in Williamsburg. But that's it."

"Come with me to Toad Hall sometime," he said. "It's a great bar. It kind of smells funny, but it's part of the charm, I guess."

I was quiet for a moment. "Well, I'm free tonight," I said haltingly. "If you are."

The corners of his mouth lifted. "If you can hang out in the city until I get out at eight, I can meet you there. Or we can go from here. Whichever."

My stomach started to do a new yet familiar flippety-flop, and I could feel the color rising to my cheeks. "I'll meet you downstairs at eight."

That evening, I wandered over to 9th Avenue and got a cheap manicure and grabbed tacos at the joint behind Port

Authority. I felt buoyant, jumbly, discombobulated, and completely unsure of what I was doing. This drink at Toad Hall didn't feel like a friends drink, and Michael, all of a sudden, didn't feel like a friend. He was more interesting than that. I started to think: *If this goes poorly, if this is a bad drink, then I won't have any friends in this town except for my roommates, and that would suck. But then, I thought, how could it be a bad drink? We're already friends.*

We took the C train down to Canal Street and walked over to Grand, where smoking patrons clustered outside Toad Hall. We ducked through the old black painted doors and grabbed the big round table at the front. Michael pulled out the copy of a Hunter S. Thompson book that he'd crammed in his back pocket and placed it on the table, and said, "What can I get you?"

Six hours later, we emerged into the wee hours of Manhattan. We had closed the place down and walked out the doors right before the bartender flicked the lights on. We covered a lot: my grandmother, his dad, peripatetic childhoods, ambitions, Hunter S. Thompson, the music we loved, the things we craved. "What train do you need?" he said, as we meandered back toward Canal. "The A, although I might just take a cab if I can find one," I said, sleepy and unwilling to face Brooklyn-bound delays at two a.m. "I need cash, though."

We found an ATM, and I slid my card into the door for

entry. Michael opened the door for me, and as I walked through, he touched his hand to my lower back tentatively, protectively, and left it there just until I got to the machine. *OH*, I thought. *Oh.*

He flagged a cab for me and opened the door, and I stood between it and the curb, unsure of what was going to happen next. "Well, thanks," I said, and I was all of a sudden very, very tired, but also very, very buzzy. "See you tomorrow?"

He held the door open as I slid down onto the Naugahyde seats. "See you tomorrow," he said, and grinned at me. The cab pulled away and zoomed me home over the Manhattan Bridge, and all I could think was: *I guess that wasn't a friends drink. Nope, definitely not.*

Chapter 7

In the Public Eye

L ET'S PAUSE HERE SO I can give you a few of my own bona fides that might get me into the wedding announcements. I went to a "Public Ivy" college, I worked at a major media corporation, my dad is a park ranger (like I said, Ira loved public servants), and perhaps most important, I am directly descended from Edward Doty, one of the two men to fight the first white-people duel of Plymouth Colony in 1621, just half a year after *Mayflower* passengers set foot on their new world. See, I have founder's blood in me too. And it's really of the purest sort.

Not really. So, this guy came over as an indentured servant, survived the voyage, got free, and proceeded to rack up a court record and bad reputation unmatched by most of the members of the colony. He was one of the first examples of white male privilege ever seen in New England, and really, what an example it was. After he and a fellow servant, Edward Leister, finished the duel—in which they only managed to land little stabs here and there, so lame—they were bound together by their heads and feet, which was supposed to last a whole day. But these two whined so much that they were released after an hour, patted on the head, and told not to do that again. Then, after Edward Doty gained his freedom, he saw the inside of a court more than just about any other white man in Massachusetts. In January 1633, he was sued three times, all over hogs. In April, he was sued again for slander. He swindled a neighbor out of land and lost that lawsuit. A neighbor sued him for stealing firewood. He sued his own father-in-law over some matter of money, and he was sued for "dealing fraudulently in a trade of bacon for beaver skins." You know the guy in Missouri who threatened Black Lives Matter protesters with his AR-15 while his barefoot wife brandished a pistol? Edward Doty was that guy, the original come-and-take-it white American man.

It may surprise you to know that I don't take my *May-flower* lineage very seriously, or at all. I mean, depending on which genealogy group you talk to, up to two hundred thousand people can likely claim the same direct lineage to that litigious idiot, and it's not really something that I find interesting about myself. This flies in the face of a deeply embodied cliché of Southern womanhood, that of knowing who your people are. One of my aunts has two shelves of black binders full of relics of dead relatives, family trees, pages from family Bibles that help her trace who we are and where we come from. We have old cardboard boxes full of faded receipts, the hospital bill from when my grandfather was born (it was thirty-eight dollars), property sale records from the 1880s, sepia portraits of vacant-eyed people staring just beyond the camera, with little clue to who these people are. Other things we have: Records of enslaved people being sold from one member of my family to another. Souvenirs from a 1906 reunion of the Confederate Veterans of America. Seven hundred dollars in Confederate money, some of it signed by the treasurer of the Confederate States of America. Tax records with one column that says *free* and another that says *Negro*. We have all that and a lot more.

So when these wedding announcements casually dropped in the fact that the bride was descended from John Jinglehopper, the first governor of South Carolina, there's no way to include the indisputable fact that John Jinglehopper (let's just call him that) enslaved people. When we asked the groom for proof of his relationship to Jay Gould, the superstar robber baron of the Gilded Age, there's just no room in the announcement for any indication of what a true villain Jay Gould was, and the DNA that was carried forth into this young groom, who was marrying a lovely woman he met while in medical school at the University of Virginia—yet another problematic place. When we included this kind of information about these people, we didn't tell the whole story. We weren't there to tell the whole story, to be fair. But maybe the announcement, and the fact that these people saw fit to include that information in the first place, told us a different story; perhaps that was more of an indictment.

But you know who could tell the whole story, and who helped lift the veil on these announcements, if you'll pardon the pun? Gawker. The same media empire that Hulk Hogan brought down, the same place that adored its stature as the scourge of big-name New York media, the same sweatshop that Nick Denton used to make millions and young writers used to make their names—at least one of whom I was wildly jealous of for about a decade—that same Gawker saw an opportunity with the wedding announcements. They already poked fun of and took the piss out of most of what New York media people thought was proper. What could be more fun than the wedding announcements?

Making original fun of something that a lot of people already make fun of is challenging, but the minds at Gawker were up to it. Two writers there, Katie Baker and Alexis Swerdloff, devised a system that Baker later called "matrimonial moneyball." It was a scoring system that owed a good deal to sabermetrics but had its own, shall we say, panache. They tried to answer this question each week: which couple best exemplifies the spirit and standards of the *Times* Weddings section, with its impenetrable cloche of secrecy? With this scoring system, they were really trying to figure out how people got in, what people should play up about themselves to increase their chances, and, every so often, to explain the inexplicable.

The system went like this: each couple would be assigned a certain point, or lose a point, based on a scorecard that took into account each usual category of information. Take universities: three points for you and your betrothed if you attended an "Insufferable," which included Caltech, Cambridge, Harvard, MIT—you get the idea. Two points for the "Demi-Elite," including the University of North Carolina—two points for me!—and Dartmouth, although I'm pretty sure most Dartmouth graduates would argue that they should be granted Insufferable status, given the academic rigor there. Anyway, two points for a Rhodes or Marshall Scholar, three points if a parent is a genuine celebrity (likely, and I'm just guessing, Kelly Ripa or higher), four points if a person is descended from a robber baron (Jay Gould!), and one point if the announcement includes any of the following signifiers: Head of the Charles, Iowa

Writers' Workshop, first novel, Foreign Service, the 6 train, Twitter, vineyard, Maine, marathon, *Mayflower* (another point for me!), Yaddo, yogurt, yurt. There's a lot more.

The Weddings desk loved these breakdowns. Ira and I read them every Monday—bless the poor Gawker editor who had to spend her summer Sundays scoring the wedding announcements—and loved what they did. Just like most people who have attempted commentary on the wedding announcements, Gawker was pointing out the privilege inherent in every single word on these pages. But unlike some commentary based in opinion, Gawker scored the privilege. We talked to these people all day long, and it sometimes dripped from their voices. While Gawker didn't hear that necessarily, they still pegged these people. The advent of Gawker's system made submitting your announcement more fraught, because what if, just what if, Gawker picked up on it and made fun of you?

People didn't care. In fact, they loved it. Not everyone was in on the joke, but it was all part of the same public and media fascination with the wedding announcements, and again, when it comes to weddings, all press is good press. It's entertaining, especially when you consider who these announcements are about. Sometimes they're about interesting people, but really, most of them are focused on good junior attorneys at law firms or finance people, pillars of society who don't do much to change it. What makes them fascinating to readers is one day, just one day, when they get to wear pretty dresses and rented tuxedos and be the center of attention, and the wedding announcements are just one more kind of attention. I get it. We all want our fifteen minutes, and for some of us, a write-up in the wedding announcements is it. And that's fine.

There's been a lot of ink and breath spilled about why the wedding announcements are good, or why they're bad, or why they should cease to exist. In the comments on a column about the announcements by the *Times* public editor, Clark Hoyt, one woman sniped that a Vows column about two former drug addicts—admittedly a detour from the usual Vows fodder—should not have been included. "The white-trashing, trailer-parking of America, brought to us wrapped in roses by the NYT," wrote ToniSuzanne of Clemson, South Carolina. In a letter to the editor, Nancy Van House of Berkeley, California, ranted that "the subjects don't pay, and the *Times* spends staff time factchecking and interviewing participants." (There goes my job.) "Do I care that two people who met at Yale and graduated cum laude—children of perfectly nice people like hundreds of thousands, millions of others in this country—got married in Connecticut?" she continued. "More important, these announcements (in the so-called newspaper of record) perpetuate values that I and many others question. The 'achievements' that you say have replaced bloodlines are overwhelmingly business-oriented. (And how much are these mostly 20- and 30-somethings likely to have achieved? And why should they get credit for their parents' achievements?)" Nancy Van House of Berkeley, California, you have a point.

The criticisms are all valid. But there's one thing that these people didn't see: how the wedding announcement fits into the glorification, almost deification, of the American wedding as a whole. The details of dresses, punch, and bouquets that were once the meat on the bones of an announcement grew into long-form stories, and those stories turned into magazines like *Brides* or *Modern Bride* or the queen bee, the truest tastemaker of them all, *Martha Stewart Weddings*. But Martha Stewart didn't coin the phrase *the perfect wedding*, and neither did wedding blogs, which bloomed into full view right around the time I started writing the announcements. In *Cinderella Dreams: The Allure of the Lavish Wedding*, the authors point out that the first evidence of "the perfect wedding" surfaced around the 1920s, when advertisers and marketers, not to mention women's magazines, started to urge couples—but again, really women—to purchase fancy engraved invitations, an expensive cake, and a designer gown. Perfection is an excuse for fancy, sometimes too fancy, to the point of going into debt that will take years to repay. I know a couple

who got married almost a decade ago and they are still—
still—paying off their wedding, which is extremely unfortunate, as they are now dancing around divorce. Another
woman I worked with at the *Times* was engaged for three
years in order to save for her perfect wedding, and I hope
she got it.

Anyway, the details that I used to hang on to in wedding
announcements as a child—those are the details that cost
so much, and in some ways have supplanted the meaning
of the wedding itself. It's ironic, I suppose, that the wedding
announcements I wrote actually eschewed those very details that bolstered the glorification of American weddings
and created a $75 billion industry that can justify not only
charging you thousands of dollars for a wedding cake, but
also $3 per slice to cut it. In 2018, the average cost of a wed-
ding in this country was $44,000, and that excludes the
honeymoon, another $12 billion industry separate from
the weddings industrial complex. It makes me feel crazy to
contemplate that yet another idea of perfection marketed
to women (and increasingly men, but let's be honest) has
resulted in some major meltdowns, an absolute ton of debt,
and things that no sane person would normally pay for or
strive for. Wedding announcements serve to glorify your
big day as a bride or a groom, but what do they say about
your marriage?

I kept delving into my assignments each week, and with each announcement, I thought about it a little more. Here's a boldface name for you that I will not reveal but who got written up in *Vogue*. This woman was the perfect intersection of wealth, lineage, and major excess. She was descended from one of the great European leaders, with a triple-barrel last name, and she was taking her new husband's last name—and it was an unfortunate one—so she was about to have four last names. That to me deserved its own matrimonial moneyball category. Anyway, she was one of those people who had appeared in *Vogue* over the years for various reasons, but none so auspicious as the occasion of her own wedding.

This story has nothing to do with my interactions with her. She was very pleasant and forthcoming with what I needed, and she made no bones about who she was and where she came from. People from that echelon of society tended to either beat their chests or hide who they were, so it was refreshing to talk to a woman who just wanted to get it done—and oh, by the way, she was being featured in *Vogue*, so this wasn't even really the most important piece of reporting about her wedding. I had a relatively awkward conversation with her father, whose heavily accented English was hard to understand, especially since it was being filtered through a satellite phone. But that's really the sum of it.

This story is actually about this woman's engagement ring: a six-carat stunner built from a diamond that belonged to her family. Her mother had given it to her fiancé before he proposed, and he had it turned into a lovely ring that could stop traffic if it caught the sun. This thing was so big that apparently it was uncomfortable to wear while doing housework—not that this woman did much housework, but I assume she washed a dish or two. Which explains how, a few weeks before the wedding, her six-carat diamond ring, which she had taken off and placed on the kitchen counter, disappeared. She and her future in-laws tore the apartment apart, pulling everything out of the drawers, turning over the rugs, cleaning out every bag and tote bag. No dice.

I have never worn, nor will I likely ever get close to trying on, a six-carat diamond ring. I'm guessing that this thing probably cost more than I have in my retirement account. I'm also guessing that you can probably see a six-carat diamond ring flashing across the room, especially if you have floor-to-ceiling SoHo loft windows, as she did. But again, no dice.

Then her very sensible mother-in-law thought to look in the trash under the sink, even though the bride-to-be swore she had put it on the counter for safekeeping. Moms know where to look, generally, and this one dumped a full bag of garbage into the tub (she plugged the drain first) and searched with gloved hands. And finally, finally, she found a dirty, probably sticky six-carat diamond ring. Whew.

I have many questions about this story, which was reported in one of the city gossip columns a few weeks before the wedding. First, how the hell did they get that story, and why was it leaked in the first place? Did the bride tell this story on the party circuit and it caught Cindy Smith's ear? Or did the bride leak it herself as a run-up strategy to her wedding, to gin up interest in her wedding announcement and coming *Vogue* feature? It was a very strange ploy for attention, and exceedingly so given this bride's serious lineage and generally balanced appearance. She wasn't a Paris Hilton, flashing her tongue and her vagina on red carpets in Bali, nor was she clamoring for the cameras at the Met Gala. She didn't even pluck her eyebrows. But I realized: once again, when it comes to weddings, all press is good press.

I HAD BEEN thinking about what to do about Michael. His hand on my back had changed things in a way that I didn't think could be reversed. I didn't think I minded; I liked it. I spun through our six-hour drink in my head over and over, at the gym and on the train home at night, trying to figure out what to do next. Since then, he had been a bit quiet, and I wondered if he was waiting for me to make the next move. And then I got an email: he had gone down to Florida to see his mom and stepdad, and just happened to be there when a hurricane came through. *It is miserable here,* he wrote, *heat, humidity, tree branches scattered like the dead.*

Romantic, I thought. *How are you?*

I was fine. I felt like I was beginning to be more than fine. I was starting to want him to come back to New York so we could continue whatever we had started that evening at Toad Hall. A few days later, my extension rang from the national desk, and I picked it up. "Hey, I'm back," Michael said. "Got plans tonight?"

I did in fact have plans that night. My friend Jenny was in town from Washington. She was a woman who always seemed to collect people wherever she went, and I was supposed to hang out with her and whoever else she'd picked up. "I do," I said slowly. "But you can come if you want."

We were just going to grab some dinner. Jenny's friend was, for some odd reason, fascinated with the Howard Johnson's in Times Square, so we were planning on ending up there. It was mid-September, meltingly hot, and ice cream seemed like the right thing to do.

"We're going to get dinner and then ice cream. Do you want to come?"

He cut me off. "Absolutely," he said.

At HoJo's, I ordered a dish of something and pushed it around as it melted. I kept casting glances at him, this generous, funny man in another T-shirt with a ratty neck, the kind that had been washed so many times that hope was the only thing holding it together. His summer haircut was growing out on his neck, and his glasses kept slipping down his dignified slope of a nose.

And then, as my friend was rattling on about something, Michael's hand slowly migrated to mine under the table. It was tentative, and then rushed, as if he had to grab it before it disappeared. And then I felt us float away from the HoJo's and into a midnight space of our own, where the only noise was the rushing of water and a steady thump-thump of hearts, and we plummeted down, down into a fizzy, sparkly pool, where our fingers entwined like roots growing toward each other.

We wandered out into the warm fall rain and made our way to the steps of the New York Public Library, where, to the amusement of several homeless people and late-night passersby, he kissed me until the sun peeped over the Midtown skyscrapers. The lions kept watch over us, and a white limousine sped past us down 5th Avenue, screaming toward the dawn. It was the beginning of something. I had forgotten about my couples and weird lavish weddings and six-carat diamonds. All I knew, all I wanted, was right there in front of me.

Chapter 8

Mating Rituals

HAVE YOU EVER stood against a long wall with other girls, waiting for a bunch of boys to run over and ask you to dance before anyone else can get to you, mostly because they don't want to get stuck with the fat girls? If you haven't, here's how it goes.

One peculiar thing about growing up in the South is the segregated ritual of cotillion, which hundreds of middle-class white children, despite years of progress, are still subjected to every year. This is a series of classes in which middle schoolers learn how to dance, how to ask one another to dance, how to treat each other with politesse, and, if your class really gets into the weeds, how to set a table, behave politely, and modulate your voice. It is a distant cousin to Amy Vanderbilt's etiquette book, the one who only shows up for Christmas and you really wish he wouldn't. Do not mistake me: the world would run a lot more smoothly if we all said please and thank you, and life might possibly feel a little more orderly if everyone could dance the fox-trot together, although who dances the fox-trot anymore? However, like so many other things of this nature, cotillion is a class signaler. White children of means were, and are, sent to cotillion to learn manners that were created by and for white people, to police each other and people Not Like Them. This is also a different thing from Black cotillions, where young women make their debut into society.

Every Tuesday night, my parents dropped me off at a dance studio across the street from the country club, where I and sixty other unwilling kids split up by gender. The woman who owned the studio and taught the class, Mrs. Shaw, was a former Miss Fayetteville and carried herself ramrod straight, like she was still trying to keep the crown on her head. She taught the girls. Another woman—tall, horse-faced, whose name I never remembered—taught the boys, who all congregated at the far end of the studio and quickly dropped their navy blazers onto the chairs against the wall. Mrs. Shaw (who was divorced but we had to call her that because *Ms.* was feminist propaganda) pulled an accordion curtain down the middle of the room, then commanded us to line up, face the mirror, and copy her spins and sashays. We were not allowed to wear pants, and woe betide the girl who showed up without tights or pantyhose. Most of the time I wore a plain black pleated skirt, Sam & Libby ballet flats, and a sweater from my mom's closet. Every so often, if I was feeling fancy, I wore this blue velvet dress with a white ruffle down the side that accentuated my burgeoning twelve-year-old curves, which, to my mind, came too soon. Women in my family have always blossomed early, and I got my first period on my eleventh birthday at summer camp. If there is a God, she's not as funny as she thinks she is.

As best we could, we copied Mrs. Shaw, who reeked of Virginia Slims and was as tanned as a leather handbag. She scanned us with a glint in her eyes, hunting for our missteps, as she and her ankle bracelet kept time. At the half-hour music mark, she paused the music. The other, horse-faced teacher yanked back the curtain to reveal a bunch of sweaty pubescent boys who had been directed to put their blazers back on, straighten their ties, and tuck in whatever had come undone during dance practice.

"Line up!" Horse Face bellowed, and the girls all backed up in a single line against the mirror where we'd just been watching Mrs. Shaw twist and contort, all the while keeping an invisible crown straight on her frosted head. The teachers stepped aside, and one of them yelled, "Go!"

What happened then remains one of the strangest things I've ever witnessed, never mind participated in. The boys hauled ass across the dance floor, Bass nubucks slapping at the polished wood, striped ties flapping in the breeze, barreling toward us like infantry into the breach. Their job was to procure a dance partner for each song, and their mission was to get to the *right* girl before someone else did. The pecking order was clear: the boys who didn't get to Annie Martin or Jennifer Barry first tried to grab Laurel Dennis's hand before someone else did, and so on and so forth. The boys would chart their path across the floor and signal with a hand gesture to this girl or that that they were the target this time; they were the chosen one. All we could do was wait for Horsey to say go, huddle against the mirror, grab on to the barre, and hope to avoid the worst, which was being left with no partner at all. This repeated itself six or seven times, until the clock chimed eight and we were released out into the cold. Once every few classes, the teachers turned the tables, and we got to race over to the boys, who were suddenly terrified of what their choices had wrought. That was when the fat girls got their revenge.

It is a curious feeling, waiting to be asked to dance. It's an even curiouser feeling, waiting to be asked to dance by a glistening twelve-year-old boy with damp hands who didn't want to dance with the fat girls but at some point he was going to have to do it because there were more girls than boys in the class, and Caroline Hamlin and Noelle Fink were always left without a partner, and had to dance with each other or the teachers, who didn't want to dance with them either. Not even the only popular fat girl landed a partner every round; it was as if these boys, who all thought they were pretty hot shit, had been told by their mothers that the fat girls were more fertile than the skinny girls, and they'd better stay away because they were not equipped to become grandmothers before the turn of the twenty-first century. This one guy, Chris Schaffer, whose dad was a big-deal dentist in town, refused to actually touch the girls he had to dance with, whom he considered beneath him socially. If you didn't swim at the country club and run up a tab on your dad's account at the 19th Hole, then your young waist was not worthy to serve as a resting spot for Chris Schaffer's tennis-tanned left hand. He would hover it an inch or two away from your body and hold it there until the number ended, and refused the handshake with which we were required to leave each other. Please remember that this was a manners and dancing class, so Chris Schaffer was freely flouting its two basic tenets: (a) we were supposed to be polite to each other, and (b) he as the male partner in this whole thing was supposed to guide, with firm but gentle pressure from his *hands*, the hapless female through the steps of the box step or the waltz or whatever we were supposed to be learning that night.

You may not be surprised to know that Chris Schaffer continues to be an asshole. I am pleased to report that he became a dentist in Fayetteville just like his dad, and is just as boring now as he was in 1991. I have no problem with dentists, but I do still have a problem with Chris Schaffer and his ilk, privileged scions of unimaginative families who never thought the word *no* applied to them. Anyway, I got two things out of cotillion: my friendship with Charlie, who I liked dancing with because all we did was laugh, and pictures of the end-of-season "tea dance," in which I am wearing white gloves and a dress my mom made me out of what appears to be upholstery fabric, and my friend Maggie is probably wearing Jessica McClintock, and we look miserable in every frame.

It is also yet one more space in my life where we were expected to build relationships, but people who didn't look like me—or us—did not feel welcome, and for all intents and purposes were not. You will of course believe me when I tell you that a few years later, in this very same class with these same teachers, a Black surgeon was told over the phone that he could register his eleven-year-old daughter for cotillion, only to be rejected when they got to the dance studio. One of the girls in the class circulated a petition demanding that she be admitted to the class, and a few kids said they would quit if the teachers didn't admit the girl, although frankly that could have been an easy out for them. The teachers eventually relented, but the surgeon's daughter decided she would rather not spend her Tuesday nights being taught the cha-cha by a pair of racists. Smart girl.

I bring up cotillion because it's the first memory I have of mating rituals, unless you count the time one early morning in the fifth grade when I walked into my parents' room, looking for clean laundry, and saw my dad roll on top of my mom. While we were ostensibly in cotillion to learn how to dance, we were really there to learn how to navigate each other as objects of—well, if not desire, then certainly of interest. Even though the girls were the targets, we had already chosen our arrows. I always wanted to dance with Charlie or his twin brother, and I had a huge crush on Jimmy Diehl that never resulted in anything. My crushes never really did result in anything, because I was awkward and outspoken and too smart for most of these guys. What? I can say that. Charlie told me in the ninth grade that I marched to the beat of my own drum, and that was what he loved about me. I am confident, however, that no other boys in my class did, and didn't for a long time. (It's fine, I'm fine, really.)

Anyway, cotillion created a bizarre foundation for my outlook on boys and eventually men, and it took me well over a decade to shake the assumption that I was supposed to hang out by the wall and wait for Jimmy Diehl to run at me for the samba. The demure-damsel thing had stuck its claws in my head and refused to let go, which is bizarre because *demure* has never otherwise ever been applied to me. Even with Adnan, I waited for him to make the first move, although the ardor we felt was equal. It rarely occurred to me that I could be the chaser; I could show interest without weathering a sense of shame that I felt down through my toes. That I could just want, and be wanted, and wanted well and fervently, without reservation, and I could return it. And that I wanted to.

I wanted Michael. We spent the next month or two in a suspended state, our feet just grazing the sidewalk, and mad for each other. We built air palaces for ourselves out of desire, maps on our skin to places of pleasure and refuge, calendars of *we'll do this and that and yes, not now but soon, soon, baby, yes, do it now, now.* We devoured each other like we were running out of time. We lazed on my cast-off futon as the fall sun peeped through the ginkgos, his lean body that I'd finally met curled behind mine, taking care to get up slowly or the futon would tip us both to the floor. We stayed up late and slept late and ate curry puffs from the Thai joint down the block and had languorous sex on the roof in the dark while sirens cut through the night. We asked a million questions of the other, demanding no answers, only the right to ask. We showed off. I cooked for him because it was what I knew how to do: roast chicken, lasagna, soup, fall things that made us feel safe. We watched reruns in his living room in Queens and wandered down to Donovan's for burgers, and came back and made love in his bedroom next to the living room while his roommates turned the TV up so they couldn't hear. We were helpless for each other, and that scared me like a plane crashing into my house. But I kept going; I wanted to see what happened next. And it all felt so fucking good.

The afternoon after our first kiss on the library steps—maybe five hours after we left each other on 5th Avenue—we met up in the West Village, where he led a literary pub crawl tour, which is not quite as pretentious as it sounds. A bunch of working and wannabe actors led tourists around the Village and told tales about places of literary prominence, like Hart Crane's apartment windows and Joe Gould's old haunt, the Minetta Tavern, before Keith McNally bought it and got rid of half the menu and added a $30 burger, which was a crime. The tales got less accurate and more drunken as the tour progressed around the Village, and it ended at the Kettle of Fish, where young Brooklyn dwellers whose parents had flown in from Wichita bought beers for their dads and sweaty glasses of chardonnay for their moms while the parents tried to look away from the Stonewall crowds out on the sidewalk for a cigarette. I quickly understood that few things that Michael said on the tour were 100 percent factual, or even 75 percent, but he was good at it. He was naturally, awkwardly funny, and as we meandered through the Village, I hung at the back of the group, watching him watch me, waiting for me to laugh, which made him stumble over his lines. We ended up at a late, boring movie on Canal Street, and we made out in the seats before we fell asleep, a little bit drunk, exhausted from our hunger for each other.

I went to work on Monday and, for the first time, checked my voice mail without dread. I didn't care what scorn or vitriol these brides and grooms had left for me. You'd think that a free service that they didn't have to pay for would prompt nothing but gratitude and respect, but that was before the announcements were printed. After the fact, the society desk was nothing more than a place to lay blame for a mistake or misunderstanding. I often wondered if these brides who called me, ranting about an alleged error in their announcement, were just venting their displeasure with the wedding, or the culmination of their fear of commitment. There was no turning back, and they knew it, so they had to vent somewhere. And that was often straight into my voice mail. Look, I know having to correct your wedding announcement—likely the most public thing about you—is not the most fun, and of course I saw the episode of *Sex and the City* in which Charlotte's announcement photo is splotched with ink, giving her a Hitler mustache. Mistakes happen. But I will tell you that in my experience, bloviating to a reporter about yourself and your family and trying to make things sound grander than they are—sometimes that can backfire.

A few examples, and I'll let you judge who was wrong. Exhibit A, the neurosurgeon who answered to a piece of fruit. She was terrifyingly smart, but if my interactions with her were any clue, her bedside manner left something to be desired. From our first call, she had decided I was to be treated like one of her interns on rounds. "Doty!" I imagined her demanding of me. "Are you too stupid to diagnose this patient? Too bad, she's dead already!" I would shake in my clogs, my shiny new stethoscope dancing around my neck, and I would bite my lip to hold back my tears as I went to call the morgue to come get this newly lifeless body that was all my fault, not, of course, that of Honeydew, the brilliant attending neurosurgeon.

Anyway, there were a few squishy details in Kiwi's announcement. One, her career was long and lauded, but we still needed documented proof, which she was too busy to provide us. Two, her fiancé, who, as I understood it, was a wine importer, had just changed companies. This normally would not be hard to corroborate—a call to HR would have done it—but for the fact that he was too busy with preparing for his wedding and importing fine Italian wines, some of which were likely to be drunk at his wedding, to give us details. And three, like so many other parents, hers were less than cooperative and refused to confirm even the most basic details. I don't know what they were so afraid of. Even if they didn't stand up to the Rockefellers or the Bushes—neither of which were in the pages that week anyway—the people who'd birthed and reared Peach the neurosurgeon were fine, upstanding people of Ohio, as far as I could tell. What was wrong with being a teacher and an accountant? But they balked at answering the questions, hedged when they could, and were all the way around un-helpful. I wrote the thing as best I could and sent it to Ira. "These people, man—I don't know what their problem was," I told him when I filed. "They just weren't helpful at all."

"Did you get everything right?" he asked, and he was right to. "I tried," I said. "I had a hell of a time tracking every-thing down, but I think I got it all."

"Do we need to pull it?"

I thought for a minute. "It's up to you," I said. "They *were* pains in the ass." Occasionally, Ira killed announcements just because the couple was too much to handle, or they lied, or didn't provide the right information, or sometimes they were just jackasses and he didn't have time for that. "Let me see it on the proofs," he said, and waved me away. Because everything was so hard to figure out, I was border-line late on this one, and he needed to rush it. I checked the proofs later, and Blueberry and her betrothed were in the middle of the second page, with their photo. Ira needed to fill the space and had decided to keep them on, so fine, whatever. However, Monday morning was a different story.

I was used to coming in Monday mornings and seeing the blazing-red voice mail light on my phone. I always had brides who wanted extra copies, or brides' mothers concerned that we referred to them as their actual legal names instead of Mrs. Jack Jeremiah Jinglehopper the Third. I punched in my code and held the receiver to my ear, and it's a wonder my eardrum survived the blistering. I stopped listening halfway through and hung up.

"So, that fruit bride is pissed," I called over to Ira.

"What did we do?" he asked, not even bothering to roll his eyes.

"I'm forwarding you her voice mail so you can hear it yourself," I said. "She is *awful*."

I waited for him to listen to the voice mail, watching his caterpillar eyebrows rise up and then up again; his mustache quivered as if someone had just farted. He put the phone down. "What did you do?"

"Remember, those were the people who wouldn't answer my questions?" I said, not a little defensively, but come on, it was the truth.

"Oh, those people," Ira said. "Well, we did kind of mess it up."

"Ira, they didn't answer the questions! The groom didn't even give me his new employer's number! The bride was a super bitch!"

"Yes," Ira said mildly, "but we still got these things wrong, according to the bride. I'll handle her. But I want you to send me all the correspondence with her before I call her back."

"I think she's in Vietnam, or on her way to Vietnam," I said. "I don't think you can call her back."

"Send it to me anyway. I'll figure it out."

Here's what we got wrong: the bride's new job title, in part because she gave it to us wrong; her wine importer husband's new employer, because he didn't give it to us straight; her mother's correct name, because her mother didn't want to talk to us; and, if you can follow this, the fellowship that she had before the new position she was supposed to start after their honeymoon to Vietnam, because *she got it wrong.*

Being wrong sucks, and it especially sucks to be wrong on behalf of someone else. I was no stranger to corrections. While rare, every single one stung, and sent me into at least three of the seven stages of grief every time. Which leads me to exhibit B: the journalist who should have gotten his facts straight. One Monday not long after my run-in with Lady Mango the mean neurosurgeon, I checked my voice mail, and there was a terse message from one of my grooms, this one a writer for one of those Big Thought Washington political magazines that no longer exist. He was a medium-sized deal in Washington and a very big deal in his head. And somehow, to his mind, we had gotten his wife's age wrong. I went back and checked my notes before calling him back, and there it was on the printed submission that Ira had marked up. According to the information they'd given us, the bride was thirty and her birthday was in the fall, so she hadn't turned a year older recently. But the groom was furious: his lovely new wife was actually twenty-nine.

"Jonah, I have the submission in front of me, and it says thirty," I told him. "I checked it with Miranda, just like I checked everything else."

I could hear Jonah fidgeting. "But she is twenty-nine."

"She told me she's thirty." For some reason, I remembered that my mom said once that they got married in April, the month before her twenty-fifth birthday, because she didn't want to get married at twenty-five.

"So which is it?" he asked me.

I choked back a laugh. "I would be happy to explore this more with you, but I think you and Miranda will have to figure this out and get back to me," I said, and I realized: this dude was figuring out he'd married a woman in her thirties, not her late twenties, as he'd been thinking, and I think his world had just been rocked a little. It's possible she lied to him, and it's also possible that he just didn't know how old she was and saw *thirty* in the announcement—the same age as he was—and his assumption that he'd married a younger, more innocent woman deflated quickly. Either way, I decided it was not my problem. I hung up and didn't hear anything more from Jonah and Miranda, the couple who maybe, possibly got off on the wrong foot. I doubt they're still married.

I think we've well established how occasionally foolish and downright awful these brides and grooms could be. But almost to a couple, with the exception of a firefighter-teacher pair or two former service members (infantry, not officers), these people came from moneyed classes. Very few of the people I interviewed had likely ever swabbed floors and scrubbed toilets after the restaurant lights had been turned off, or got summer jobs for any reason other than to build character and stay out of their parents' hair. I am not immune to that judgment; I mean, the reason I worked during the summers was to save money for boarding school, not to help my parents pay the rent. Nor did I think most of these people had never done hard work in some way. But the nets that kept them safe were tightly woven and reached far into the recesses of American industry and finance. And when it came time to perform the ritual of marriage, those nets were what helped write the checks for the catering deposits, the synagogue deposits, the dress deposits and the limo rentals and when the bride's mother wanted to complete her fine-china registry of twelve place settings because how could her daughter throw a proper dinner party with only nine? The money helped make it special, as did the old family friends and connections happy to call in a favor or two. I often wondered what these brides and grooms would do with a wedding in which they had to make their dresses themselves, work deep into the night for overtime to pay for their wedding barbecue, and ask for a portable speaker for Christmas so they could have music at their reception.

Michael's roommates Mark and Jessica were planning one of those weddings. They were college sweethearts, and Mark and Michael had moved from Florida to Long Island City together with all their worldly goods crammed in a U-Haul. Mark had proposed to Jessica with a ring that was given to him by his magician mentor, who wanted it to go to a good home, and it did; its tiny diamonds twinkled from Jessica's manicured hand as elegantly as any bauble from Harry Winston. Neither of them had any money, and neither did their parents. Mark didn't know his biological father, and his mother was a hot mess; Jessica's parents had long since split and were still acrimonious a decade after their divorce was final. But they were bound and determined to have a real wedding, despite their parents' shortcomings and their bank balances, which rarely reached four figures, and sometimes not even three. A theater friend of Jessica's made her a strapless ivory dress from material they picked up in the garment district, and Mark was going to wear a suit that doubled as a performance outfit, so he could write it off. The wedding was planned for April, a lovely spring weekend at her mother's farm on the Florida Panhandle, and Michael had already asked if I could go with him. I didn't want to say no. But I wasn't quite ready to say yes.

None of this is to say that Mark and Jessica's wedding had any more meaning than those that I wrote about for the Weddings pages. I wondered, though, if they had more money, how they would spend it. Would they splash out on platinum rings, or would they have seafood instead of chicken? Would they have a ceremony at City Hall and a reception at Cipriani, not bothering with schlepping down to rural Florida, where rental folding chairs were one-eighth of the cost? After all, the weddings that I wrote about are not, and have never really been, the average American experience. Consider my parents' own wedding. Yes, it was a different time and place, but some people in 1977 were spending boatloads of cash on their weddings, even though mine did not. And while I'm sure many Americans got married on the weekend of April 9, 1977, the *Times* didn't reflect that fact; instead, all but two of the announcements were of engagements, indicating that these brides and grooms were waiting for the wedding social season to begin. They weren't dependent on the academic calendar, as were my parents, who were teaching public school in rural Virginia. (Relatedly, an ad from the United Nations in that particular issue of the *Times* asked readers to "Take a chance on fairness" to promote women's equality, advertising the UN's designated Decade for Women, which ran through 1986. After 1986, everything was going to be copacetic and women of all colors and creeds would make equal pay and be able to walk down the street at night without their keys tucked in their fists, hahahahaha, everything is still terrible.)

In 1993, I was a bridesmaid in my aunt Jinny's wedding, on an unseasonably cold day in January. My grandmother made Jinny's gown, and my mom sewed my puff-sleeved bridesmaid dress, which, this time, was definitely made out of upholstery fabric. We all chipped in on assembling the celebrations, and my dad and uncles spent three hours doing the rehearsal dinner dishes in our bathtub. Our family wedding photo is straight out of the *Onion*, not *Martha Stewart Weddings*. My aunt Alice repeated her Grim Reaper pose from 1977 and looks like a fourth-grade teacher with a bunch of kids buried in her garden. My mom had forced a purple clip-on tie on my brother that barely reached the middle of his round little six-year-old belly, and because he was down front at the bottom of the altar, the only person to see him cross his eyes and stick out his tongue was the photographer, who I think was doing this as a favor for my aunt. Although my aunt and uncle were livid with him for most of the next decade, the rest of us treasure this photo. I hope my brother counts it among his proudest moments. They never got a real honeymoon; my uncle was in the Army, and the following weekend he hit his head after jumping out of a plane, and it took him years to remember his own wedding. Despite all that, they're still married, and as far as I can tell, they love each other more all the time.

Anyway, all I'm saying is, despite an industry pretty much dedicated to encouraging us to believe otherwise, these fancy weddings don't mean anything unless the love is real. And that's the crux of it all, right? As my first husband, Hugh Grant, said, you have to love someone with your whole heart. If Mr. Washington Writer didn't know how old his wife actually was, what else was he missing, even with their reception at the Harvard Club? Was the Fruit of the Month Club neurosurgeon angry at me, or angry at herself? (I think likely a combination of both.)

These questions nagged at me, and the nagging got louder once I started writing for the Neediest Cases campaign, just like Helene the climber clerk, who had won the competition for the coveted reporter slot and was safely ensconced on the business desk, where the deputy editor known for his extreme womanizing had to tuck his tongue back in his head every morning when she walked in. This guy was the worst. A brilliant journalist, to be clear, a champion of writers who could talk a story onto the front page like no one else. But otherwise, that man never met a skirt he didn't try to look up. Once, when he was still a clerk, Michael had to vouch to George's wife that he had been making phone calls to reporters, not other women he was sleeping with or attempting to sleep with. Years later, I worked with him briefly, and the first thing George would do after he dropped his bag at his desk was to dial an internal extension and mutter into the phone, "Bizday is in the house," and then a few hours later he would disappear for a very long "lunch" after dialing that same extension. He eventually resigned after an internal investigation; at least two women had accused him of engaging in inappropriate communication, which is a very *Times*ian euphemism for who knows what, although I'm sure we can both take a good guess. It appeared he and his unstoppable penis had finally gone too far. To everyone's extreme bafflement, he is still married, and I hope his wife has no shortage of side pieces to keep her busy. Does that count as love? To them, I guess it does.

With each Neediest story, I explored a corner of the city where my weddings work, and my own little social existence, didn't take me. I wrote about a teenager in Brownsville who needed new shoes. I wrote about a Gambian boy in the Bronx with a lethal heart condition who had lost his mother, and whose favorite treat was a spoonful of sugar mixed into a glass of milk. I sat with a deaf man who needed a blinking door signal to let him know when someone was downstairs. I met a motherless young poet who needed seventy-five dollars for the orientation fees for college. "You got to hustle for everything," she told me.

What were these people doing on Saturday mornings, as the couples I wrote about prepared for their weddings in their suites at the Four Seasons? Surely many of the families I wrote about could be counted upon for generous contributions to the Neediest Cases fund, which could help pay the deaf man's rent, or refill the young poet's meal card. But poverty and trauma aside, the refrain I heard when reporting out these stories was love. The teenager needed to work to support his mother, and needed the shoes to do it. The Gambian boy's milk was given to him by his father, for whom he was everything in the whole wide world. The people I wrote about needed—my God, they needed more than I could even fathom—but they also wanted and loved, and loved well. It wasn't some O. Henry story, although some of these certainly carried a whiff of that. It was love unadorned, naked as anything offered by a new mother. It was perfect.

I have been rich in love all my life, both giving and receiving, from my parents and brother and aunts and uncles, from friends and more than friends, and it is a wonder to be able to say that. The more I discovered about Michael, the more I saw that he held ten thousand leagues of love and seemed ready to plunge deep into it with me. Even though I knew what it was to love and be loved, I didn't know this fervor, this passion, and the pace that pushed it harder, rushing toward something glowing but unknown. So I freaked out, because I don't know, when you're twenty-five, what else are you supposed to do?

One November weekend, not long after we had started spending practically every night together, we were cozied up at a bar with some college friends of mine. Shots happened, more shots happened, Rob was bombastic, Jess was drunk, and it was the usual circus of yelling and one-upmanship. It was deeply comforting. Even though Michael thrilled me, and I was glad to know I thrilled him, I found myself growing uneasy. It was too much too fast. (Yes, I know I was obviously chickenshit and too dumb to recognize how good I had it.) At any rate, Michael joined us after his shift ended, and he and Rob instantly fell in step together, matching each other shot for shot. I was proud to introduce him to some of the people who knew me best, as an adult out of the nest, as a journalist and a writer, and as someone who wanted more all the time. Rob put his arm around my shoulder at the bar and said, "Doty, I like him." And that puffed my chest a little.

But. But but but. The more shots were poured, the looser everyone of course got, and the night got long. Right before we headed for the 7 train and back to Woodside, Michael put his arms around me, kissed my cheek, and said, "I'm either going to marry you, or this is going to end very, very badly."

Whatever I had been drinking evaporated out of my head and was replaced by cold fear. What did he mean? He was going to marry me or kill me? Obviously that was not going to be the case. But all of a sudden it became clear: the heat of the first few months together was supposed to sustain this until we met our graves, and I wanted to run out of the door right then, screaming into traffic. So I did the next best thing. The next morning, I called my friend Jake, a reporter who had just moved back to North Carolina, and asked if I could come down for the weekend. "I need a break," I told him. Since we'd met my freshman year of college, Jake had fielded many of my breakdowns, over boys and everything else, and he said, "A break from what?"

"I'll tell you when I get down there," I said.

Then I went cool on Michael for a couple of days. I avoided him at work, I returned only one or two of his many calls, I declined his usual invitation to stay over. I needed to get my head straight. I had no plans to break up with him, but I needed to slow things down. My need for him was evolving into something that felt permanent, and it scared the everlasting holy shit out of me. And instead of facing it like a grown-up and talking it through, I decided to just get on a plane, because taking the E train to the airport and fighting the TSA at rush hour felt more pleasant than that.

"So, I'm going to North Carolina tonight to see my friend Jake," I told him after he'd finally tracked me down in the newsroom. "I just need to go home for a few days."

Michael was suspicious, and he had every right to be. "Who's Jake?"

"I told you about him. My friend," I said. "Don't worry, I am not going to sleep with him." (I was not, did not, and have never, just to be absolutely clear on that point.)

"Why do you need a break?" he asked. I could tell he didn't finish his thought. *From me*, his eyes implored. *Why do you need a break when things are so good?*

I knew those were his questions. And I really didn't have an answer. All I knew was, the idea of forever with him scared me in a way that I'd never known. I didn't have the words to tell him how terrified I was. And so I didn't say anything.

He walked me to the elevator and pushed the down button for me. "Well, I'll see you when you get back, then." It was a question more than a good-bye. People were around, so he didn't sneak a kiss to a spot right below my ear, as he'd done so many times in quiet corners of the newsroom. The door dinged, and I walked through it and turned back to him with a short wave. He didn't wave back, and I thought: *What did I just do?* But I kept going downstairs.

CHAPTER 9

At Last, Sort Of

I CAME BACK. I called Michael from the taxi stand at the airport. "Do you want to come over?" he asked, and I knew everything hinged on what I said next.

"Yes," I said, shakily, resolutely. I wasn't sure what I was going to say until he asked me. The stand operator pointed me to a cab, blew his whistle twice, and waved more cabs down the curb. "Sixty-first Street in Woodside," I told the driver.

"Sixty-first and what?"

"I'll show you when we get there," I said, and I strapped in. We barreled down the BQE past St. Michael's Cemetery, where a photographer had once given me a tour after we finished a Neediest assignment. "Lots of neediest in there," Ashley had said while we made the loop around the graves. I was fascinated by how cemeteries seemed to thrive in a city that probably had to dispose of dozens of bodies a day, but where we were all crammed in, each longing for our own bit of green and sky. Why were New Yorkers just not all cremated? I guessed the people who opted for coffins and mausoleums were used to living on top of others, and didn't mind doing it for eternity.

The cab finally pulled up to Michael's house in Woodside, a two-story thing that he shared with three roommates in their upstairs apartment, two people in what amounted to cells in the basement, and the owners, Nafiz and Shirah, who lived on the first floor. They were lovely people, Indian immigrants who were generous to the young strivers living above and below them. During the blackout of 2003, Michael and his mother, who was visiting from Florida, had to walk across the 59th Street Bridge to get home. Peggy, who had hypoglycemia and the beginning of multiple sclerosis, had reached her breaking point and couldn't walk anymore. Nafiz found them in the dark among the throngs, piled them into his minivan, and brought them home, as people who lived along the 7 train, the immigrant express, streamed across the bridge. They were much better people than my Brooklyn landlord, who refused to fix the giant swelling coming from our kitchen ceiling that we had nicknamed *the polyp*, which she claimed just added character. But the other thing that Nafiz and Shirah owned was a very loud parrot that didn't bother Michael. His mom and stepdad were bird people, and he lived for years with a lovebird named Scooter, who specialized in flying into the ceiling fan, and a neurotic African gray parrot named Gizmo, who was in such a sad state that he picked off all the feathers on his chest. It bothered me, though, in part because I am terrified of birds and don't need to be in the same house with them, even—or really especially—if they're behind bars. As far as I could tell, this parrot's cage was right under Michael's bedroom, which made for some interesting evening serenading.

Michael was waiting for me on the stoop, and he took my bag and led me upstairs without a word, into his room, where he sat down on the bed and stared at me, his palms out, waiting. I sat down next to him, and his old Salvation Army bed creaked like it always did, reminding me that everything we said and did, good and bad, could be heard out in the living room. "Why did you leave?" he said, after we sat a while in quiet. I thought about leaning against him, but I felt the ice between us.

"I needed space," I said. "What you said about marrying me—it was a lot to think about. And it scared me."

"What? When did I say that?"

"At the bar the other night. You said that you were either

going to marry me, or this was going to end very badly. And both feel insane to me, and I freaked out, and I needed to get out."

Michael rubbed his head, which I noticed was shorn close again. He and Mark must have gone down to Astor Place for cheap haircuts while I was gone.

"I didn't mean it in—well, I meant it in the sense—I don't know what I meant, really. But I wish you'd told me that you got scared instead of just freezing me out and flying to go see another guy."

I rolled my eyes at the thought of Jake as the other guy, and Michael put his hand on mine. "Cate, please, *please* don't roll your eyes at me. You left without a word, pretty much, and what was I supposed to think? I thought you were going to come back and I wasn't going to have a girlfriend anymore."

"I didn't mean that," I said. "I was rolling my eyes about Jake."

"Yeah, but who's Jake? I don't know him. I mean, you left and didn't kiss me good-bye. You didn't bother to say goodbye. You didn't say anything. So you tell me what I was supposed to do."

Michael pulled his hand away and rubbed his head again. "What do you want to do for dinner?" he said. I looked at him, surprised. "Look," he said. "You're here, and we're going to wrestle this thing to the ground, and I missed you, and you must have missed me or you wouldn't be here, either that or you're here to actually break up with me. So, which is it, and what do you want for dinner?"

"I want curry puffs," I said. "And I want you. That's all." I took a breath. "And I'm sorry."

"It ruined my fucking weekend, you know."

"Well, you'll have more," I said tartly. "If it helps, my weekend wasn't all that great either."

We edged closer to each other on the bed. "Oh, yeah?" Michael asked, and he took off his glasses and laid them on his desk, on which he'd written *Free Farts*. "Jake's not that good in bed, huh."

"Fuck *off*, he's a *friend*," I said, kicking off my shoes. I saw where this was going, and I wanted it. "For what it's worth, he told me I was being a chickenshit."

"He was right." Michael pulled my hair aside and started kissing my collarbone. I thought of his lovely shoulders beneath his T-shirt and the collarbone he broke when he was skiing in Utah, when he didn't have health insurance, and the emergency room doctor set it the best he could without charging Michael more money. It ached when it rained. I had started to know these things without thinking about them, like directions on how to get home. "Wait, stop," I said, and pushed him back. "Listen. I am sorry. But this is a lot and it's scary to me, and it's got to be scary to you too. Right? I mean, you said 'married.' That's—that's a lot."

"Yeah, I know, and I had had a lot to drink, and you were a little drunk too," Michael said, a little exasperated. "I know that I love you"—we had already said the L word, which also terrified me, but again, it just felt so good—"and that you say you love me, and we have extremely good sex, and your face is my favorite thing in the world, and so I don't know. I will do my best to never hurt you, and I will back off. Is that OK?"

I screwed up my mouth so I wouldn't smile. "Yes. That's OK."

"I mean, if I'm being honest, it sounds to me like it's more than OK," Michael said, and he smiled. He kissed me again, this time on the mouth, gently, and then hungrily, and I kissed him back, hungrily, and then stopped. "Wait," I said once more. "Go slow. Please."

WE DID GO more slowly, even though we spent the next two days in bed, getting up only to eat Thai food and then, the next morning, to grab an Irish breakfast down on Wood-side Avenue, before watching a movie and falling back into bed until dark. We were really good at having sex, eating, and having big, loud discussions, and all of it left their mark on the space between us, a space that got more crowded with love and fear and doubt. I wondered when it would tip in one direction or the other, or if the glass would fill one way, and then another, until it all overflowed together, mixed into a potent brew.

I wasn't kidding when I said my weekend hadn't been that great. I had gone back to Chapel Hill, where I spent so many days and weeks with Adnan, rolling through coffee shops, driving around in the dark, where I had first really fallen for someone. Every ramble down Franklin Street brought his voice back into my head, and every sip of beer at He's Not Here made me remember something of him that I had put away for safekeeping: a note left after a date, or a song that sent us off to sleep. After we split and he left the country, I didn't trust myself to fall again, especially so quickly, and so hard. I wondered, though, if the ease with which I'd fallen in step with Michael meant that maybe I didn't really love Adnan after all. Maybe it was all smoke and no fire. Maybe it wasn't real. But it sure felt real, and if it wasn't, what was? After all the encounters I'd had with brides and grooms, and the disasters I saw in the making, I just wasn't sure.

Right before Michael and I started dating, I had begun to look into master's programs in international affairs. I dreamed of being a foreign correspondent someday, or maybe an aid worker in a war-scarred country, rising to be chief of mission, driving around in a Toyota Hilux, fighting with governments and agencies to get aid to those who I thought needed it the most, hosting the occasional secretary of state and having illicit international affairs. I didn't know—and didn't think to find out—that (a) that fantasy was rooted in some major colonialism that I hadn't yet recognized, and (b) many of the foreign correspondents at the *Times* started almost the same way I was starting: writing Neediest Cases stories, picking up assignments, writing and writing and writing. You didn't need a master's degree to cover wars and recovery. In fact, most of the people covering the Iraq War had been recruited from Metro beats, like City Hall and the cop shop. One of them had been kidnapped along with a photographer and held for a few weeks, and when they were released, as the story went, they went back to the heavily guarded bureau compound and fucked like proverbial rabbits for a week, giving no thought to their partners stateside. This rumor went around as proven fact, and I guarantee it was judged by very few fellow journalists back in the newsroom. War and kidnapping put more flexible morals like fidelity aside. I told you, journalists are weird creatures, and that's what makes them such good storytellers. They ask what others won't, they go where others won't, they do what others would not, to tell a true, good story. The whole "fake news" crowd can absolutely, 100 percent, without a shadow of doubt, lick my ass.

Michael burst into my dreams of becoming an international woman of mystery and slowed them down a little. I knew I had something good with him, even though I was scared. But I also knew that I had something good with myself. I had big things to accomplish, big things to think about. I carried—and carry—the usual self-doubts that most women have: am I making the right choices, do I look better in dresses or jeans, did I insult that person ten years ago, what if I never weigh the same again, can I please never weigh this again. But I do not doubt my brain, and I did not then doubt that I was in New York, in the place that I loved, to do something big, even if I didn't know what that big thing was, or even how to figure it out, or what *big* meant.

If you look at great romantic partnerships across the decades—of people who accomplished big art, big thoughts, big changes—it was the women who fell behind. We all know this. When I thought of the women I grew up reading about, the woman had to raise the children, pay the bills, and get up before dawn to write, while the man, of course, just took his sweet time, smoked his pipe, stunk up the house, and thought big thoughts while gazing out the window, marking the time by the mailman.

These women marked time differently. Their clocks ran by the school bus schedule, the milkman's schedule, when it was safe to have sex with their husbands and not produce another child, when it was time to get their roots done, when to start dinner, when to bake the birthday cake, when to buy bigger underwear for their children. "I have found the warm caves in the woods," Anne Sexton wrote in "Her Kind," "fixed the suppers for the worms and the elves: whining, rearranging the disaligned. A woman like that is misunderstood."

Any woman trying to do something can tell the same basic story and fill in her own particulars—how her days and months and years were spent in service of others, of her own blood or not, while fighting the tide to find the right words, the right thoughts, to find the goddamn *time*. Women's time has always meant less than men's time, which is hilarious, since we've always had to pack in so much more. All of this you of course know, but I was slowly figuring it out. So the partnerships I knew about that I wanted to emulate were those in which the women made the work free of evident burden. I wanted to be Georgia O'Keeffe in New Mexico, Martha Gellhorn without Hemingway, Julia Reed with her exacting wit and shoe collection. I had no intention of being a Camille Claudel to a cruel, thieving Rodin. I wanted to be Sexton's possessed witch, haunting the black air. The worms and the elves could find someone else to take care of them.

I worked with some of these women, older women who had reputations for severity, emotional obtuseness, even cruelty. The cruelty label was almost never fair, but the severity one was. Most of these women had a good two decades on me, and they'd come up in the business when newsrooms were sexist, condescending backwaters. One woman had started her career abroad, seeing more opportunity for women in war zones, where derring-do wins the day, over domestic newspapers, where she had a very good chance of being relegated to the women's pages, writing about women's interests, like weddings. This woman had been held up by the Khmer Rouge and escaped from Pol Pot's clutches; she had more smarts and adventure in her right hand than most people do in a lifetime. Another woman, whose moods changed with what bills were before the Senate, ate exactly one cup of nonfat vanilla yogurt for lunch, taking the tiniest of nibbles to stretch it out, and looked at me with unvarnished scorn when I mentioned one day, on a lark, that I wanted to be a travel writer. "That's not important," she said, and walked away.

She hurt my feelings, but I also knew what she meant. We were there to do big important work, to chronicle the world, and maybe to change it as necessary. But she seemed myopic to the different ways that could happen. I understood why: she'd come up as a woman among many, many men, who'd sharpened her elbows with their demands, their me-firsts, their aggression, their many looks down her blouse while she was banging away on deadline.

Often, these women, who frightened me daily with their brains and intellectual brawn, were divorced. Or they'd married late, deep into their careers, or they had partners in different cities. A few had had famous affairs. Some had come to the newsroom while married, and their marriages ended not long after. One woman and her husband were hired at the same time, and a few months later, they split. She ended up with a new last name, that of an editor on a different section, and that wasn't the first name change to happen there under similar circumstances. Custody arrangements and summer camp decisions and *please can you take the girls tonight, I have a late press conference* were wrangled in the stairwells between reporters and editors, layout people and photographers. Two women who worked in the same section got into a fistfight in the bathroom over a husband who, as far as anyone could tell, couldn't yet choose between his wife, the assailed, and his mistress, the assailant. The assailant eventually won him away from his wife, if you can claim that a victory.

So I watched a lot of commitment falter, and some grow stronger, and some remain out of sight. Some, I was growing to admire. Needing more editing help, Ira had hired a retired copy editor named Abraham, who, with his flop of gray hair and daily bow ties, resembled a slighter, gay Hal Holbrook. Abraham lived two blocks into Hell's

Kitchen with his partner, Kenneth, a former reporter, and he walked home every day for lunch. Kenneth cooked. I learned quickly to tune in around ten thirty to their whispered phone arguments over what would be served.

"We had tuna *yesterday*!" Abraham whispered into the receiver one morning. "I do not want—Kenneth, calm down—I don't want a tuna *melt* when I just had tuna *salad*!"

I pulled my shirt up around my face so I wouldn't laugh. Two desks down, April's shoulders shook, and her earrings tinkled.

"Why do you need another avocado? That has nothing to do with a tuna melt!" he continued. "Kenneth, I will bring something—fine, I'll just go to *McDonald's*." Abraham slammed down the receiver, pulled on his double-breasted blazer, and stomped out to the elevator bank. Tony just shook his head. Abraham came back an hour later, and I don't think he brought Kenneth an avocado. Despite the daily drama, I loved Kenneth and Abraham. I loved their long partnership, and I wondered about their lives together as gay men through Stonewall, the AIDS crisis, through "don't ask, don't tell," and finding their way to each other in a newsroom where their love and the strength of their partnership was ignored, shunned, or frowned upon. They were committed, no matter what, even if the menu was wrong that day.

But they also had the advantage of being white men, for whom this particular world was built, although who they truly were likely hindered who they wanted to be.

I talked to a lot of women who were doing big things and who happened to be getting married. One thing about the Weddings desk: if you want to talk to a lot of smart, accomplished women, to try to understand things that you don't know about yourself yet, it's a pretty good gig. And this stuff plagued my brain. I knew there was no way to settle it down 100 percent, but I wanted to know what other women did and thought. How did they reconcile their desire for partnership with their bedrock need to be themselves, to be the smartest voice in the room, to make the art that changed the world? Or to be more blunt, how did they get their own shit done while making space for someone else?

One day, my assignment list included an announcement for a woman who was a very big deal at Google. Her résumé was fierce: time in government, chief of staff to a cabinet member, two advanced degrees and one terminal degree, smart move after smarter move, lots of volunteer work. She was a few years older than me and was likely making ten to twelve times my salary. She was marrying a man who had built a start-up, sold it for millions, built another one, sold it for more millions, and was then running the show at a big tech company whose products the *Times* used. Her name

wasn't household yet, but it was going to be, in a big, turbulent way—in part of her own making, and in part because
her life to come would split from the path in ways she would
not likely have imagined. But even without that look into a
crystal ball, I wanted to know more about her. This accomplished woman, who glowed from her engagement photo—
eyebrows aligned with her fiancé's, of course—was entering into what she hoped was a permanent partnership, in
which both people were the job and for whom life could not
come at them fast enough.

I called the groom first. "I'm so glad you called!" he said,
and I could hear some jostling in the background. "We're
leaving for Arizona tomorrow, and this was one of the last
things on the list to take care of."

"I imagine it's quite a list," I said, and noted that he seemed
to take ownership of the all-mighty pre-wedding checklist
that so many brides kept in their heads. "It always is."

"Yeah, and this is a busy week for her, so I'm trying to
wrap a lot of it up," he said. "She's been running this show
until now, but she's got a lot of shows to run."

"I bet. Can you tell me about her?"

It was, in the realm of the announcements, off topic. We
were there to fact-check this guy's age, employment, education, and lineage. But his admiration for the woman he was
about to marry reverberated down the line, and I wanted to
know more. You might think that that would be standard

practice the week before someone gets married, but trust me, most of the grooms I spoke with radiated nerves and a wish to get off the phone, not adoration for the person whose hand they were about to take.

"She's brilliant," he said. "I mean, you've got her résumé, right? She's just brilliant, and she's kind. She's so kind. She makes time for people. It's hard to do that in our business, but she does. She knows how to use time right."

"It must be challenging to see each other," I said. "You both seem to lead such big careers."

He laughed, and I heard a loud zip; he was packing for his wedding, I thought. "It's definitely hard, and it'll be harder when we have kids," he said. "But we'll work it out. She's a big gun, and I know when to get out of her way, and she knows when to get out of mine."

We went down the checklist of questions, and I asked for his college credentials. "You guys have to ask for that?" he said, and laughed.

"Yep. You didn't know this was actually a job interview."

He laughed again, and we hung up. Next up was the bride. Her assistant put me on hold for maybe ten seconds, and then I heard the clatter of a phone being yanked off its cradle. "Hello! Hi! I'm so glad you called!" She was thrilled to talk to me. We went through the questions, and she put her hand over the receiver to yell for her assistant to email over pictures of her diplomas on the wall.

"So, can you tell me a little about him?" I asked.

"Ooooh, how much time do you have?" She giggled, and I knew this was not the same poised woman who appeared in trim Ralph Lauren gabardine before thousands at annual stockholder meetings. "He is so generous," she said. "I just adore him. I mean, obviously, right? But he's so considerate. And of course he's absolutely brilliant."

"He said similar things about you," I said.

I almost heard her blush. "Well, he's very supportive," she said.

"You both have such demanding careers. I imagine it must be hard to see each other as much as you'd like."

"We do, but that's how we like it," she said. "And you know, he always has my back. He always wants to know what I need."

Well, if that isn't the sexiest thing, I thought. A man who asked you what you needed, and not just what you wanted for breakfast. "It sounds like you balance each other out."

"What's balance?" she said, and laughed again. "It ebbs and flows."

I thanked her and hung up. *What's balance*, I thought. It was a good question. What did I mean by *balance*, anyway? Did I mean a partnership in full, or did I mean my needs first, his much later? Not long after they got married, I ran across a picture of their wedding. They're dancing together, her ivory slip dress draped off her slender shoulders, her mink hair grazing them. They're looking at each other with more than love, more than lust, more than understanding. It is a calm assurance that they are exactly where they need to be, and nowhere else, other than right by the other. It's as if every molecule of oxygen between them is there to be shared, to give life to and salve them both.

A few months later, a Vows column landed on my desk. "Young people," Ira said. "They're obnoxious, but the story isn't bad. You free tomorrow night?"

These two people were getting married on a Thursday night on the sidewalk in front of their favorite jewelry store. They were self-described raccoons, always drawn to the shiniest objects, and I wondered if they meant each other too. I interviewed the bride first, who had moved to town from Los Angeles, where she worked as an executive assistant to a Famous Movie Producer. The story was complicated, but not really. She was the girlfriend of this guy's best friend from college, but after they started hanging out, they fell in love. Fair enough. Love knows no bounds, and a cross-country boyfriend is no match for the guy right in front of you, showering you with roses, affection, and fancy dinners. But their relationship, and their impending union, had caused ire in their circle of friends, to say the least.

I thought Rhett and Scarlett were destined for divorce. They had to be. They'd only known each other a few months before they decided to hitch up for life; the way they talked about their impending marriage, it sounded like an act of defiance more than an act of love. Scarlett gushed about Rhett the same way I would talk about a hot dog with extra mustard, and Rhett didn't really have much to say about Scarlett. It was entirely possible that his affection for her was founded upon her perky rack and her Hollywood connections. He had built an education business targeted to New York's neurotic parent class, and judging by the ring he gave Scarlett, it seemed to be working pretty well, even though we were on the edge of a recession.

The next night after work, I walked over to the jewelry store, a famous place at a famous intersection where rich people, or just people willing to go into a lot of debt, bought large jewels and silver baby rattles. At least one moron had named his child after the store. I waved at the freelance photographer whom Ira had tracked down last-minute to shoot this thing, and he said, "So what is this mess about?"

I gave him the backstory, and he snorted. "Yeah, that'll last," he said. We watched as the groom paced in front of the store, the display windows stripped of their jewels for the evening, their glow bouncing off his gelled head. A few of their friends milled around the sidewalk, and I leaned up against the building, not wanting to interrupt, waiting to watch this thing go down.

A silver limo pulled up, and out stepped Scarlett, wearing go-go boots, a miniskirt, and a halo of tulle around her head, like a pompadour from a Sargent painting. The driver held the door for her while she paused to survey the scene, like Annie in *Father of the Bride*, except that instead of three hundred black-tie guests in a church, Scarlett's witnesses were a few friends on light and music duty; some tourists with backpacks and FAO Schwarz bags; the jewelry store security guards, who seemed to be on extra alert for this event; and the photographer and me, two invited interlopers. Rhett stood up straight, and a friend started playing a song on their portable CD player. Scarlett did her best imitation of a bridal march across the twenty feet of concrete, under the lit paper lantern held aloft by a guest, joined hands with Rhett, and they were pronounced husband and wife as traffic honked and a 5th Avenue bus lumbered past, as the city twinkled at them, as it does for lovers sometimes. Scarlett turned to her friends with a possessive grip on Rhett's pinstriped arm, threw her bouquet up in the air, and howled into the night. It felt like a fitting beginning, I thought, if not necessarily an auspicious one.

I talked to her a few days later, after the dust had settled, and asked how she felt about it all. "Married! I feel married," she said. "I'm a wife. That's crazy, right?"

While I agreed with her in my head, I laughed and said, "That was the goal, right? How do you think the ceremony went?"

She was quiet for a second, and when she answered, she

was more subdued. "I wish our friends had understood why we did this," she said. "I just couldn't turn my back on it." Scarlett and Rhett's mutual friends had not looked kindly at her shifting amours, and the whole thing had caused a bit of a rift. "But!" She cheered up. "But I'm married to Rhett now!"

I agreed. We got off the phone, and as I settled in to write, I went back over my notes. These two people from opposite coasts, with little more shared than a friend and a love of spontaneity, had, at least for the moment, found utter happiness in each other. I was absolutely positive that they would be divorced in a year. I never could get to the bottom of their particular rush to the altar; they couldn't speak eloquently enough about it for me to make sense of it, and it's possible that their families and friends didn't get it either. But they seemed to hear each other perfectly, and that was enough to try out a lifetime together.

I went home that night, back to my apartment, a rare night away from Michael, but I wanted to get my notes straight without distraction. My roommate Rebecca was watching HGTV from the couch that we had recently rescued from the sidewalk, and she was eating popcorn off her chest, too lazy to sit up straight and eat it from the bowl.

I adored Rebecca. She gave absolutely no fucks and wanted what she wanted, which, boiled down, wasn't a lot, but it was enough for her: Pete, a little money in the bank, lobster night at the Park Slope Ale House, and more Pete, and maybe later, a full service of Mottahedeh Tobacco Leaf china. This is the same girl who kept a bag of Reese's cups open on the kitchen counter, and when she passed through the kitchen on the way to the bathroom in the middle of the night, she would grab one or two for the trip. The fact that we had candy wrappers in the bathroom trash can repulsed Michael, but Rebecca was unapologetic, and I found no fault with the practice. We paid our rent on time, we all got along and knew when to fight it out and when to let it go, and we had loud roof parties where flirting was the background music and guts were spilled, along with lots of cheap wine from the 7th Avenue liquor store.

Rebecca and Pete were edging toward marriage. They'd known each other since kindergarten back in North Carolina, and she was ready to get this show on the road. Pete was saving up for the ring that he knew she wanted, and in the meantime, they spent nearly every weekend together, emerging occasionally from her bedroom to watch TV and eat takeout. We all spoke each other's language.

"How was it?" Rebecca had been fascinated by this assignment. "Did they actually show up?"

I dropped my bag and coat and sat down on the floor, and plowed my hand into the popcorn bowl next to a half-drunk bottle of red wine. "Yep, they actually went through with it. She wore go-go boots."

"Shut *up*. Who are these people? What is wrong with City Hall or a church or the Elks lodge?"

"I don't know," I mused. "But they do seem to love each other, or at least like each other enough for a while."

Rebecca finished her cleavage popcorn, sat up, and brushed the crumbs to the floor. "They're definitely getting divorced," she said. "Hold on. I'm getting you a glass so we can finish this bottle."

I chewed my popcorn and thought, and Rebecca came back with the bag of Reese's cups and a giant glass for me. "My mother would kill me if I got married like that," she said.

"Mine would too, I think. Although, you know, her mother got married up here by herself, no sisters, no family, nothing," I said. "But that was during the war."

"Think about what these people don't have," Rebecca said, as she poured enough wine in my glass for two people. "There's no support system here, their friends don't like them, they only have each other, and they don't even know each other. I'm not trying to be ugly, but it just seems hard to me."

I wondered. Rebecca's mother would absolutely kill her if she pulled a stunt like that, which was moot because she would never consider it. She and Pete had known and loved each other for so long that imagining their future together, for her, was like breathing. There had never been any question about their commitment, or what their future would be. She already knew what she wanted to carry for her bouquet: a magnolia bloom from the tree in her grandmother's yard, with a family locket wrapped around it. The only hurdles left were for Pete to get that ring and Rebecca and her mother to plan the epic wedding they both wanted, with a Methodist ceremony and a reception at the local art museum. Her engagement was likely to be announced in the local paper, as well as the nuptials themselves, and her mother had already picked out the photographer for Rebecca's full-length wedding portrait. For someone who ate chocolate on the toilet and popcorn off her boobs, this was serious business.

I ate a Reese's cup and washed it down with a sip of red. "It's not what I want, that's for sure."

"Have you figured out what you do want?" We had talked a lot about how afraid I was of it all. Michael was a fixture in our apartment, and had quickly gone from a visitor to a member of 537 who was expected to contribute, clear the table, and just accept the candy wrappers in the bathroom. He was the one who had hauled our new, less disgusting couch up the three flights of stairs, and we ate a lot of takeout on the roof together, with Rebecca and Pete and Layla and whoever else was around. I nodded hesitantly. "I just need him to back up a little," I said. "I mean, he was talking about marriage."

Rebecca ate another Reese's. "Yeah, but you said you were both drunk, so it doesn't count. And anyway," she said, "would that be the worst that could happen?"

It was a good question, and I didn't know the answer. But I was maybe starting to have suspicions that it wasn't the worst thing that could happen.

CHAPTER 10

Tchoupitoulas

Y OU WANT TO go on a trip with me?" Michael said over the phone, and I laughed. It was the tail end of August, hot as unmitigated hell, and I had no plans to go anywhere that didn't have air conditioning.

"What do you have in mind?" I asked, and I twirled back and forth in my old chair. It was early in the week, when I did the bulk of my cold-calling with these brides and grooms, and I was glad to have something else to think about for a minute. By the August of my second season on the society desk, I'd started to look at these brides and grooms with annoyance; the thrill of romance had faded a bit, even though my own was in full throttle.

"How about New Orleans?"

"Say what?" I stopped twirling. "What about New Orleans?"

A nuclear explosion had just gone off in New Orleans in the form of Hurricane Katrina, and as Michael worried about his dad and stepmother two hours east in Mobile, the levees broke. The waters rose, and people climbed into their attics and onto their roofs, waiting for help that wasn't on the way. We watched CNN as people huddled without enough food or water in the Superdome, as the Lower Ninth and Arabi and Chalmette and Treme took on enough water to rip family pictures off the living room walls, as the National Guard moved in and smoke rose above another city that we could never know fully but still loved.

Like every other big news outlet, the *Times* was scrambling to get as many journalists as possible on the ground in New Orleans. Metro reporters and correspondents from around the country had been yanked from their regular assignments and told to get their asses down to New Orleans, by air or by land, and do it now. But they still needed a place to stay, and it wasn't like the Hotel Monteleone had availability, with nightcaps available at the Carousel Bar. So the national desk dreamed up a scheme, and they had tasked Michael, the hotshot, to execute on it.

"So, they want me to drive an RV from New Jersey to

New Orleans, park it on Canal Street, and set up a bureau," he said.

I laughed harder. "What, there aren't any RVs in Texas that you could drive over the border? Or in Mississippi? I mean, anywhere?"

"Bridget said she couldn't find one south of Baltimore," Michael said. Bridget was the national desk's shy, stalwart administrator, who did all the advance work for the political conventions, cleaned up everyone's expenses, and took care of the things that no one else wanted or knew how to deal with, like finding a place for twenty-five reporters to use as a base camp in the middle of a natural disaster. She had her own secret romance inside the building that everyone knew about. For almost a decade, she had been in love with an older man who worked on the thirteenth floor. He had shaken free from a marriage gone sour but his children disapproved of another union. They rode the train home together every evening to Long Island, and I would see her waiting by the turnstile for him, her pale Norwegian cheeks scarlet with the mere thought of him emerging from the brass elevators. She acknowledged his existence to me exactly once before they finally got married; a few years after Katrina, we were driving through the night in Denver, waiting for the Secret Service to sweep the convention center before the Democratic National Convention, and she turned to me at a stoplight and said, "I miss my friend."

"So what does this have to do with me?" I asked Michael, although I already knew the answer.

"They want a second clerk to go, and I'm not going to do this drive with anyone but you," he said. "I'll probably stay down there for a bit, do some reporting, help out. You should come too." He had his business voice on, and I could feel him champing at the bit to get going. Like any good journalist, he wanted to be there yesterday, to get the dirt in his boots.

I cradled the phone against my neck and threw my hands up in the air and whooped. "When do we leave?"

"Tonight, if we can."

I hung up with Michael and turned to Ira. "The national desk wants me to go to New Orleans tonight," I said. "Do you mind?" This was a tricky thing. August traditionally had been a slow month for weddings, but this one wasn't, and Ira needed all the help he could get, or at least that was what he said. But I knew the news desks would overrule the society editor's demands any day, and I also knew an adventure and a good assignment when I saw it. There was no way I was going to miss this one, not that I had given any thought to what driving an RV entailed, especially driving an RV into a disaster zone.

Ira sighed a very deep sigh, rumbling with discontent over a news desk poaching me. He already knew he couldn't say no, though, and the fact that I had thought to ask was a courtesy. Ira knew I was packed and ready to go in my head. "Yes, I suppose," he said, exhaling another big sigh. "Give me what you haven't finished and I'll give them to Tony."

I had already shuffled my stack back into the week's manila folder, and I slid it across the desk. I rummaged around for a reporter's notebook and ran downstairs to Bridget, who had a plain envelope of thousands of dollars in cash for us, and warned us to keep every receipt. Everyone had heard the horror rumors already: There was no gas south of Maryland, or no cash left on the Gulf Coast. Civilization as we understood it ended at the Mason-Dixon Line, although frankly, a lot of people probably thought that anyway. "Should you maybe get a lot of gas in New Jersey and bring it with you?" an editor asked as Michael, Bridget, and I huddled by the desk.

Bridget raised her eyebrows; she was used to this sort of unhelpful suggestion. "How would they do that?"

"You could get some gas cans or something, and fill them up in Jersey," he said. "Just keep them in the back of the RV for when you need them."

On its face, having extra gas in case of disaster is, of course, a good idea. But I was not about to follow through on the suggestion that we turn our rented RV into a mobile bomb, with dozens of gallons of gas bumping around in the back over a thousand miles of 110-degree asphalt. Sometimes it really showed who had come from elsewhere and who had probably never been west of the Mississippi, and this was that dude, which, I have to believe, impeded his effect as a national desk editor. One time I went to the Minnesota State Fair with a bunch of *Times* people—it's a long story why—and they all had an eye-opening, wondrous time on the Tilt-A-Whirl and the Ferris wheel, especially the guy who had never in his life eaten a smoked turkey leg on a midway.

Bridget wasn't buying it either, but she had the good sense not to show it. "Great idea, Lane," she said, and turned back to us. "You aren't going to do that," she muttered. We both shook our heads.

Three hours later, we piled into a Town Car on the way to pick up an RV in Branchburg, New Jersey, with the hopes of making it to Virginia before midnight. We had both dashed to our respective apartments to throw a few things in a bag, and Michael had grabbed a bunch of his CDs for the road. I flipped through his black nylon book. "*Titanic, the Musical*?" I howled. "I'm not listening to this shit."

We agreed on many, many things, but I was not down with his musical tastes, and he felt the same about mine. How was he to know that Joni Mitchell taught women of a certain age to feel, as *Love Actually* tells us, or that Erykah Badu was basically perfect, as was Mos Def? I kept flipping.

"I am *definitely* not listening to this," I said, pointing to a Boyz II Men compilation album. Their end of the road for me was in the eighth grade.

Michael, though excited and focused, was cranky. He didn't like being distracted from his mission, and what I didn't know was that he was nervous about driving an RV thousands of miles through these United States, which of course didn't stop him from saying yes; you always say yes to an adventure, we both knew. But he once did $1,500 worth of damage to his dad's clunker Oldsmobile just by taking it through a car wash, so his driving record at that point was a bit, shall we say, fractured.

"I don't think you're going to have a choice in this," he said. "If I'm driving, I'm listening to what I want." Remember, this was before Bluetooth and Spotify, so creating a road trip playlist, especially a last-minute one, was a bit of an ordeal that required bringing a bunch of organized CDs, changing them mid-drive, and putting them back in the Case Logic so they wouldn't get scratched. The hardships, I tell you. I rolled my eyes, wished I'd had the sense to bring my own music, and squirmed in my seat, ready to get on the road.

We got to the RV rental center, and they parked us in front of a twelve-inch TV/VCR combo so we could watch the eight-minute video that would tell us everything we needed to know about driving this RV, which loomed just outside. The workers had pulled it around front for us, and it had a big mural of Mount Rushmore on one side, right below the company's 1-800 number. We loaded our stuff in the back, checked the mirrors, and gingerly pulled out onto Route 22, headed west, then south toward New Orleans.

Michael took the first driving shift, and I settled into the role of navigator and DJ. Bridget had armed us with maps of every state between us and Louisiana, but we knew where we were going, more or less. We were drawn toward south and home and knew the way. And as he eased into driving and found his comfortable speed, I reached across to his captain's chair and rested my hand on his shoulder. The sun caught the antique aquamarine ring that Michael had given me for our first Christmas together, plucked out of a jeweler's window in Park Slope. We had miles to go before we slept, and many more to go after we woke, but we were both happy in that moment, on the road together toward a purpose.

That month marked a year of full-fledged dating for us, and we had found our comfortable silence and routines that showed us the way back to each other at the end of each day. Michael had moved uptown to a tiny one-bedroom in Harlem, but it was *his* one-bedroom, and he was proud of it. It took me a long time to learn that he had spent his childhood in deep poverty, his dad working odd jobs just to make ends meet. To Michael, something as simple as fresh garlic felt like a luxury; so many of the things I had grown up taking for granted, like a whole gallon of milk in the fridge, were the things he saw least. I loved learning about him, and I asked him all the time: *Tell me about your dad. Tell me about living in a cabin with no heat in the dead of winter. Tell me about when you were six years old. Tell me.*

This was a hard thing for him to do. Michael had worked so hard to escape the clutches of his father, a hard-drinking, hard-talking man who lived in his books and smoked a tremendous amount of a few different things. I had heard enough to know not to ask too much. Gary was supposed to come up to New York in September for the wedding of a *Times* reporter who used to work in Mobile with him, and he was very excited to meet me, the woman who had made his beloved son so happy. It was to be a black-tie affair downtown, and I had a beaded cocktail dress on order from Lord & Taylor. Michael, not willing to rent a tux, bought a new suit. Gary, I was informed, would be wearing his dressiest plaid button-up shirt, a knit tie, and sandals with socks.

Barreling down the highway toward the Gulf Coast, I could feel Michael's tension rise. We had no plans to stop in Mobile, and it didn't make sense with the roads anyway. I had come to understand the things that drove him, and one was to not be like his dad, and to be near his dad as little as possible. But I also knew that the pull between them was the devil's magnet. As the afternoon faded on our second day on the road, we neared Montgomery, and I asked, "Should we go through Mobile and call your dad?"

"No," Michael said, a bit sharply. "Let's go toward Meridian and find a place to pull off."

I pressed just a little. "But we're kind of close."

"No. Just no."

We kept going into the night and ate a road dinner of garbage snacks we picked up at a Walmart in Chattanooga. We dropped down through Hattiesburg, and the roads going south emptied, except for power trucks and semis laden with supplies for the storm zone. Katrina had taken out the power and road signs, so we had to light the way forward ourselves, and we hoped we were still pointed in the right direction.

Around midnight, we followed a caravan of Alabama Power trucks to the parking lot of a gas station that had lost its canopy to the storm. Michael parked the RV between two trucks, and we hopped out to stretch. The air, so close to the storm's path, was fetid. It felt old, cruel, laden with something dark that we didn't quite understand. I grabbed a bottle of water, and we brushed our teeth behind a rusted propane tank, spitting into the grass and wiping our mouths with a shared napkin. I leaned against the fuel tank and looked up at the stars. Without the streetlights and ambient light from the highways, the stars were on unbridled display, and they were a swath of cream across the night sky. We were so tired, so very, very tired, and we still had a few hours to go before we got to Canal Street. Michael wrapped himself around me, and I leaned my head against his chest, thinking just for a moment that we were on a really good date that ended with stargazing, not a humid night spent not touching each other on cheap, rough sheets that smelled like old tires. We went back to the RV silently and got into bed, knowing that the next day, we and the Alabama Power guys were headed into hell.

EVEN THOUGH WE were destined for New Orleans, Bridget had seen into the future and understood that this story was not a one-week deal. She had rented out an old plantation in Baton Rouge that had been turned into a weddings space, complete with slave quarters decorated in old Southern style, with carved mahogany four-poster beds, pineapples everywhere, and not a whiff of repentance. The *Times* planned to use that as a home base away from the chaos in New Orleans; the men got the big house, and the women took over the slave quarters. The younger reporters slept on the air mattresses, and the older hands claimed the four-posters. We were going to rest there, and I spent the last three hours on the road dreaming of a hot shower in Baton Rouge, a thought that had never before crossed my mind.

We pulled into New Orleans midday, and after we parked the beast and shook off the road funk, I was directed by whoever was in charge to take their SUV and drive around the city with a columnist named Dave, whose gruff demeanor both amused and scared the hell out of me. I was to drive us back to Baton Rouge, and he was to write his story on the way so he could file when we got there.

We got in the car, and he said, "You know where you're going?"

"No, but I can figure it out."

Dave was tired, and I think being saddled with a clerk who didn't know where she was going made him more so. "OK. We're going to look for bodies. Did Krista tell you that?"

Krista, an editor who set up shop in the RV, had not, in fact, told me that. It was a peculiarly awful thing that Katrina had done: it had made a city that loved its own unable to bury its dead, instead leaving them to rot by necessity on a street in the French Quarter, on front porches in the Bywater, in attics and front rooms and bedrooms, just behind the doors of candy-colored shotgun houses. Dave was there to bear witness for these people, their bodies grown stiff in the unrelenting heat, and by proxy, so was I. This was a far piece from my brides and grooms, who, in the late heat of summer, were holding their weddings in freshwater locales like New Hampshire and Vermont. This was not that.

"Turn left here," Dave said, and pointed to the street sign.

"Chop-pi—how do you say that?" I asked.

"Chop-ah-too-lus," he said, writing something down. "Do you know much about Bruce Springsteen?"

I was in the middle of a Springsteen training camp that Michael had devised for me, with the understanding that to know him, I had to know Bruce. Before this, I had not cared about or given a single thought to Bruce Springsteen, but Michael made it quite clear that Bruce lit the way for him when others could not. "I'm learning about him, but Michael is a big fan. Rabid fan, I should say," I said.

"Rabid, huh." I felt like I had said something wrong and wondered why he'd asked in the first place. "Pull over here."

I found a spot in front of a shotgun house with iron bars on its windows, and we opened the gate and walked slowly up to the porch, where an occupied body bag rested on a worn-out glider. Someone had decorated the bag and the porch with Mardi Gras beads, and a warped piece of poster board was woven through the porch railings. *Claude H. Johnson died here, August 31,* it read. *Rest in Peace. Call 911.*

Dave took notes, silently, and I watched where he looked, wanting to learn. A photographer named Kenny had been there for a few minutes already, and he rested in a small bit of shade and wiped the sweat from his face. He smelled terrible. I remembered that he had been sleeping on a cot in City Hall for three days; he needed and deserved the Baton Rouge shower far more than I did.

"There's another I want to check on," Dave said, and I followed him back to the car and pulled back on to Tchoupitoulas Street. We kept the windows rolled down, looking for a hint of a breeze, already embarrassed by how we smelled, and we passed a house whose gate hid what sounded like a hundred barking dogs, abandoned but locked up for safekeeping. An ASPCA van idled nearby, and we trusted that they were on the case. We took a left on Poydras Street, and then a right, and then another right onto Union, where Dave asked me to pull over again. There on the cobblestones was another corpse, this one barely covered by a blue tarp. It was marked by orange traffic cones, and it was rotting in the heat and sun. There was no one to come pick up this dead man and treat him properly, and so there he rested.

Dave took more notes, and we got back in the car once more. "Let's get out of here," he said, and I nodded. I turned the car north toward Baton Rouge, toward a plantation with mossy oaks, air mattresses, and hot showers, where he could file and I could rest and figure out what to do next. Michael, I knew, was out with another reporter, and I didn't want to bother him. In this place, where people were drowning and dying and help was not on the way, we knew the jobs we'd been sent to do. We knew that, and we loved it, just as we loved each other.

I checked in with Ira when we got to Baton Rouge after I finally showered off the day. "All OK up there?" I asked, trying to inject some cheer into my voice.

"Oh, yes, all is fine," he said. "How is your grand adventure?"

"It is quite the adventure," I said. "Do you need me to make some calls from here?" I felt guilty about leaving him in the lurch, even though I knew there were plenty of people to take my place temporarily.

"No, no, just come back safely," Ira said. I loved that about him, because I knew he meant it. Everybody there did. Say what you want about the vicious liberal media, but they—we—meant it when we said *be safe*, because we knew what could happen. We had all known colleagues to be injured in car crashes, kidnapped, held at gunpoint, blown up, murdered for nothing. Daniel Pearl's widow, Mariane, appeared in the newsroom sometimes—she was a friend of the executive editor's—and when she came through, everyone grew quiet, especially when their little boy was with her. We knew what could happen.

I took a walk around the grounds and watched a science reporter named Ralph pitch a one-man tent in the grass, preferring his own space away from the air mattresses and the snoring. This was the thing I had gone to journalism school for, I thought: running to the storm, not away from it, into the storms we cause and the storms we endure. Why was I still reporting on brides and grooms? I thought back to the first story I had ever written, about the drugs that saved the lives of HIV patients, and I wondered, really for the first time, what needed to come next.

I FLEW HOME a few days later. Michael had been called back on a different assignment, and our friend Lila, another clerk, was coming down to replace me. Ira had stomped his feet a bit and wanted me back after all, and although I was loath to leave, I was glad to be going home. I got on the last flight out of Baton Rouge that evening, a giant 767 filled with aid workers needing a break, journalists, and refugees from the storm. I was in the next-to-last row of the plane, and behind me were three little boys, all wearing brand-new purple polo shirts and khaki shorts. Their mother was across the aisle, and her weariness rose from her like steam. She had nothing to carry, and neither did the boys.

No one on that plane could do anything but stare at

the seat in front of them. Everyone was worn down, their edges exposed, weary from days of heat and anguish. Everyone, that is, but these three boys, who were extremely pleased with the plane, the snacks, the flight attendants, the barf bags, and the tray tables, which they kept flipping up and down. The flight attendant tasked with keeping an eye on them didn't have the heart to tell them to stop, and neither did my row mates. They wiggled and squirmed and laughed at the pilot when he came on the speaker, and their mother closed her eyes, taking the hour in the air—a scant hour—while the rest of the plane could watch her boys.

We began our final descent, and the flight attendants took their seats. And then the youngest boy yelled to the plane at large, "I gotta poo!" He started to get up out of his seat, and the flight attendant on watch unbuckled and ran over. "Son, you have to sit. We're about to land," she said firmly.

"But I gotta poo," the little boy insisted. "I gotta poo *bad*."

I started to laugh, and so did the man next to me. The little boy looked at us, confused; what was so funny about his needing to poop?

"You really can't hold it?" the flight attendant asked, looking toward the front of the plane where the other attendants were sitting. The pilots had already dropped the wheels, and I could smell Dallas's smog.

"No! I gotta POO!!" the boy yelled, and desperation rose in his little voice.

The flight attendant picked him up and shoved him into the toilet, and stood there, watching him to make sure no disaster ensued. I laughed until I cried, and I felt a little bad for laughing, and then I realized that I needed to cry, and this was as good a way as any. Everyone on that plane would probably have benefited from a good sob, and at least this was entertaining.

Michael met me at home that night, and we sat together in his dark, cool living room and watched a movie. We didn't have much to say; we needed each other in the cool quiet and didn't need to say anything at all. The air between us said everything, and that was enough.

"GARY, ARE YOU about ready? We need to leave in fifteen minutes," I yelled from the bedroom. It was the afternoon of our friends' black-tie wedding, and I had been tasked with getting myself and Michael's dad, Gary, downtown. Michael was working a Saturday shift and was going to change at the office, and so I was taking this particular one for the team.

Gary had flown in from Mobile a day or two before, and he had pretty much tripped over himself to hug me on the curb at the airport. I had many preconceived notions about him from Michael, but I wasn't prepared for his outsized presence, which set Michael on edge from the moment we gathered him at LaGuardia. He was immensely proud of his son, and he loved talking about Michael in front of him. Michael hated it.

"Gary, did you hear me?" I zipped up my dress and headed into the living room, where he had been sleeping on Michael's fold-out. Before I tell you what happened next, you should remember: this man weighed three hundred pounds if he weighed an ounce; it was unreasonably hot that September day; and I loved Michael with all my heart already, so there was no backing out.

Gary hummed a lot, and I mean a lot, and he was humming to himself as he prepared for this wedding. I guess the humming was too loud for him to hear me, otherwise maybe he would have been more modest. But he didn't hear me, and so when I rounded the corner, this is what I saw: a sweaty fifty-six-year-old man with a ponytail and skinny legs, humming, holding open the waistband of his saggy old gray underpants, and liberally dousing his balls with baby powder. Clouds of baby powder hung in the air above the coffee table, which of course was coated in it. It was like watching the Swedish Chef. I turned on my heels silently and ran back into the bedroom, where I stayed until it was time to go.

"You owe me," I hissed when I found Michael, after I'd wrangled Gary out of the apartment and into a cab and convinced him that he could wait until we got downtown to smoke. "You owe me so big, I can't even tell you."

"What happened?" he said, and immediately started laughing. I was so mad, but he did look great in his new black suit.

I waited for Gary to walk off for a cigarette, and then I painted the scene for Michael. "In his *underwear*!" I said. "There's baby powder everywhere!"

Michael sighed and pulled me toward him. "I love you very, very much, and I am so sorry," he said. "But I am also sorry to say that this was bound to happen. It won't be the last time you see Gary McElroy in his dirty old underpants."

As it turns out, it was not, in fact, the last time I saw that man in his underpants. But as we made our way up to the wedding—which was perfect, even if the strap on my dress broke and fully exposed my right boob to the bride's brother—I knew this was just one more bizarre feature of the life we were making together, little by little. We ate Jordan almonds and toasted our friends' love and good fortune, and underpants or not, we had found shelter from the storm.

CHAPTER 11

Fairy Tale of New York

ICOLE, YOUR ASS is *huge*," her mom yelled. My friend, the Nicole in question, was up for display on a painted plywood platform in the middle of a dressing room at Kleinfeld, trying to find her wedding dress. This being her first foray into the bridal industry, she didn't know that her hunt would involve her standing nearly naked, topless and in a thong, with her mom, her sister, and me trying to look everywhere but at her body, which she was trying to cover with her hands, fruitlessly. Had she known, she would have worn full-coverage underwear, or maybe have just canceled the whole thing altogether and ordered a cream silk dress from J.Crew, as everyone else seemed to be doing then. It would have been less painful than this ordeal.

There was a time when Kleinfeld, that storied New York

wedding gown emporium that dresses thousands of brides every year, wasn't a short wander from Chelsea Market, nor did it have its own TV show or a well-groomed fashion director named Randy. But if you were in the know, it was still very much A Thing to get your dress at Kleinfeld. Women would often fly into JFK and take a cab straight to the showroom—which was not a tony Manhattan address but rather in the outreaches of an outer borough—and then head directly back to the airport after they'd chosen a dress. Manhattan people who didn't want to pay for a cab or a car service had to take the R train to 86th Street in Bay Ridge, the next-to-last stop on the line, and walk north four blocks to Kleinfeld's showroom at 8202 5th Avenue (that's 5th Avenue in *Brooklyn*, for those of you keeping score), where the sidewalk traffic was a little different than the 5th Avenue most tourists saw. Nicole and her mom lived way uptown in Washington Heights, so they had gotten up even earlier than I had for their trip down the entire length of Manhattan and across most of Brooklyn. I had it easier and had stumbled down to the subway at eight thirty, a light coffee and an everything bagel in hand. Nicole had made an appointment for nine thirty and, with the knowledge that she'd get charged if we were late or didn't show, made a point of calling me early to make sure I was up. I was up. The whole thing was actually my idea.

I should back up. Not long before this, Nicole called me

and asked if I was going to be at work the next day, because she had something to show me. "What do you mean, you have something to show me?" I asked.

"It's . . . it's a change," she said. "A big physical change."

"Did you cut your hair?" I asked. Nicole occasionally grew her hair long and donated it. But I knew instantly what this physical change was about, and it involved her boyfriend of not that many months: David, a tall, rangy guy in finance with lovely blue eyes and a big laugh, who absolutely hung on Nicole's every word. They met through a mutual friend, a guy who Nicole and I had gone to boarding school with, and instantly fell for each other. Michael and I had gone with them to Massachusetts back in the fall on a lover's weekend to show our new boyfriends where we had gone to school, zooming up I-95 in her mother's inherited old navy blue Cadillac. Michael and I were still cautious of each other, learning the moves and figuring out the questions we needed to answer, but Nicole and David were already rock solid. He gave her diamond solitaire earrings for Christmas, big enough to catch the light, and a scant while later, followed them with a three-diamond platinum ring. Which, of course, was the physical change she wanted to show me.

She waited downstairs in the *Times* lobby for me, and I grabbed her outstretched hand as soon as I got through the turnstile, gleeful and sad all at once that my friend, with whom I had traveled and cried and eaten bad dining-hall food and listened to the *Stealing Beauty* soundtrack about a thousand times, was doing this big thing that I couldn't get my head around.

They were on a fairly tight budget for the wedding, and they were also in a relative rush. David had gotten a job with an Australian company, and they were supposed to move to Melbourne in early summer, just in time for winter Down Under. They had to get it all done and get out of the country, in a matter of months. Nicole was deep underwater with her loans from Barnard and had little money to spare, and while David had done well on Wall Street, he was an early recession casualty, so until the new Aussie job started, they weren't exactly flush. Her dear sweet dad lived in the woods in Massachusetts and drove a bus for a living, so he couldn't contribute much. Nicole's mother came from some sort of Spanish millionaire family and wore on her person some of the most fabulous jewelry I have ever seen, but she never seemed to have much actual money.

Rosa was a goal in and of herself. She had lived all over the world, raised children on a kibbutz in Israel, and smoked joints with Allen Ginsberg in Colorado, and she had the jewelry and the stories to show for it all. I never quite understood how she got her money, but she always seemed to be coming into enough funds to get her through a year or two. Nicole and I were both scholarship kids in high school, but her mother still found the cash to spirit them away to Antigua for Christmas break. She knew when to get away and how to do it, and insisted on it, even with almost no money in the bank. I loved her. She was intimidating, worldly, and well traveled, and she judged frequently, harshly, and with surgical precision. Which brings me to Kleinfeld.

I feel responsible for the Kleinfeld meshuggaas. Given the state of things, Nicole and David had decided to get married at his parents' house down South instead of attempting to throw a party in New York, and they figured they could do the whole thing, soup to nuts, for ten thousand dollars. Nicole had started looking around the bridal stores in the garment district and perusing the racks at Lord & Taylor. She had exactly one thousand dollars to spend on this dress, and less would be better. She sort of had an idea of what she wanted, but she knew that whatever she wore, unless it was a turtleneck sweater, her mother would make a comment about her upper arms. One day after a fruitless search at Loehmann's, another place where, with its communal dressing rooms, your ass was on display if you wanted to try things on, we stopped at Starbucks so Nicole could get a consolatory Frappuccino, her only vice.

"Why don't you try Kleinfeld?" I asked. "I think a lot of the brides I talk to get their dresses there."

"It's so expensive," she said. "I really cannot spend more

than one thousand dollars on this dress. The food is already costing more than we thought." I knew David's parents were helping them some, but I also knew that this relatively tight budget weighed on Nicole. She hadn't ever fantasized about a big wedding. But she wanted a nice, pretty wedding, where her guests felt comfortable and fed, and she didn't have to worry too much. A thousand dollars is a lot for a dress anyway, but considering that Manhattan brides spend an average of almost $3,400 on their dresses, she was looking for a bargain-basement deal, at least in the eyes of bridal shops. She held on to the fantasy of the perfect dress, but she was also stressed out, and her mom, who considered the entire exercise exceedingly bourgeois, was not helping.

"Look at their website and see what their price ranges are," I said. "I mean, this is the biggest place in New York, right? Surely it's not all for millionaires."

She called me later with an update: we had an appointment with the Kleinfeld team at nine thirty on Saturday, as soon as the doors opened. "This is the way to go," she said, reassured by her conversation with the receptionist and somewhat confident again that the perfect wedding dress was within her grasp. "I had to give them my credit card to hold the time, though, so we have to show up."

I assured her that I had nowhere else to be that Saturday but with her in Bay Ridge. A few days later, I met them outside the subway, and we walked up to Kleinfeld. We passed a tuxedo rental shop, a tailor, another tux rental joint; these places' fortunes must be intrinsically tied with the women who swanned in and out of Kleinfeld, I thought. We walked into the hushed showroom and were immediately handed glasses of champagne, and a tall, loud woman in a black suit ushered us into a large dressing room, where Nicole was measured, prodded, and commanded to disrobe. "What size bra?" one woman demanded in a deep Russian accent. "I'll get you a good strapless. You'll need it."

"All my clothes?" Nicole asked.

"Yes, yes, all of it. You can't try on beautiful gowns in jeans," the Russian woman said, and closed the door behind her as she went to retrieve a strapless bra, size 32B, that I hoped had been washed.

"Honey, you've got nothing we haven't seen before," another saleswoman said. "Go ahead. We'll get you a robe."

Nicole looked at me in the three-way mirror, and I grimaced. "Maybe wait until she comes back with a robe?" I said. But Nicole was cowed by the efficiency of these women, who had seen it all before and would see it all again. She stripped down and got up on the plywood pedestal, cupping her hands around her boobs protectively. It was cold in the dressing room, and she looked as miserable as a person could possibly be at nine thirty on a Saturday while looking for the dress that would transform her into a bride.

Then her mom piped up. "When did your ass get so fat?" she asked. Nicole closed her eyes, looking deep within herself for any sense of serenity. *"Mom,"* her sister said. "She looks great. Ignore her, Nicole. You look great."

"I never was that big when I was your age," Rosa kept on. I fidgeted on my own ass, which was at least two sizes bigger than Nicole's, not knowing what to do. "Do you want your sweater?" I asked her, trying to be helpful. Nicole shook her head at me in the mirror, determined to soldier through and ignore her mother as best she could. The remaining saleswoman looked uncomfortable. "You have such lovely little breasts!" she interjected. "They'll look great in your dress."

If it were possible, Nicole would have fainted with misery right then and there. All I could do was sit there and wait for this Russian woman to come back with a strapless bra and please, dear God, a robe for my friend, who was already self-conscious of her tits and her ass—I mean, Jesus, who isn't—and had walked into a massacre. She was like a troop swimming for shore at Normandy, her chest wide open for incoming fire. Finally, the Russian woman came back with a strapless bra and a short robe. She harnessed Nicole into it and commanded her to get her breasts right— "Like this, you understand," she said, leaning over and shaking her chest perpendicular to the carpet—and the dress parade began.

[251]

The options were limited. Kleinfeld could dress any-body, but they were better at dressing people who had more money to spend. Nicole settled on a plain white V-neck dress with tiny beaded trim and a short train that ran right up against a thousand dollars, tax included. As the woman totaled up the damage, Nicole put her clothes back on and leaned her head against the wall. She was exhausted and could not wait to get the hell out of there.

"And another three hundred for the alterations," the saleswoman said. Nicole sat back up. She had reached her breaking point. She had finally found a dress for under a thousand dollars, and she had humiliated herself in front of her mother, her sister, one of her closest friends, and three intrusive saleswomen to do it. "I'm sorry, that isn't included?" she said.

"No, honey, alterations are very difficult," the woman said, and then her tone frosted over. "But if you just want to buy the dress and do the alterations someplace else, that's up to you." It was absolutely Nicole's funeral to ruin this white satin dress that she would wear exactly once, even though the saleswoman agreed that yes, of course, she could cut it off and dye it and turn it into a perfect cocktail dress.

"Yes, I would prefer that," Nicole said. She handed over her credit card, and we got out of there as fast as we possibly could. It was past lunchtime, and the weak March sun was harsh over the Bay Ridge rooftops. Nicole looked at me, and I raised my eyebrows at her. We didn't say a word. Fantasy: zero; stone-cold reality: one.

EVEN THOUGH IT was before the official beginning of the wedding season, I had already rejoined the Weddings desk. Ira was ramping up his staff, expecting a busy year, and whatever I was doing had ground to a halt. So I agreed to go back upstairs to the fifth floor, to the smelly, windowless submarine, where tales of romance rang against the dirty old walls and Abraham grumbled daily about what Kenneth was planning for lunch. I wasn't in the mood to go back, and that was because I was not in the mood for romance. This time it really wasn't my fault. It was Seth Rogen's.

One night, Michael and I decided to go see a late movie after work, and we settled on *Knocked Up*. You're likely familiar with the plot. A lazy stoner dude and an ambitious, beautiful woman have a one-night stand, she gets pregnant, and for some inexplicable reason, she decides to not only keep the baby but try to build an actual relationship with this guy out of what started as a drunken fumble. Seth Rogen is the stoner dude, and Katherine Heigl is the upwardly mobile woman who, understanding that her on-air career pivots on how she looks, attempts to hide her pregnancy from the E! News brass who hold her professional future in their hands. Unlike *Four Weddings and a Funeral*, this movie does not hold up, at least for me.

Don't misunderstand me. I love Seth Rogen, and Katherine Heigl's character is grossly mistreated. What is wrong with expecting that your baby's father should provide more than a cast-off crib he found in an alley and wiped down with Purell? So what if he finds redemption while she's howling in the delivery room, smacking down her dickish obstetrician and taking command of the situation, as men are still somehow, wrongly, expected to do? Anyway, at the end, he's still kind of a man-child, although now one with a child; they'll probably split before the kid gets to preschool, and she'll marry an entertainment attorney and move to Brentwood; the end. We walked out of the theater and grabbed a taxi uptown, back to Michael's bachelor apartment in Harlem.

But as our cab rattled up the West Side Highway, Michael couldn't look at me. He stared out the window at the sailboats moored out in the Hudson. I didn't know what was going on in his head, but he was curled into the corner of the back seat, wrapped up in himself. He didn't want to dissect the movie like he usually did. He didn't want to say anything at all. I was tired too, but I was also confused by his rapid descent into a dark silence. I had assumed that I'd stay at his apartment, but I decided to go home, to my own

new single-person studio on a cliffside street that over-
looked the Hudson River. "Can you make a second stop?
187th and Cabrini," I said, and knocked on the plexiglass
divider between us and the cabbie, who didn't want to be
heading that far uptown to begin with and didn't want to
go farther north still.

That snapped Michael out of his silence. "You're not
coming over?" he said.

"No, I have some things to take care of at home," I lied.
"And you seem tired."

"I'm fine," he said, and reached for my hand.

"You sure?"

The cab pulled up to 150th and Broadway, and he got
out in front of the corner bodega. "Love you," he said, and
slammed the door. I went home and sank into the quiet of
my own space, with my own little couch and my own clean
bathroom with the pink tile and the steam pipe that reverberated the bathroom sounds of my downstairs neighbor,
Melvin, who was not well, physically or mentally, but was
still protective of me. One evening, he heard two guys in
my apartment—Michael and our friend Joseph, who had
come over for dinner—and the next day, he showed me the
baseball bat with the nails stuck in it that he'd have no
problem swinging at the head of anyone who threatened
me. I missed my roommates and Brooklyn, but I loved my
little apartment uptown, and I loved Melvin, even if I could

hear everything he did in the bathroom, including the time I heard him yell "Cannonball!" just before he flushed the toilet. I loved my quiet little street and its stone wall where teenagers gathered at dusk to smoke pot, its views of the river and the George Washington Bridge, and the Palisades beyond. Mostly, though, I loved that everything was mine, and no one else's. Michael had a drawer and a toothbrush, but the four-poster bed and the sheets on it were mine, and the coffeemaker was mine, and the sun streaming through my window in the mornings was mine. The only thing I didn't like was my upstairs neighbor, a dude whose chosen music for his one-night stands was Evanescence.

Michael was uncharacteristically quiet over the next few days. We talked a few times, but he clearly wanted to get off the phone. We met for coffee up in the cafeteria, but he just looked out the window. "You OK?" I asked again. He nodded, and I gave up and headed back to my desk and my stack of announcements.

This week, among the usual bankers and junior attorneys at Beezus, Barnes and Boggletank, I had two that were very exciting to me. One was a do-gooder in the White House, and I always got a thrill when calling the White House. The second was a feminist scholar whose work I had read in college and who published constantly. She and her fiancé were both heading into their second marriages. She was older, maybe my mom's age, maybe a bit older, and had the crazy hair you'd expect of an Upper West Side white-lady feminist scholar who wore chunky jewelry and a lot of linen. She was certainly an archetype, but I was curious: why was she getting married again?

When Gloria Steinem got married in 2000 for the first and only time, feminists and nonfeminists, women and men, came for her. Camille Paglia called her marriage "proof positive of the emotional desperation of aging feminists." Feminists—first-, second-, and third-wave—questioned her motives. It was for immigration purposes—her new husband was born in South Africa and had spent most of his life in the United Kingdom, and he needed an easy, legal way to stay in the United States. Or it was because she was lonely, because obviously what postmenopausal sixty-six-year-old woman didn't pine for a man's dirty socks on her floor? Or it was because she was casting off a more severe and completely faux tenet of feminism that rejected male partnership recognized by the state.

Steinem ignored the criticisms and basically gave the finger to Camille Paglia. "I'm happy, surprised and one day will write about it, but for now, I hope this proves what feminists have always said," she said. "That feminism is about the ability to choose what's right at each time of our lives."

She spent three years with her husband, until he died of brain lymphoma. At a fund-raiser in 2002, the year before he died, he hung back and held her tote bag as she mingled.

"I'm Gloria's guy," he said, understanding that she was the big gun, and his job was to have her back. Who wouldn't want that?

The Feminist's first wedding announcement had appeared in the paper back in the 1980s, on the same page as those of the descendant of an industrialist whose name was plastered on buildings in at least four countries, several writers, a famous geologist, a former professional ice skater, and a bunch of debutantes. The man she was marrying, the Professor, was a bi-continental brain whose social theorizing had gotten his name into the paper several times before he married the Feminist. I was nervous to call her. Not him so much, really, although I always felt intimidated by people of letters. I wasn't brushed up on my feminist theory, and not that it was going to come up when I talked to her, but still: we were about to talk about marriage.

"So nice to talk to you!" she said breezily, with an air of humor that I hadn't expected from such a Serious Person. "Isn't this fun? This is a fun thing to talk about."

"Well, it isn't abortion rights," I tried to joke.

"Thank God, no," she said. "I don't want to talk about that today. Christ. How can I help you?"

We did the checklist, and she pointed me to her first

wedding announcement as proof of her divorce—"not that you asked," she joked—and then I said, "I've been looking forward to talking with you, honestly—I love your work, and I'm so glad to be able to write this."

"I appreciate that," she said. "I'm probably going to get letters about getting married. Oh, well."

"Like Gloria Steinem?" I asked.

The Feminist laughed. "That was such horseshit," she said. "It's just no one's business. Even if it's in the *Times*."

"Do you think you'll write about it?" I asked.

"No," she said, almost sharply. "We're both public people, and this is private. Would you?"

"I'm not married," I said.

The Feminist laughed. "You're too young," she said. "But if and when you do, try not to write about your marriage. Keep each other's secrets, as much as you can."

I remembered what a very funny woman once said, that everything is copy. This very smart woman was saying that not everything was copy; some secrets should remain that way. I wasn't sure which was right. But I thanked her, and we hung up after she promised to fax over a copy of her diplomas, which, again, who cared, but I had to ask. Then I called the White House.

I always loved calling the White House, and I used to do it a lot. I loved the excitement of getting the switchboard operator and of, at least momentarily, being on the line with what felt like the center of the world. It didn't matter what administration I was calling; then, at least, I felt like I was calling people who mattered, and who were there to help others. This particular bride had worked on the presidential campaign and ran Latinx outreach, working to register young voters and crafting immigration policy plans. She was so young, but so many dreamers are.

"How is your planning going?" I asked the Woman Who Wanted to Save the World.

She sighed audibly. "There's just so much to do still," she said. "I thought we'd be done by now."

"When do you leave?" They were getting married in Dallas, where her very large family still lived. I had already talked to her divorced parents, and her mother sounded flustered to be talking to the *Times*, especially about the wedding circus that she was marshaling in her daughter's absence. Her dad didn't sound too high on the whole thing, especially since her fiancé was nearly ten years older. But I didn't tell her that.

"Friday, and I'm not even packed yet," the Woman said.

"Is the president coming to the wedding?" I joked, and then felt like an ass. But she laughed.

"No, he'll be at a trade meeting in Mexico next weekend," she said. "Not too far from us, but no."

"So, how long have you known Isaac?" Her fiancé was a political veteran, a Hill operative, and, as Google told me, didn't necessarily work for the right side all the time, or at least my right side.

"A few years. We met doing outreach in the swing states," she said. "You know what it's like on campaigns. You see people all the time with the same interests. It just kind of happened."

I took notes and thought: *This girl sounds tired.*

"When did you get engaged?"

"On July fourth," she said, and I rolled my eyes a little. "We watched the fireworks from the White House, and he got clearance to propose to me in the gardens."

"That's so romantic!" I gushed. "Not everyone gets to do that."

She laughed a little. "Nope. How could I say no to that?"

Well, I thought, *you could have said no, even if the Secret Service were milling around.* "No, it would be hard to," I said. "Do you think you'll stay in the White House after the election?"

"Well, it depends on what happens, obviously, but I don't know," she said. "I feel like I want a smaller stage for a while, and Isaac wants kids." She paused. "We want kids."

Oh, lord, I thought. But I wished her luck and got off the phone. Maybe this practical woman didn't gush; maybe she was more private than that. Maybe she already knew to keep her fiancé's secrets. But I just kept thinking that happiness sounds like bells ringing, and hers were quiet and still.

I decided it was time to confront Michael. Regardless of what was going on in his head, the silence was worse. In some ways, he was giving me a dose of my own medicine. We both tended to go into our heads when things got hard. Not necessarily the things between us, but external things, like work and family mess. But this silence was different. It felt directed at me, and I couldn't figure out what exactly I had done. A few nights later, we ordered pizza, and I sat down on his disgusting sofa. We bought a cover for it at IKEA, but it kept getting twisted up, and finally he gave up on it. It was half on the couch and half entangled in the fold-out. It was a mess.

"So can you please tell me what is going on?" I asked. Michael sat on the floor in front of the TV, his knees pulled up to his chest. "I don't know what I did, but this is getting weird. What is happening?"

The air in the room became cloudy with fear, mine and his. I didn't know what he was about to say, but he did.

"I can't do this right now," he said.

"What do you mean, *right now*?" The skin on my neck began to burn. "This, like this"—I gestured to the space between us—"or what?"

"This," he said. "You and me."

What the fuck, I thought. "OK. So, you're dumping me."

"*No*," he said, and he put his face in his hands. "No. I don't want to lose you. But I just need some time. I feel fucked up right now, and I need to be by myself."

"What fucked you up?"

He paused and looked up at the ceiling. "You're going to laugh if I tell you."

"I want you to hear me on this," I said, my voice trembling. "I am not going to laugh at you, but I need you to tell me what it is." *He met someone else,* I thought. *He's moving to Peru. He's gay. He's gay and moving to Peru with his new hot Peruvian boyfriend.*

"That movie."

"What movie?"

"*Knocked Up.*"

It was my turn to rub my face and look at the ceiling. "*Knocked Up.* Are you fucking kidding me?" I said. "What about that movie is bothering you? It's a movie. A *movie.* With idiot men and lots of pot. What the fuck?"

I knew I was perhaps belittling Michael's pain at that moment, but all I could think was, *I'm going to kill Judd Apatow, and I don't know him, but I'm going to kill him.*

"Nothing about that movie bothered you?"

"Other than the misogyny, no," I said. "I mean, what was it that was supposed to bother me?"

"It's not scary to you, the idea of having kids and getting married, all of that? How is that not scary?"

I started laughing. "That's what you got from that movie? I thought it was just supposed to be a funny movie with dick jokes."

Apparently, somehow or another, Michael had seen himself in Seth Rogen's character, disregarding the fact that he was neither a pothead nor unemployed. The idea of committing to a woman and child—the idea of growing up—crept into his consciousness as the credits rolled, and he walked out of that theater with a newfound fear of life, the future, and life with me.

"So, you need some time because of a movie," I said. "What am I supposed to do? Are we breaking up, or is this a 'break'? I mean, I don't get what you want from me."

Michael was quiet, and his eyes were red. "I don't really know what I want from you either. I know I don't want you to go. But I need to go into the dark for a while."

I got up and threw my pizza in the kitchen garbage and put my shoes on by the door. "You know, when you figure out what it is you want, you let me know," I said. "I'm just going to go home, because you obviously don't want me here. And I don't want to be here."

Michael just looked at me and didn't say anything. I was waiting for him to do the whole *wait, don't go, I need you, I made a mistake*, but he didn't. We stared at each other.

"I love you," he said finally.

"You sure about that?" I said, and closed the door behind me, which I felt was as cinematic an exit as I could muster. I imagined him collapsing into tears after I left, not even able to make it down the hall to his bedroom, but I knew it was far more likely that he was going to watch re-runs of *The West Wing* and eat the rest of the pizza. I walked up to Broadway to wait for the M4 bus, forcing myself not to cry at the bus stop because honestly, this whole thing was such a cliché that I wasn't willing to go to *that* level of cliché. I called Nicole.

"So, I think Michael maybe just dumped me?" I said, and my throat ached.

"Ohhh, bunny," she said. "What happened?"

I repeated the whole scene to her, and she was quiet for a minute. "He probably just needs a little bit of time," she said. "He was probably telling you the truth. I mean, I get it. It's scary, the whole getting married thing."

"But not once have I ever said I wanted to get married," I said. "He was the one who brought it up, a long time ago! I was the one who freaked out!"

"Well, maybe this is his turn to freak out," she said. "Maybe this is your turn to see what he does."

And that was when I started crying. "But what if he doesn't come back?"

"He might not," Nicole said. "But that'll be OK too. You'll be OK. But I don't think that will really be the case. He just needs to have a big freak-out, figure out his shit, and then he'll be back. And in the meantime, you get some time to yourself."

Time to myself. Even though I had pushed and pulled against the idea of committing, against the idea of marriage, to the point of being pessimistic about my own job, I didn't think I really wanted time to myself. I realized that I had started to look at our future together like breathing, just like Rebecca and Pete did. I had assumed that we had cleared the initial hurdles, and that even though I didn't really want to get married, we were still heading toward a life together. But maybe I had been wrong.

"Do you want me to come over?" Nicole said. "I can get a cab."

"No, I'm going to take a shower and go to bed," I said. "But thank you."

I trudged up the stairs to my apartment and opened the door, and considered flinging myself on my bed, just like in the movies. But I was starving. I hadn't eaten my pizza, nor had I eaten lunch, and there's not much that has ever subdued my appetite. I decided to order from the Indian restaurant on Fort Washington Avenue and eat it on the stone wall. It was a pretty spring evening and the street didn't smell too much like pot smoke, so I placed my order, grabbed my wallet and keys, and went downstairs to wait for the delivery guy.

I leaned out over the wall toward the river and breathed

in the spring. I had battled allergies since I had moved to New York, but this year, they stayed away. My body had gotten used to this town, and so had my brain and heart. It is perhaps one of the biggest clichés in modern literature to talk about New York City as a romantic partner, but it had become one of my two loves. It was adoring, nurturing, infuriating, messy, loud, coddling, affirming. The traffic went *ca-chunk ca-chunk* over the GWB, and sirens flew by on the Henry Hudson Parkway, right below my street. Two teenagers snuck into the shadows at the end of the stone wall right next to a brick house that had been built to hang off the cliff, and I saw a lighter flare up and then a pin-sized glow. The girl hopped up on the wall and the boy tucked himself between her legs and wrapped one arm around her, and they shared a joint and took no notice of me, giggling to themselves. I flagged the delivery guy on his bike and paid for my food and unpacked my pakoras and saag paneer on the rough top of the wall.

What was I going to do without Michael? I hadn't known this town without him. Not really. Most of my memories here—a Neko Case concert in Battery Park, burgers at Chumley's, the snowstorm that left six-foot drifts along the streets, that time we saw Robert De Niro—they were with him. I hadn't had much of a chance to do things on my own, as me, in the city I had dreamed of since I was eight years old. This "break," as I guessed we were going to call it, was my chance to be by myself, do exactly the things I wanted to do, even if that was just nothing at all.

But what if he doesn't come back?

THE NEXT FEW months were, shall we say, complicated. We decided to take a break, like Ross and Rachel, and I hated even knowing who Ross and Rachel were and that they took a break at all. We agreed that we wouldn't see other people, and neither of us really wanted to. We wouldn't run away from each other at work, but we wouldn't hang out for a while. That was the plan, at least. Sometimes we met for a drink on Friday evenings, but mostly we stayed away and just checked in every now and again.

I was lonely. But it was a satisfying loneliness, if that exists. Loneliness by definition is empty, alone, devoid. But I wasn't. I missed Michael horribly, during the day and at night. I missed our lazy Saturdays, our wanders, our long quiet breakfasts. I missed his voice, his listening to me, only me, his hand on my lower back, protective and searching all at once. I started to hate my job, not just because I didn't want to talk to brides and grooms anymore but because I didn't want to be in the same building with him and not *be* with him. I wanted him in my very breath.

But I felt half full just the same, and it was because I was learning this place and this life as me, just me. I started doing things by myself and not worrying. I spent whole days at the Met, wandering the Costume Institute because that was what I wanted to see, not the Temple of Dendur (which, fine, it's impressive, but it's the same thing every time). I went to the Town Shop on Broadway and got fitted for a bra, and for the first time in my life started wearing the correct size. I met Nicole for pedicures and long lunches, and one day I walked from 190th Street to West 4th Street, just to do it. I spent hours exploring Chinatown, and I spent more hours going from museum to museum uptown, just because I could. I picked through the treasures at Jean's, a silversmith in the diamond district that had hundreds of thousands of dollars' worth of serving pieces just hanging from the ceiling like smoked meats. I wrote voraciously. I wrote for the *Times*, and I wrote for myself. At first, it felt like I was just trying to fill the time. And then it didn't.

After a few months, Michael and I started hanging out more, and then sleeping over again. It was awkward. Michael really was in a tough spot. Unbeknownst to me, he had been spiraling into the deepest depression of his life just before we went to see *Knocked Up*, and that movie was the lit match on the coals. He decided to go to therapy, not just to figure out what he wanted with us, but what he wanted in general. The stories about his family are his to tell, but he had had a difficult childhood, tougher than I knew or would know for years, and much of his freak-out about Seth Rogen had to do with being a father. If he committed to me, he reasoned, then that meant he was likely committing to be a father, although we had never really discussed kids or whether we wanted them. And he could swallow a lot of things, but he could not swallow the idea of being like his own dad. It wasn't just Seth Rogen's man-child either. There's a scene in a Vegas hotel in which he's stoned, in his boxers on the bed and watching Steve Martin wrangle children in *Cheaper by the Dozen*, and Paul Rudd, still wearing his fancy suit from their shroom-fueled night at Cirque du Soleil, asks him: "Do you ever wonder how someone could even like you?" That one line knocked the breath from Michael and crystallized for him years of sadness, confusion, and uncertainty about what was next. So he went to therapy, and I went to the gym, and we had Friday night fights that started with takeout and usually ended in bed.

Our friend Lila asked me one day if I wanted to go to the New Yorker Festival with her and her boyfriend, and I said sure, why not. "Great," she said. "I really want to see Judd Apatow and Seth Rogen."

"Wait, what?" I said.

"Yeah, one of the movie critics is interviewing them on Sunday," Lila said. "Should I get tickets?"

"Yes, please," I said. "Get two for me."

I went downstairs and found Michael on the business desk, where he was learning to design pages. "So, the New Yorker Festival is next weekend," I said, leaning over his desk.

"Oh, yeah?" He wasn't paying attention to me. He was trying to get two columns to line up and it wasn't working. He kept slamming his mouse down.

"Judd Apatow is going to be there with Seth Rogen. I guess they'll be talking about *Knocked Up*."

Michael stopped abusing the mouse and looked at me. "Are you serious?"

"Yep," I said, and I flashed him a big grin. "Want to go with Lila and P and me?"

Michael narrowed his eyes at me. "I have to work."

"It's Sunday. You don't. Don't you want to ask Seth Rogen about his process?" I was daring him and being super mean, and I did not care.

He turned back to his monitor. "I'll think about it."

"Lila got you a ticket."

"Oh, yeah? Tell her thank you."

I walked off and thought, unjustly, *What an asshole*. I mean, come on. The people who made the movie that scared the shit out of him were doing a question-and-answer session fifteen blocks from where we were standing, and he didn't have the balls to even show up, much less ask a question. Although, to be fair, it's mostly assholes who ask questions at events like that, guys who like hearing their own voices booming through a microphone, and they don't even pose questions, more like statements that attempt to show off their brains and sensitivity but all they really do is show their ass.

Anyway, Seth Rogen hosted *Saturday Night Live* that weekend, and he was funny, obviously. I don't remember much about it, only that I watched it at Michael's apartment and he was nervous the entire time. I knew he had real problems to deal with, and together we had a lot of shit to work on, but it was just a little bit fun to watch him squirm. The fear that this was all for nothing haunted me day and night, but I decided that I might as well get some entertainment out of it.

The next day, I got up, drank some coffee, and got ready to go downtown to the festival. Michael was still in bed.

"I'm leaving in about ten minutes," I yelled from the bathroom. "You sure you don't want to come with me? There's a ticket for you."

"No" came faintly from the bedroom. I went back in to get my shoes, and he had pulled the covers up to his nose. The room smelled like depression.

"Come on," I said, and shook his foot under the cover. "This is a once-in-a-lifetime chance to ask Seth Rogen questions."

"No," he said again, and turned on his side. I shrugged,

walked out the door, and took the 1 train down to Columbus Circle, where I met Lila and P. We headed over to the
theater on West 58th Street, and it was mobbed. The first
thing I did was walk straight into Bill Hader, who is extremely tall and was doing his best not to make eye contact
with anyone. The second thing I did was go downstairs to
find the bathroom. I went down a tight, windy set of stairs
to an equally tight, windy passage with red carpeted walls—
it was very bordello chic—to the restrooms. And there, standing in front of the women's room, in a faded navy polo shirt
and looking stoned or hungover or both, was Seth Rogen.

I had no idea what to do. But this was my chance. This
was my moment to say, *Hey, Seth? Cate Doty. You don't know
me—I mean, obvious—but wow, do I have a funny story for
you. Sure, you've got time for this. Trust me, it'll be the story
you tell onstage in about twenty minutes, the one about the
crazy girl who stopped you in front of the bathroom before you
went onstage and blamed you and Judd Apatow directly for the
demise of her relationship. Interested? You could tell it on* Letter-
man *too. Totally fine with me. Even though I may die alone, an
old hag who once had love but lost it to the sands of time, I am
giving you this gift to use at will. Bless you.*

I should pause here to note that I never did, nor do I
now, bear any ill will toward Seth Rogen, or Judd Apatow,
for that matter. They have nothing to do with Michael's reaction to that movie. He bore responsibility alone, and if I

ever were to run into Seth Rogen or Judd Apatow, I would not mention this story at all. I would only thrust a copy of this book into their hands and run like the wind.

Anyway, I did not, in fact, seize my moment. I tossed away my shot for glory and vengeance. Instead, I waved like a moron and said, "Hey, man. You were great last night."

Seth Rogen looked up at me and, as graciously as he could, given that we were standing outside a bathroom and he was probably hungover, said, "Um, thanks."

I wiggled by him to the bathroom because I really did have to pee. When I came out, he had disappeared. "Well, shit," I said to no one in particular.

Did I chicken out? Sure. Do I regret it? You bet. Did I ask a question after the interview with Judd Apatow, surrounded by hundreds of people crammed into a poorly air-conditioned theater? Not a chance in hell. Am I glad I'm telling you?

What do you think?

CHAPTER 12

Catherine

MY EYES FLUTTERED open at six thirty a.m. on Father's Day. My flip phone was buzzing on the rusty radiator cover, where I'd left it in its cradle to charge. Michael had gotten out of bed to pee, so I threw myself over to his side of the bed and grabbed the phone. My mother was calling. My mouth went dry; I knew why.

"Cate?" It was my mom as I'd never heard her: hollowed, lost, a person without country. "She's gone."

"Oh, Mama." A hammer force came out of nowhere and stole my breath, yanking it out into the room along with a strangled cry that did not seem to come from me. I pulled it back into my lungs and felt it rattle in my chest. "OK."

For months—or perhaps years—we'd been keeping vigil

as my grandmother slipped away from us, first into the impenetrable forest of dementia, and now into the beyond. She had been in a hospital in North Carolina for several weeks, her organs shutting down one by one, just as her senses had quit on her before she was ready. Catherine loved the smell of frying fish, the taste of freshly churned peach ice cream, the vinegar snap of a summer cucumber-and-tomato salad. But dementia often takes the sense of smell first, and with that went her ability to taste anything deeply. Long before she stopped eating to prepare for her final breaths, she lost the desire to eat, and one more flicker of the intellectual fire and passion for everything that had buoyed her for more than eighty years, through wars and love, marriage and loss, was gone.

Her last days drew out in a hospital bed in Morehead City, a port town on the coast. My mother spent months ping-ponging between my parents' house in the Shenandoah Valley and my grandparents' ramshackle beach cottage, a sloped-floors affair that rested on land once worked by people enslaved by my grandfather's ancestors. The house was the top floor of an old military barrack that somehow my grandfather had hoisted onto cinder blocks, and around that he built the beach refuge to which my mom and her four sisters—and eventually all the grandchildren—gravitated. My grandparents retired to the coast after decades in Fayetteville, home of Fort Bragg and the 82nd Airborne, and Catherine spent hours every day in a floral slipcovered recliner, doing crossword after crossword, Sudoku again and again, reading *Reader's Digest* and *National Geographic* cover to cover. But one day when I was in college, she put them down and started spending her hours gazing out the porch door to the White Oak River, just beyond the bluff.

The turning point came midweek, and my dad warned me that I'd need to get down to North Carolina soon. She got worse on Friday evening, and Saturday felt like a ticking clock; but no word came at lunchtime, or when we went to dinner at the Italian place on 86th Street, or when we'd parked it on the couch to watch a movie. No word came while I brushed my teeth, wondering whether I should put on a black lace nightgown. No word came as I drifted off to sleep with my back turned to Michael, listening to the late flights descend through the night to LaGuardia. But the dawn broke warm and blue, and the sun glowed against the renter's cream walls of my studio apartment.

"OK. Where do you want me to go?" I asked my mom. I didn't want to know about Catherine's last moments then. I'd get all that later. All I wanted to know was where my parents wanted to pick me up.

I could hear birds chirping through the phone, and I knew she was standing outside in her garden. I saw her there among the rosemary and coneflowers, and I could hear the breeze rustling through her purple irises. I pictured her in her blue floral robe with the tiny lace trim and slippers, steadying her hand to call me, and drifting out through the kitchen door to her garden, to breathe the early-summer air grown newly harsh and unknowable: the air of a life without her mother in it.

"Fly to Richmond, and we'll pick you up there," she said.

"OK, thank you," I said, and reached down for my laptop on the floor. "Mama, are you OK?" The stupidest, most obtuse thing I had ever said.

I heard her open the screen door and let it slam. "I'm fine," she said with an unintentional coldness that I deserved, full stop. "Call your daddy when you've booked something."

She hung up, and I dropped my phone. I pulled the duvet cover all the way up to my chin and slid down, and thought: *I should be sad.*

Michael came back into the room and crawled in next to me. "My grandmother died," I said casually, and yawned and stretched, like a baby up from a nap.

He sat up on one elbow and reached around my waist. "Oh, baby," he said. "I'm so sorry." He pulled me close from behind and rested his chin on my ear, and I stared out the window, unwilling to look at him.

The truth was, I didn't want to hear it from him, and I was afraid to as well. We were in a tentative détente after weeks of fighting, crying, both of us walking away and drifting back to each other. I'd thrown my keys at his head. We were cruel to each other, intentionally and not. Even though we had decided to spend the weekend together, I didn't know what to think. I worried that we'd fallen back together out of habit, or worse, out of fear. I wasn't sure if the devil I knew was better than the one I didn't.

But I couldn't think about that then. I opened up Orbitz, booked a 10:30 flight to Richmond, and called my brother to let him know, since I knew my dad wouldn't pick up. I didn't know what to do next. "I should pack," I said.

Michael already had his jeans on. "Let's go get breakfast first," he said.

THAT SPRING HAD been a season of loss. It seemed like every other week, a friend posted a memorial of a grandparent on Facebook: a memory of summers at a lake cottage accompanied by a scan of a faded snapshot, or a story about a favorite recipe, or just a link to an obituary. Sometimes it was a veiled *good fucking riddance to that bastard.* Now it was my turn, and I had nothing to broadcast. I wondered if I'd been stunned into silence, or if I just didn't want to talk to Michael. But I couldn't say a word as we walked down Cabrini, dodging families on their way to Father's Day breakfasts. I thought of my grandfather, now widowed after sixty-two years of marriage, alone in the beach cottage. I thought of him sitting on the long screened-in front porch that overlooked the vast front yard edged with live oak trees, and beyond that, the river that flowed south to the Atlantic.

I wondered about the other couples and families as we stood on line. Where did they come from, and how were they made? A cul-de-sac in Youngstown, or a bungalow in Atlanta, or did they carry the proud badge of the lifelong New Yorker, which I envied? I watched the couples order: the woman impatient for the man to make up his mind, even though he'd had ten minutes on line to decide. Two girls, fingers entwined, ordering the same thing. A man in cargo shorts and a little boy who was hopping on one leg. "What do you think Mom wants?" he asked the kid. The kid shrugged. We got to the register and ordered two sausage, egg, and cheese on rolls. I pumped half-and-half into my paper cup of coffee at the station by the door and mindlessly dumped in too much sugar.

Sugar: my first taste of it was on my grandmother's lap. I was five months old, and it was the first time my parents had left me with her and my grandfather. She fed me chocolate ice cream from her bowl after dinner. Catherine raised five girls and had no modern qualms about limiting sugar, waiting to introduce foods, worrying about allergies. To her, I was her first grandchild and her namesake, and by virtue of that—and also by being a human being—I should eat ice cream. So I did, happily, and my mother rolled her eyes when she heard. Catherine's discipline for me was not about caloric intake or healthful eating. It was about thinking and using the sense that God gave me.

Think: that was what she did, all day, and she judged those who did not use their brains for good and in full. When I was fifteen and about to go away to boarding school, she gave me a silver necklace that spelled out *think* in tiny hieroglyphs. She hammered me—all of us—incessantly to think, to use our brains, to go look it up in the encyclopedias in the basement. When I was ten, she gave me a subscription to the *Christian Science Monitor*. "There's good writing in that," she said.

As we all watched her descend into the airless cave of dementia, memories ricocheting without rhythm in the darkness of her deteriorating brain, my mother keened alone in her car for her brilliant mama. We ached as a woman who forbade anyone in her house from using the word *moron* lost her ability to follow a conversation, to remember why she came in the room, even to read. She was brilliant.

I saw Catherine last on Valentine's Day, at the cottage. She sat in that floral slipcovered armchair as my grandfather ate an apple in his Naugahyde recliner, his partial plate clicking in his mouth. My mom and I sat together on the couch, quietly, and my grandfather watched a basketball game. I wondered, somehow, if this was going to be the last time I saw my grandmother, and stored that lament away.

"I'd like to go to Alaska," my grandfather said after a cruise ship commercial finished playing. "I'd take a boat out and see all the glaciers."

"Would you?" Catherine said. "I've already been to Alaska."

My mom looked at me sideways and stifled a horrified laugh.

"You have?" she asked her mother. "When did you go to Alaska?"

Catherine thought for a second. "I went with the Coast Guard when I was young," she said. "Before I married your daddy."

What the hell, I thought.

"How did you get there?" my mom asked.

My grandmother leaned forward conspiratorially in her chair. "The Coast Guard took me on a *submarine*," she whispered.

My grandfather slammed down the footrest of his recliner and threw his apple core in the metal garbage can full of his used tissues and old newspapers. "Honey, you have never been to Alaska," he said.

Catherine sat up straight. "Yes, I have," she said. "I went when I was twenty-two years old with the Coast Guard."

"Catherine, no, you *haven't*. That is a dream you had. I know you've never been on a submarine."

She stood up, unsteady on her bare feet, and shook her right pointer finger at my grandfather. "Yes, I have. I know you don't believe me, and I don't know why you don't," she said, livid. Her voice shook, and she turned her face away from him. She stomped over the brown linoleum floor back to their bedroom and slammed the door.

My grandfather looked at us and dropped his head, broken and frustrated. "I don't know where she got that idea," he said. "I know full well that the Coast Guard never took her to Alaska. She ain't ever been on a submarine either."

"Daddy," my mom said calmly, "it's probably from reading all those *National Geographics* over the years." As much as it pained her to watch her mother slide away, it was worse for my grandfather. His beautiful girl, his wife of sixty-two years, was going out to sea without him, and he could not follow.

Out to sea: the Coast Guard was how my grandparents met. In 1942, the Coast Guard, needing recruits, flung its arm open to women and called them SPARS, like the Navy's WACs. My grandmother, a recent summa cum laude graduate of Birmingham-Southern College, joined up after months of being back home and taking her place once again as the baby of the family, whether she liked it or not. Her sisters, Elizabeth and Margaret, were serving in the Red Cross in the South Pacific, and her brother, Richard, had joined the Navy. Catherine, twenty-two and wildly bored, took the bus from Birmingham to Atlanta and signed up for an adventure at the Coast Guard recruiting office. In August she boarded the *Birmingham Special* to Pennsylvania Station, hauled her trunk through Midtown over to Hunter College, and joined the 1943 class of the Coast Guard SPARS: female recruits tasked with men's jobs as the world burned.

After boot camp in the Bronx, Catherine took her place at the Coast Guard supply depot near South Street Seaport. Her chemistry degree qualified her to work in a laboratory and test uniform materials for flammability, and so that was what she did five days a week, never knowing until then how much fabric the United States military needed. After work, she and her girls tried as many restaurants as they could before collapsing into their bunks at Hunter each night. They went to Harlem and ate oxtail stew and collard greens, which hearkened to her of home. They went to Chinatown and slurped noodles, the first Asian food she had ever eaten. She got chastised by a patron in a restaurant in Greenwich Village for eating fried chicken with her fingers, and she fired back, "Well, how would *you* do it?" She ate sandwiches at an automat, rode the subway to Brooklyn and back, dipped her toes in the water at Coney Island.

In January, Catherine took a ride upstairs on the elevator at the supply depot. The doors opened on the second floor, and in stepped Carpenter First Class Richard Riggs, native of Swansboro, North Carolina, but lately of Greenwich Village, tenth of twelve children, cabinet builder for the Coast Guard, and a handsome devil. He was suave in his uniform, and she glowed in hers, her shapely legs peeping from her modest skirt and her apple cheeks from above her navy jacket. Richard, known as Chips because of his carpentry work, smelled of tung oil and sawdust. He took his place beside her in the elevator and grinned. The doors dinged at all the floors, but I doubt they heard them.

A little over a year later, on March 4, 1944, Paul Robeson played Othello at the Shubert Theater, just across 44th Street from the *Times* building. Georgia O'Keeffe exhibited a new series of desert paintings at a Madison Avenue gallery, and the Metropolitan Opera's matinee was *La Bohème*. Shirley Jackson published a new short story in the *New Yorker*, and the Jockey Club, 250 Park Avenue, solicited donations of binoculars for the Navy. A lot of things were happening in New York that Saturday, but the most important thing was that Chips and Catherine got married at a church on East 29th Street. Chips had once dated

Fiorello LaGuardia's secretary, so he figured that the mayor could marry him, but nothing doing, it being a Saturday. So Catherine and Chips walked up to the Little Church Around the Corner, also known as the Church of the Transfiguration, although few people ever called it that. The story went that the rector there would marry pretty much anybody, no blood tests or parental release required. So my grandparents took their place in the oak pews of the Holy Family Chapel and watched as couple after couple got married, signed the register, and floated back out into the bitter March wind. Many of the couples married on the weekdays were half servicemen off to war. Many of them did not return.

Chips slid a gold ring onto Catherine's finger, and they were declared married by the Rev. Dr. Randolph Ray, who, in his book *My Little Church Around the Corner*, estimated that he had married hundreds and hundreds of couples over the years. The new Mr. and Mrs. Riggs signed the register, and went outside to find a late lunch. That night, Catherine moved her things into Chip's apartment on West 13th Street. A month later she was pregnant, so she resigned from the Coast Guard—per their requirement—and went about setting up house for her family in Astoria, where they could get more space, cheaper. She gave birth to my aunt Alice in January at the naval hospital on Staten

Island, and they spent that spring sitting on the stoop, watching Queens go by. On the weekends, my grandmother ate a lot of Greek food with Alice parked in a buggy; Chips was on mysterious missions during the evenings, helping pull Nazis out of Long Island Sound and dispose of them off the books.

As the war wound down, Chips and Catherine knew their time in New York was over. More babies were wanted, space was tight, and they needed family around for help. Chips shipped out to California for one last assignment, and Catherine packed up the baby and their things and moved in with her mother-in-law, who, by all accounts, was a piece of work. Rena Freeman Riggs had unbendable ideas about how to raise children, how to cook, and how her baby boys should be treated. Catherine had fierce ideas about those things too, but, powerless in the face of her husband's backwards clan and exhausted from young motherhood, she crept into her books until Chips came home. When he finally alighted from the train in Wilmington several months later, sewn into his uniform against theft was a heavy solid gold necklace with matching earrings: a trinket he'd found in Long Beach for his best girl, who he knew was chafing under his mother's hounding.

It was perhaps not what she'd expected. But then, what did she expect? I wondered. Although she married for love, hers was not the generation to put its romance eggs in one basket. As an eight-year-old, I helped out at her bridge parties, refilling candy dishes and taking dirty plates and glasses to the kitchen. I listened as she bid for tricks and counted for scores. I was bored by the details of the game and comforted by the droning of these women's voices. She surrounded herself with brilliant women who in a different time would have run the world, but at the beginning of the feminist revolution, they taught school and raised children, played golf on the weekends, cleaned the kitchen in the evenings while their husbands played secret boys' club at the Masonic lodge. My grandmother said that she was pretty sure all these men did at their meetings was roll around on the floor in their pajamas.

Whatever she expected, what she got was sixty-two years, five girls, two bankruptcies, a few trips to Spain, and a husband who mourned her long before she died. Her slide into dementia was long. Two weeks before the September 11 attacks, my grandfather had emergency triple-bypass surgery in Chapel Hill. My mom and her four sisters sat in the waiting room for hours; my aunt Karen kept bursting into tears, which annoyed everyone else, and they told her to go out into the hallway and do it there. Alice hobbled outside to smoke, and Gail and Jinny read all the magazines and paced. My mom and I sat next to my grandmother, who held her old-lady purse on her lap and gazed vacantly at the wall. "It was like she was just waiting for the bus," my mom said later. "She had no idea where she was."

Where she was: Off the Alaskan coast in a submarine. On a boat on the Nile. Back in New York, eating fried chicken with her fingers. Plucking muscadine grapes off the vine that covered the back fence, peeling back the leathery skins with her brother and chewing the flesh inside. On a sailboat with her Mariner Girl Scout troop on the Gulf Coast. Playing golf with Mrs. Wands and reading the newspaper at the club afterward. She was many places. But she was not with us.

And then came Father's Day, and a dawn that washed everything clean.

I SHOVED CLOTHES and makeup into my backpack, distracted, and Michael called me a car service. He carried my things downstairs, and we sat on the stoop, waiting for the Town Car. I could still taste the sausage from my sandwich and regretted not brushing my teeth again.

"Call me when you land," he said. I nodded and leaned against him. I breathed in his beard. "Did you get your phone charger?" he asked. I nodded again. We leafed through the Sunday paper, and I flipped past the Style section. I didn't need to see my couples that morning. I knew who they were and didn't care how they'd fared on Saturday night, as I waited for my grandmother to die.

A beat-up black Lincoln pulled up and the driver waved at me, and we carried my things to the car. "I love you. You know that?" Michael said. "I love you so much."

"I know," I said, and my lungs emptied of breath again. "I love you."

Three hours later, I was on the curb at the airport in Richmond. I'd left a temperate spring day in New York and flown into a listless heat for which I was not dressed or prepared. I'd also realized on the plane that I had forgotten to pack anything to wear for the funeral, although I did remember my phone charger.

My parents pulled to the curb in their Jeep, and my brother hopped out of the back. We didn't say anything; what could be said? He threw my things in the boot, and I crawled in the back. My mom was in the driver's seat.

"Are you OK?" I asked her, as she looked in the rearview mirror. She nodded. Her face was washed in new grief, pale and exhausted, but she still wore red lipstick, and that made me feel better. *She's OK*, I thought. She did not reach for me, and I did not reach for her; I knew that if I touched her, a dam would burst that could not be resealed, and we had miles to go still. I settled into the back seat for the drive down to the coast, and I forgot to call Michael.

AS IT HAPPENED, a couple who got married at the Little Church Around the Corner right after Chips and Catherine was featured in the *Times*: "Aurelia M. Giorni Wed to Army Man; Becomes Bride of Wilton T. Entwistle in the Church of the Transfiguration," trumpeted the headline at the top of page 15 of the late city edition of March 7, 1944. The announcement is a classic of its form. It includes all the details of class, lineage, education, and employment, noting that the bride was descended from Bertel Thorvaldsen, the Danish sculptor, and that she was given away by her uncle, the commissioner of highways for the state of New Jersey. But it also listed what the bridal party wore and carried. The bride carried a bouquet of white camellias and freesia, while the flower girl carried "a basket of pink sweet peas and blue lace flowers."

The new Mr. and Mrs. Entwistle radiate something from their picture, but I'm not exactly sure what. The groom's uniform peeps out from the neck of his military-issue overcoat, and he's looking at something above the camera off in the distance, not sure whether to smile. The bride found the lens, though, and has a tight grip on her new husband's arm, her wedding ring in plain sight. The groom had recently finished an Army civil engineering program, so his deployment date was probably not far off. The bride and groom knew they had little time to waste; on the day they were married, the *Times* noted, American forces fought "the greatest air battle in history almost from the coastline to Berlin and back." Allied forces were determined to grind the Third Reich into submission, and on the other side of the world, Merrill's Marauders had reaped havoc in the Chinese-Burma-India theater. While most of the brides and grooms I wrote about faced looming deadlines and irate clients, these brides and grooms faced the distinct possibility of never seeing each other again, only days or weeks after their weddings.

One day, not long before my grandmother died, I took a long lunch from the desk and wandered over to the church on East 29th Street. I buzzed the door to the rectory, and a man in short sleeves and a clerical collar let me in. I told him what I was there to do, and his face reflected understanding, and that he'd heard this story before. "They're all back here," he said, and waved his hand toward a storeroom next to his office.

He opened the door and there, in neatly labeled boxes, were hundreds, if not thousands, of records of weddings performed at the Little Church Around the Corner. They were organized by the groom's name, so I pulled down the box marked "RI." And there it was: the yellowed card that my grandparents and their two witnesses had signed on March 4, 1944, along with the Rev. Dr. Ray, that recorded the occasion of their wedding. It was probably the last thing my grandmother ever signed with her maiden name, although I'm certain she had to work to remember to use Riggs for quite a while after.

I sat on the carpet and held the record for a while. It was no thicker than an envelope, but to me, it was as weighted as a family Bible. I put it aside to make a copy and sifted through others. Roger Riley of Wilmington, North Carolina, and Jeannette Lyons of New Orleans, married on Thursday, September 28, 1944; their announcement appeared in the *News and Observer* of Raleigh, and the groom reported for duty at Lake Placid after their honeymoon tour of the New England states. Maurice Hiram Wertz of Lake Worth, Florida, and Betty Jane Worley of Perrysville, Ohio, married on Saturday, February 6, 1943; he survived World War II but died back in Florida at fifty-two after a short illness, leaving only Betty behind. Or Lieutenant William LeRoy Messmer of Detroit and Mary Lucille Rider of Norfolk, Virginia, married on Saturday, February 17, 1940; he has a park named after him in Detroit, just across the E. Edsel Ford Freeway from his old neighborhood. And Elmer Miller of Staunton, Virginia, and Maybelle Burgess of Hartford, Connecticut, married on Saturday, February 20, 1943; their announcement was featured in the

Groom Riggs - Richard. Date March 4th 1944
Bride Bullock - Catherine Craig
License 5799 - Mar. 4, 1944 (1:08 PM)
DO NOT FILL IN ABOVE THIS LINE

Church of the Transfiguration
1 EAST 29th STREET
NEW YORK, N. Y.

Date March 4th 1944 Hour 3 PM.
GROOM'S FULL NAME Richard W. Riggs
Residence 117-W. 131st. N.Y. N.Y.

Occupation Armed Service
Where Born? City Swansboro State N.C.
Bachelor or Widower   Color or Race White   Citizen of U.S.A.
Date of Birth (Month, Day, Year) Aug. 28, 1916
Baptized? Yes In what Denomination? Baptist
Father's Christian Name John C. Riggs
Mother's Maiden Name Rena W. Freeman
Parents' Residence Swansboro, N.C.
Address after Marriage 117-W. 131st N.Y.C.

BRIDE'S FULL NAME Catherine Craig Bullock
Residence 148-W 10th St. N.Y.C

Where Born? City Birmingham Ala State Ala.
Maiden   Color or Race white   Citizen of U.S.A
Date of Birth (Month, Day, Year) Feb 5, 1921
If a Widow, give Maiden Name
Baptized? Yes In what Denomination? Presbyterian
Father's Christian Name Willa T. Bullock
Mother's Maiden Name Adelaide C. Sherman
Parents' Residence (Deceased)

OFFICIATING CLERGYMAN Randolph Ray

We, the undersigned, solemnly swear without evasion or reservation, that the above statements are true, that we are not divorced, that our Parents or Guardians are aware of this marriage, that we are of legal age, that there is no impediment nor objection to our marriage, and that we are entering into it of our own free will.

Groom Richard W. Riggs
Bride Catherine C. Bullock
Witness Charles Golder
Address 621 East 179th St N.Y.C
Witness Claude Dobie
Address 139 E. 35" St NYC.

Hartford Courant, on a page titled "Feminine Topics," and even though their residence after marriage was 18 Gramercy Park South, they were both buried in Thornrose Cemetery in Staunton, right across the street from my brother's house.

These people went to war, came home, or never left at all. They married and loved and ached, they fought in the night, they sent their children to school in the mornings and agonized over bills, illness, the possibility of nuclear war. Maybe they played bridge with their friends in the evenings; maybe they reminisced about that really great meal they had in the West Village the night before they got married. They all came from elsewhere, though, and somehow had made their way to the oak pews on East 29th Street. They signed their licenses, brought their witnesses, maybe had a bouquet for the ceremony, maybe had a drink or two after. Just like my brides and grooms stood each week on the edge of forever, so did they, and the decades ahead weren't written. I rested on the floor for a while, lulled by the humdrum of the air conditioner, and listened for the young voices that had rung out long ago with hope and love with the bloom still on it.

AT THE FUNERAL, I sat behind my grandfather, who'd aged a decade since Valentine's Day. He shook on his feet, and he slumped forward, his shoulders without strength. As a bald minister took the pulpit, I sweated in my polyester funeral getup that I'd bought at Sears, the only place near Swansboro that sold anything resembling decent clothes. *I should have just worn jeans*, I thought, as I tugged at the cheap fabric of my skirt.

Next to me, my brother was sweating in his suit, and my cousin Lisa fanned herself with the funeral program. It was murderously hot outside, and the air conditioning could only keep things at a low boil in the sanctuary. My uncle by marriage sobbed and gasped for breath behind me, and as sweat trickled down my neck, I got unreasonably angry in my head. *She's not your grandmother*, I thought, cruel in grief, forgetting that she had served as a keystone for him too. *You aren't named for her. She's not your mother. Shut up.*

Before the service started, I stood with my mom at the sanctuary door, greeting people I'd never met and losing their names immediately. A great-aunt named Mary rolled up in her wheelchair and grabbed my hand. She held on to it tightly and looked at my mom. "My word, she favors her," she said, cocking her head at me. My mom nodded, and I saw her fists clench.

"You mean Catherine?" I said.

"Of course," Aunt Mary said. "Your cheeks. You look just like her."

My stomach quaked, and I felt my throat seize. "Thank

you," I said, and loosened my hand from hers. I hustled through the church kitchen to the azalea garden for some air. *I cannot cry*, I thought. *I will not cry. I cannot do this. She is still here, somewhere.* I sucked the heavy air into my lungs and went back into the sanctuary just as the organ began to play.

My mom and her sisters took their places in the front pew, and my grandfather sat in the corner. He stared at the program, unwilling to look at the minister as he spoke platitudes about a woman he barely knew. *How do you bury a wife?* I thought, as my uncle howled in my ears. But then I realized: Chips had lost Catherine long ago to the water, where her gaze landed each morning, where she was happy and free, and remembered all as it had happened. He had let her go. And now her sails were full with fair winds, and he was left on the shore, ready to follow. But he could not.

I HIT THE button for 2R, and Michael buzzed me in. I had decided to go straight to his apartment when I landed back in New York. I needed him, even though we were in a tight spot. I needed him to tell me that this was all OK: this grief, this interior cruelty that bubbled inside me like lava, making me hateful; this inability to cry, even as I watched my stoic mother weep. As the pallbearers had rolled my grandmother's coffin outside to the hearse, my mom and her sisters huddled together, reaching for the American flag draped over the box carrying their mother. I breathed in the air as the coffin passed, wondering where my grandmother had gone, and did not cry.

Michael opened the door and took my backpack off my shoulders. I stood in the doorway, not knowing what to do or where to go. He held out his hand to me and pulled me inside. And then my knees gave way completely and I collapsed on the floor in a mourning heap.

"My mother doesn't have a mother anymore," I sobbed. He closed the door behind us and curled up on the floor with me, and all the longing and grief and cruelty poured from me. I wept onto his blue T-shirt for my mom, and I wept for my grandfather. He loved Catherine then just as he had the day he met her. They were both strangers from the South, in an unfamiliar place on a grand adventure, and they'd found a home in each other's arms, six decades before Michael and I had ever met, in the same city on grand adventures. "I wish she'd known you," I told Michael as my sobs quieted eventually, wrapped in his arms against his front door. "I wish you'd known her. I wish she knew I loved you."

He kissed me on the forehead. "I wish I'd known her too," he said gently. "But I'm so glad I know you."

I kissed him. I kissed him again, and again. We climbed

onto his disgusting Salvation Army couch and made fast, fevered love in the dark. Afterward, I lay there on his chest, our legs and fingers entwined, and I thought: *This is where we should be. No matter what. Here is home.* And I decided to fight for it.

CHAPTER 13

I Am My Beloved's, and My Beloved Is Mine

MICHAEL IS MISSING," Erin said. It was right before lunch on April 24, the morning of our wedding. I was trying to write a check to the reception shuttle driver without messing up my fresh ballet-pink manicure. I paused before signing my name and looked at her. She was standing in the middle of the bed-and-breakfast suite we'd shared the night before, the last room I was to sleep in as an unmarried woman. We had already popped a bottle of champagne, and shoes and clothes were strewn everywhere. My mom had not yet shown up with the wedding dress that she'd spent all night finishing. My wedding ceremony was supposed to start in five and a half hours.

"What do you mean, he's missing?"

"Mark said he and Jack were looking for him to make sure he was OK, and he wasn't in his room," Erin said, holding the phone away from her like it had germs. "He isn't in the hotel, and he isn't answering his phone. They can't find him."

She sat down next to me on the bed. "I'm sure he didn't go anywhere."

I laughed as annoyance crawled up my spine, and finished writing the check. "I know he didn't. Where would he go?"

Erin seemed to think it was a foregone conclusion that Michael had become a runaway groom, or had been hit by a car in a crosswalk, or had choked on his morning pancakes. In any event, she had fast-forwarded to a bridegroom absent from the altar of our wedding ceremony—a ceremony that he'd scripted front to back and for which he'd created a production binder, like it was a play. She was clearly shaken. I was just irritated.

"I'm sure he's fine," she said, patting my shoulder awkwardly.

I rolled my eyes. "He didn't go anywhere. He doesn't have the car keys, and he has no idea where he is, anyway." After nearly six years together, I knew three things: one, there was no way Michael wouldn't show up for this wedding; two, he had zero sense of direction and couldn't escape even if he wanted to; and three, he did most of his processing in a bathroom, where he probably was, somewhere two of his closest friends hadn't thought to look.

The day for which we had planned and saved and spent and dreamed and fought was here, finally. I hadn't slept the night before and was running on coffee, champagne, and cured meats from a fancy deli platter sent by thoughtful friends. We held the rehearsal dinner at an old, dank-smelling swim club in Charlottesville that at one point allegedly had been a speakeasy. My future mother-in-law had strewn rose petals and Christmas lights everywhere, and we had barbecue, slaw, an enormous chocolate cake, and a slide show and speeches. I told everyone that it was a casual affair, but they all still showed up in dresses and ties—all except for the fashion-executive wife of a friend, who took the casual message to heart, showed up in fancy jeans, and looked like she wanted to melt into the floor as women in sheath dresses filled the room. I wore a dress from Target and yellow Louboutins that I'd gotten off eBay. My hair was terrible, but I felt good. We'd run through the ceremony, delivered most of the welcome bags, done a walk-through of the venue, and divvied up tasks for the next day. We were on our game as much as possible, I thought.

The night before we got married was an embrace, cut through with cheap wine, old stories told by dearest friends, and gentle skewering of us. Giddy and full-hearted, I accidentally outed my friend Ramona's early pregnancy in front of a long table of old friends. Michael had a little too much to drink and, teetering, took a drunk selfie with his grandmother. My father-in-law made fun of my politics. My dad's sister wandered around the entire time with chocolate frosting on her face from ear to ear, just thrilled to be at a party, and no one had the heart to pull her aside and wash her face. I left with Erin to finish the table assignments and entrusted Michael, who I knew wasn't fit to drive or be left alone, to his friend Carlos, who swore he was on best-man duty and wouldn't let anything happen to Michael or to disrupt our wedding day.

Apparently that was a mistake on my part.

THERE'S SOMETHING CRUCIAL missing in a wedding announcement. There's no public document of the jitters, the hangovers, the things that go wrong, the mud on a dress hem at the end of the night, the joy and the gentle sorrows. After all, your announcement has been written and gone to press hours, even days before you walk down the aisle. It's being inked as you're doing your makeup, perhaps, hair in rollers, dress drifting from a personalized hanger. The print editions are being bound and thrown onto trucks, to be dropped across the city overnight, maybe as you're still dancing, or on your way to a magnificent hangover, or eating late-night catering leftovers from a foam clamshell, aching legs nestled against your new spouse's on a hotel floor.

So the wedding is announced after the date, but, unlike everything else in the paper of record, the wedding itself isn't actually reported. What are the things we don't read about in a wedding announcement? Are they what is lost to memory, or are they the most important thing? What isn't reported? Sometimes they are the funniest things, or the strangest things, or the most joyful things. And sometimes they're the things we want to remember the least.

One Monday morning months before my own wedding, my desk phone rang. On the line was a bride whose announcement had run in the paper that Sunday. We'd talked a couple of times before they'd left for Mexico, and I liked her. She was sweet, a little awkward, wildly smart, and so excited to talk about her wedding. Like so many brides I talked to each week, she'd been a bit harried, but in a wondrous way, as if she couldn't believe her luck.

High Society had just married a commodities trader from Deer Park, whose parents owned a faltering salvage company. She was an associate at a white-shoe law firm in Midtown, recruited straight from Penn Law, and had grown up in Merion, Pennsylvania, which, as the crow flies, wasn't that far from Long Island. But High Society's world was far different from Himself's. Her parents probably spent more just on their horses than his parents made in a year, or maybe two. He was a public school kid; she was a Country Day alumna. They met at a bar uptown right after she joined the firm. He charmed her with fast talk and spontaneity, and they were engaged within a year.

The picture she submitted showed two people in cashmere sweaters, eyes at exactly the same level, a bucolic wintry day filtering through the picture window behind them. Himself had gotten into manscaping, and his eyebrows were pencil thin. I'd wondered what they looked like in their natural state. High Society probably never knew.

As I'd written in her announcement, the wedding was set for Saturday evening at an expensive resort near Puerto Vallarta that Himself had campaigned for. High Society had wanted to get married at her childhood Episcopal church in Merion, with a tented reception at her parents' horse farm, but Himself had pushed hard, dreaming of hot pictures from their beachside honeymoon that he could show his bros back at the trading desk. So the Riviera Nayarit in April it was. Shoulder season, but that meant the rates were lower, which Himself liked. High Society's parents, her radiologist father had indicated during his interview with me, were somewhat resigned to the whole thing.

The line was a little fuzzy; she was clearly still in Mexico.

"Hi, Cate," she breathed down the phone. She sounded tired. "This is High Society."

"Hi!" I said brightly, making a mental note that she didn't use her married name. "Congratulations! How was the wedding?"

"Well," she began, and stopped. I could hear her breathing heavily, almost like she was gasping for air, and my heart sank a little. There was no way this was going to be a good phone call.

"I was wondering," she said haltingly. "Could you take our wedding announcement down off the website?"

"Um," I said, scribbling *CAN WE REMOVE AN AN-NOUNCEMENT FROM YESTERDAY?* on a sticky note and passing it to Ira over my desk. He read it and instantly shook his head no. "I don't believe so," I said. "They're public record and part of the news report, so we could correct it or add an editor's note if something was really wrong, but we can't remove it necessarily. Can you tell me why you want to take it down?" I spoke as kindly as I could, because she'd started crying.

"Well—" She paused to take a breath. "I found out on Saturday night that Himself had been cheating on me, so we're getting an annulment as soon as we get back to the States."

"Oh my God," I said, and gave Ira a "holy shit" look. "I am so, so sorry to hear that. I really am." I didn't know what to say. I was instantly on fire with rage for her, for her months of dreaming and joyful planning, dress fittings and parties and practice writing *Mrs. Himself* for her parents' many thousands of dollars. No matter how difficult these brides and grooms could be, every single one of them was taking a leap of faith, and we cheered them on—or at least we cheered on the ones who weren't total jerks. This was a violation of one of my own, the young women who'd thrown caution to the wind and sought love at some cost, and I was furious.

But I was also curious.

"Can you tell me what happened?" I put on my gentlest reporter's voice.

She took a deep breath. "Well, it's kind of funny—"

"You don't have to tell me, honestly," I said. "It's none of my business." But in some way, I felt it was. I'd spent quite a bit of time with this woman's relationship.

"No, no, I don't mind," she said. "I should have known. Or I should have suspected. But I didn't want to."

The night of her wedding, after the toasts had been drunk and shoes had been removed, High Society and her maid of honor had gone back to the bridal suite so she could change into a lighter dress for an after-party. After the maid of honor had unhooked High Society's dozens of buttons, she'd gone to the bathroom, leaving the new Mrs. Himself to shimmy out of her Monique Lhuillier with the ribbon sash. As she stood by the bed, thousands of dollars of satin and tulle around her feet, she heard a phone buzz. Her maid of honor had left her BlackBerry on the nightstand. She picked it up absently, out of habit, and saw a text message from "H.S.<3" on the screen.

THAT SUKD, it read in all caps. *U WERE SO HOT THO WISH I MARRID U ISNTED. U COMING TO THE BEACH????*

"Wait," I said as she told me this. "You wrote it down?" She'd read out the message to me from a resort notepad, spelling and all.

"Well, yeah, I'm an attorney," she said. "I know he can't fucking spell, but I think he actually may be stupider than I knew."

Whoa.

High Society confronted the maid of honor after she came out of the bathroom. The alleged friend, drunk, confessed the whole thing. She and Himself had been sleeping together since the engagement party at Christmas, when he had walked her out to her car across the icy lawn, and they'd kissed behind her Land Rover, out of sight. It was a total meet-cute—except that Himself's fiancée and the maid of honor's best friend was inside with her family and Himself's parents, drinking to good fortune and the fairy tale realized.

"So what are you going to do?" I asked.

"Get an annulment and move out," she said. "Or maybe

he should move out. He makes more than I do. He can afford a nicer place anyway." They'd been squeezed into a studio on the Upper East Side that High Society had rented after law school. Ever prudent, she had wanted to begin saving immediately for a house, probably a center-hall colonial near her parents in Pennsylvania. Himself had seen his future, I guess, and it was full of equestrian meets, school fund-raisers, and summers in Bay Head.

"Did you have any hint that this was going on?" I prodded carefully. "You said you should have known, but I think probably everyone says that. Should you really have known? I mean, would anything have given it away?"

High Society was quiet for a moment.

"He never held my hand when we were alone," she said finally. "He would grab my ass or kiss me or whatever. But you know when you're just sitting on the couch watching TV, and you just want to hold hands? He wouldn't ever do that. He'd grope my boobs or something."

Her tone shifted to a boardroom crispness.

"So, of course the first thing on Google you see now is my wedding announcement," she said. "And it isn't true. I married him, but not really. Can you take it down?"

"You know what, let me transfer you to Ira," I said, waving at him over the divider, not eager to be the bearer of hard news myself. "I hear you, I totally do, and I'm really sorry. But he has to make the call."

I punched in Ira's extension and hit the transfer button. "Ira Goetz," I heard him say, and I walked away, preferring not to hear him turn her down, however gently. That was the last I heard from High Society, who, I assume, never legally changed her name to Himself's. Her announcement is still available for public consumption, although it's not the top link about her anymore. I Google her sometimes. I want to know that humans are capable of recovering from horrible humiliations and wretched heartbreak. She's changed firms, made partner, remarried, and has an address in Bronxville, where, I am sure, she's a PTA leader, fervent soccer mom, and member of the local club. I hope she's doing well.

WHAT ARE THE things that don't end up in a wedding announcement? Cake disasters, lost rings, rained-out receptions. Or worse: infidelity, family secrets revealed at the worst times, fights, runaway brides, runaway grooms. If you're lucky, though, it's the good stuff. The funny stuff that's worth remembering, like awkward toasts or split zippers, or the kindnesses, like your friends decorating the reception hall while you gad about, trying to calm your nerves with manicures and milkshakes. Or it's the silly things, like a groom gone missing temporarily.

Michael and I got engaged the previous March on a windswept cliff in Ireland. It was exactly as romantic as it sounds. We were on a trip with our parents and my brother, who had all gamely come along because they knew this was it, the trip that would cement our families together, and anyway, we'd been dancing around it for half a decade, so they might as well witness a damn miracle. In a nod to tradition unusual for Michael, he announced his intentions to my dad and brother and asked for their blessing on a walk through Prospect Park after Christmas brunch. Not long after, my mom began asking what kind of wedding I would want if, and she only meant *if*, we ever got married, and did I know that the University Club up at Columbia might be a good place? I did not know that. I kept my head down about it all and tried to pick up some speed on my runs through the park.

My brother and I used my frequent flier miles to save some money, so we flew over by ourselves on Delta, while Michael (who still deserves a drink for taking on this particular task) had to get our parents from Brooklyn to Newark, pile them onto a Continental narrow-body jet in coach for six hours, and restrain himself from killing them all while his stepfather and my dad politely disagreed over who was better equipped to drive on the left side of the road. Meanwhile, Steven and I got upgraded to business class, where my brother, who had never before left the country, giggled every time the flight attendant offered us warm nuts. As we taxied out from the gate, I sipped some champagne, worked on a handful of warm nuts, and wondered if I'd return to America a betrothed woman.

The first thing that happened after we all reconvened at our rental house was that Michael got food poisoning. Deep, unforgiving, relentless, projectile-vomit-inducing food poisoning. He ate a chicken salad sandwich for lunch on some little touristy island, and by the time we settled in to a pub in Westport, he was faintly green from the neck up. A little girl stood behind her father at the bar, staring at us and picking her nose, and as he watched her I could see the bile rise in his throat. We were fifty feet from the hedge that marked our driveway when he yelled, "Pull. OVER." He threw open the back door to our rental Nissan before the car stopped and firehosed chicken salad and breakfast and God knows what else all over the grass and the inside of the door. When we finally got back home, Steven washed down the car while I helped my future husband inside. His mom took one look at him, smiled sympathetically, and washed her hands of it all. He was mine, and my problem now. Even now, he refuses to eat chicken salad on vacation.

A day or two later, he recovered nicely, and we ended up in a seaside town that during the summer served as a resort village for Dubliners. In March, though, nearly everything was shuttered but a gas station and a tiny hotel with a pub downstairs. We rambled along the shore, looking for sea urchins, and found steps headed up the cliff. Steven started to follow us up the stairs but then immediately thought better of it. He huddled with our parents down on the sand as they waited to see what I'd say.

We marched up the cliff and realized we were trespassing on an old golf course; signs everywhere warned us off the greens that likely hadn't been played in years. Along the edge of the cliff were weathered headstones, worn so well by the winds that anything carved on them had been lost to time. Michael was talking, but I disappeared for a moment: who were these people under the earth, and what had become of them? The early grass was thick and springy, a verdant trampoline that propelled us up the path to the edge. I felt as if I had been spirited up to the top of the cliff by people I had never known, a springtime earth that told the same hopeful story every year, and the hands of a person who I loved so much that I didn't have to think about it. It was as bedrock as the cliff we stood on, and as revelatory as the Atlantic winds that tangled my hair into knots. As these cliffs just were, it just *was*.

I was so blissed out by being at the edge of that cliff that I was only half listening to what Michael was saying, but when we stopped at the very crest, I realized what was going on. He drew a ring from his pocket and held it out to me. "At the end of it all, it's just us," he said, the words catching in the back of his throat. I put my hand on his chest to steady myself and started laughing, for joy and for a promise, out of relief and out of love, and also out of regret and guilt that I had missed the whole first part of his proposal. But still, I laughed, and then we laughed together.

And then I looked at the ring and thought, *Huh*. It was one of the ugliest things I had ever seen. It had this weird, square, composite-diamond thing going on in the center, with some diamond chips sprinkled up and down the band. It was fine for other people, but it was—how should I say this—not for me. I came back down to earth for two seconds to wonder what the fuck he was thinking about, but we'd fix it later, and why did he buy me a ring in the first place, I didn't even want a ring, but whatever, it's fine, it's fine, holy shit, we're doing this.

I didn't even say yes; I didn't need to. I buried my face in his jacket, and he wrapped his arms around me and nuzzled his chin into the top of my head. We stayed there long enough for our hearts to calm themselves, for the clouds to clear and the poles to change their pull. It felt like everything on earth had changed in a hot second, and yet everything was more or less the same, except one small, essential thing. We were going to do the thing. Michael slid this incredibly tacky ring on my finger, and we ran back down the path to our families at the bottom of the cliff.

We sheltered from a coming storm at the tiny hotel's pub and drank yet more champagne, and rested there for dinner. I ordered fish and chips and a double whiskey. As its warmth reached into my fingertips, my mom, who was sitting at my side, turned to me. "What are you going to do about that ring?" she muttered. I looked at her, appalled that she knew exactly what I was thinking.

"Mama!" I said.

"Cate, I don't know where he got that idea. I sent him all sorts of suggestions, antique sapphire rings and ruby rings. Never anything that looks like that." My new engagement ring sparkled under the pub lights like an unwanted disco ball.

I shushed her and said, "I don't know what to do." Michael, sitting on the other side of me, only let go of my hand long enough for me to eat. The two of us closed down the pub that night, a fire dwindling in its hearth and anxiety worming its way into my happiness. Joy is rarely simple.

"There are two things you can do," my mom said the next day as we took a car ferry across the bay. "One, you can tell him, and you know that's going to break his heart. Two, you can just lose it."

Appalled again, I said, "I can't do that to him."

"Well, you can't wear that," she said, pointing to the ring that was so ugly I'd turned it around so I didn't have to look at the setting. "You could also do what Pippie did and bang it up with a hammer so you'd have to get a new ring." That was true. My dad's grandmother, Willie McConnico Doty, hated the simple five-prong setting that her engagement diamond sat in, preferring the more ornate basket filigree settings that all her friends were getting in 1922. So she took a hammer to her ring, told my great-grandfather that one of the prongs had broken, and got the setting that she wanted. This was the same diamond that my mom wears in the same simple five-prong setting that my dad gave her, which Willie, whose friends called her Bill, hated so much.

None of these suggestions felt palatable, but something had to be done. She was right. I didn't want to wear an ugly ring for the rest of my life, and in fact, I hadn't ever given much thought to an engagement ring at all. I just assumed we'd exchange wedding rings and that would be that. But now that I had this ugly thing on my finger, heavy with the expectation of *till death do us part*, I had to fix it. So I told him. If you ever want to feel like the asshole that you really are, try telling someone who just gave you an engagement ring that they chose poorly. Very, very poorly.

"I didn't even want a ring," I told Michael that evening after dinner. "This is just—it isn't my taste. I'm really sorry, but it just isn't."

Michael, lying on the bed in our hotel, immediately teared up. He had planned this trip and that moment for months, and I had just punctured his gilded cloud of betrothed bliss. Turns out, he'd just gotten engaged to a jackass.

"I thought you wanted a ring!" he yelled. "I thought that's what everyone did!"

"I already have a ring that you gave me," I said, pointing to the aquamarine on my right hand. "I just want a wedding ring from you. That's it. I just want you."

I paused. "Did you have any help picking this out?"

Michael had climbed under the covers by this point. "Luther went with me."

"Luther?" I yelped. "What the hell does Luther know about jewelry?"

"I don't know!" Michael sob-yelled. "He's an artist and has good taste and I thought he would be helpful!"

He held his hand out to me. "Give it back to me," he said bitterly. "I won't make you wear this ugly ring."

I felt like throwing up. "I want to wear your ring. I am so excited about wearing the ring you give to me. But this is just—this is not me."

"You've been quite clear," Michael said, a cold wind blowing. "I hear you."

I took the ring off and put it in his outstretched hand. "See?" I held up my hand with my old ring. "This is all I want. You and this."

That did not make matters better. It took him a solid day to come back around, a day that I spent traipsing around Kenmare by myself, which, I have to say, was a nice break from all the hullabaloo. He found me at a tea shop on the high street, tucked into a corner with a book and dreams of our wedding already shaping themselves. I was fully on engagement cloud nine, even though I felt horribly guilty about wounding him. At least I didn't have to wear that ugly ring.

He ordered a pot of tea and a scone and grabbed my hand with the aquamarine on it. "This is all you wanted, isn't it," he said quietly, holding my hand in the light. I nodded. "Well, I wanted to give you a ring. I'm sorry I didn't choose the right ring for you. But I want a new ring that's ours. OK?"

I nodded again and held his hand to my face. It still felt cold, but I knew the thaw was coming. "You know I want to marry you, right? A ring has nothing to do with it," I said.

"I do know that," he said. "But I want to mark this beginning with something new."

We were quiet for a while. I thought about how silly this all was. It was a tempest over a ring, of things. I mean, good lord, there was a recession on and people were losing their jobs and children were hungry, and we were both furious about a piece of jewelry. But that damn ring felt atomically heavy, and heady too. I knew that Michael would never cheat on me with a friend. I knew that he would never deceive me, suck all our money up his nose, tell his friends what we did in bed, or do anything to jeopardize this. He knew the same. And I think that's why that ring felt so heavy: it was laden with all the knowledge, all our hopes, all the trips we were going to take, the fights and the makings-up, the hours and days of the life we were building together. Even though it was just a cheesy engagement ring.

We left the tea shop and meandered back to our hotel, not quite ready to walk hand in hand again. But we both knew that would come again. It always did. And that was the whole point.

THE FIRST THING I did after clearing customs was buy a stack of wedding magazines. But only the tasteful ones, of course. I flipped through *Brides* and *The Knot* and recognized a few of the couples from my job. But then I opened the bridal book of common prayer: *Martha Stewart Weddings.* Yes, I thought. My people, the ostentatiously betrothed. And I was one of them at last.

The year of planning went swiftly—and I cried through a lot of it. I cried when we picked out a new engagement ring from the jeweler in Park Slope who had sold Michael the first one. As she polished up the vintage ring I chose, she whispered, "This one fits you better." I howled when I tried on my wedding ring when Michael wasn't home. I sobbed on the couch by myself when going over the guest list and when writing my vows. I wept when we fought over what kind of ceremony to have. I teared up on New Year's Eve when I realized it would be my last as a technically single person. I read a lot of Laurie Colwin, for whom commitment was a recently acquired dark forest, where no map could show the delights and dangers ahead. "Woe to those who get what they desire," she wrote, and I believed it, and I cried. Everything I thought I'd ever wanted was barreling toward me, and I cried.

I kept thinking of the Feminist, the Taste Maker, the Smooth Operative, the Fruity Neurosurgeon, and High Society—all the brides I'd spoken with over the years. After all this, the fighting and making up, the lazy brunches and trips to Florida, the talking and talking and worrying and talking some more, would it be worth it? Would I end up like High Society after all, even though not a cell of me believed that was possible? After all, neither had she. Would I swallow my ambition for domesticity coupled with a career worth living, because after all, neither of us could lean in at the same time? Was all of this for some warped sense of being on display, or just an attempt to add to history and propagate the species? Or was I on track for a Jo March–like destiny, domestic bliss with my bearded soul mate, occupying the vaunted post of marriage? So I cried. I worried, and I planned, and we drank a lot of Prosecco, and I cried.

I did dry my eyes long enough to build a registry, and I stocked up on most of the things de rigueur for a middle-class couple: the German knives, the oiled butcher block, the high-thread-count sheets, the overpriced bakeware. I assiduously avoided the KitchenAid stand mixer, not sure how on earth I would fit it on our three inches of counter space. I agonized over china: were we the type of people to need only one pattern of dish, or did we need the china we'd use daily, and then other fancier plates to roll out for holidays? This was a question that followed me everywhere I went, on the subway platform, falling asleep at night, brushing my teeth. Just as the details of my couples' weddings and relationships summed up who they were, so did our wedding registry. Were we deeply practical, a little bit fancy, or unsuitably pretentious? The one thing I did not worry over was our silver pattern. I hearkened back to that day in Bromberg's seventeen years before and added ten full place settings of Kirk Stieff Repousse to the list. I didn't care if it was impossible to polish, a bit pricey, and just too much in general. The heart wants what it wants, and mine wanted matching hollow-handled knives, individual fruit cocktail forks, and a small tomato server. A letter opener would be nice too.

We submitted our wedding announcement in March. I

typed it up, printed it out, and walked it over to Ira's desk. I placed it on his keyboard without a word. He laughed.

"I've been wondering when you were going to come by," he said. "I'm giving this to Tony. Do you have your transcripts?" He was joking. Sort of.

"I'll send you a copy of my diploma," I said, as I wondered if I knew where it was. "Michael graduated magna, so he'll send you his transcript."

"Good enough," he said. "I need your picture ASAP."

That evening, I warned my parents about the line of questions that they'd have to answer in order for our announcement to be printed.

"I'm happy to answer any questions they have," my mom said.

"They're going to want to know what you and Daddy do for work," I told her. "Are you OK with that?"

"Why would I not be OK with that?"

"I don't know. They're kind of invasive," I said. "I ask them all the time, but I don't know that I'd want them asked of me."

I could hear my mom rolling her eyes. "I'm fine with it."

Her tune changed in April.

"These questions are very inappropriate," she said while we were on the phone for the fifth time that day, two weeks before the wedding. She wanted to know why Tony needed to know what kind of woodworking she taught and whether she was still working. She wanted to know why the *Times* thought my dad's former and current employment was relevant.

"And why do they need to know about Edward Doty? Of course you're descended from him," she said. "We've always known that."

We did, but no one in our branch of Dotys was a member of the Mayflower Society, or the Pilgrim Edward Doty Society. We had binders of genealogy, some family Bibles, and a whole lot of stories. But there was a gap in the trace. Somewhere in the early 1700s, our alleged line moved to Louisiana for a brief period of time, and then somehow migrated up to Kentucky, where they had a whole passel of children. But which person was ours? Whose direct DNA did I carry in me?

I chose not to worry about it and left that detail to my parents. I did a lot of that, those thirteen months. I also left a lot of the bills to them, and most of the logistics. My mom had come strong out of the gate with wedding plans after we got engaged, and beware, the person who tried to distract her, which included me. So I listened, and I cried, and the year passed quickly as we came to the edge of Laurie Colwin's dark forest, which might hold the worst we could imagine, or the best.

OUR WEDDING DAY broke early for me. I didn't sleep the night before, consumed with nerves and wonder and jitters. I watched the sun rise into a gray dawn that didn't portend well for our outdoor ceremony at the home of a long-dead American president, complete with slave quarters rebuilt for educational purposes. I forced down an English muffin with marmalade, and it felt like sandpaper. But I went along with the morning. I took a bath in the claw-foot tub, carefully shaving my legs, leaving my armpits for just before the ceremony. I laid out my underpinnings and jewelry: blue lacy underwear, an armored tank of a strapless bra, the aquamarine earrings that Michael had given me the night before as a wedding present. I gave him bookends of the marble lions at the New York Public Library. The library's lions stood guard over our first kiss and, I figured, Patience and Fortitude would be necessary as we faced what might come.

And then Mark called.

"He isn't missing," I told Erin as we left for our hair appointment. "He was drunk last night, so he's probably hungover somewhere. Where the fuck is Carlos?"

It was a good question. Erin called him.

"Carlos? Where the fuck are you?" she yelled into the

phone, while Michael's very Christian aunt piloted her rental Lincoln to the salon. Her daughter Marie was my junior bridesmaid and, at twelve, possessed more poise than I could ever claim. "I'm going to cut you if you don't find Michael."

I hit her on the leg and gestured to Carole and Marie, who were staring at us in the rearview mirror, aghast.

Erin paused, listening to Carlos. And then she started to laugh. "Why are you in a hot tub?"

A hot tub? I mouthed to her. She made a gagging face. "OK, so Mark and Jack are worried that Michael ran off, so can you call them and let them know that you're in the hot tub? Thanks."

She hung up the phone. "They're in the hot tub? Like, the hot tub in the hotel?" I asked.

"Yeah. So, Michael's a bit"—she glanced at Carole—"hungover, and Carlos thought he'd feel better if he got in the hot tub, so they're there in the hotel, and Mark and Jack just didn't think to look there, apparently."

Carole started laughing. "Sometimes men just don't know where to look."

I immediately wanted to run to Michael with some ginger ale and an aspirin. "Can you imagine being hungover in a hot tub! All those swirling jets, and he has the worst stomach. He's just cooking himself."

"I think that right now, that is not your problem," Carole

said. "He got himself into it, and it's Carlos's job to fix it. Right now, you need to get your hair done."

I sat back into the cream leather of the seats. Erin started laughing. "Dude, I am so glad I'm not Carlos right now. I hope Michael doesn't puke in the hot tub."

The rest of the day floated by. A woman named Sonam forced my hair into an updo, and my exhausted, wonderful mother showed up with my dress at four o'clock. My friends helped me into it, pinning my brown ribbon sash into an intricate bow, and putting toupee tape on my shoulders so my straps wouldn't slip. My bridesman, Jake, drove us to the ceremony, and as we wound our way up the mountain, the clouds cleared.

Here's the thing I didn't mention before. One afternoon in Washington, right before I moved to New York, I got an email from Michael about something, I forget what— probably more flirting thinly disguised as a work request. But as I typed out a response, I started thinking about who this guy was, and who he could be: was he a friend, someone I could talk to when, inevitably, things went south with Adnan? I liked his emails, and I liked that he seemed to know me and wanted to know more, even just through our email volleys. I thought about this. And then a thunderbolt came down to earth and burned itself into my skull, and I realized something as true as the earth's curve: *I was going to marry this guy.*

So I did. We met under the ash trees at five o'clock. Michael wore a bespoke gray suit that hewed closely to his slender body. I remembered our first unofficial date, when I saw him naked onstage, and it felt like a million years ago. I was more familiar with that body now. I couldn't tell if he was hungover, or nervous, or joyous, and as we joined hands, I realized he was all those things; he was, in fact, everything.

Our friend Dave, the columnist, led us down the bridal path, and we said our vows in front of 114 people who remain our whole world. Then the skies opened, and we dashed for the reception in the covered pavilion. It poured; we ate cake; we danced, and danced, and drank, and danced some more. We crawled into bed at two a.m. after a stop at the dive bar across the street, where my friend Charlie—on whom I had a crush in 1992—got me exactly what I needed: the world's largest glass of water. We finally made a run for it through the rain back to our room, where we made happy, fast, exhausted love before Michael rubbed my aching feet and removed the thirty-two bobby pins from my hair. And then we rolled over on our sides, held hands, and drifted into marriage together.

I didn't need the world to know about this love. Neither Michael nor I cared if it was officially "announced" or not. But the next morning, we got a text from friends who were already on their way back to New York. It was a picture of our wedding announcement from a copy purchased at the airport Starbucks. So maybe I did feel a twinge of pride to see us written up in the *Times* after all. We were in the middle of the first page. We laughed, packed our bags, and headed out toward the airport and the life ahead of us.

We'd made it. And I knew that he was worth it. We were worth it.

EPILOGUE

The State of the Union

So, WHAT HAPPENED next? We boarded a plane to Barbados, then a smaller one to Bequia, a tiny island in the Caribbean, where we stared at the blue water for a week and didn't try to make sense of anything other than where to go for dinner. We drank a lot of rum, wandered among the goats on the island, and brushed dried seaweed off our feet in the evenings, all the while letting the thing we'd just done permeate our salty skin, fill the air in our lungs, weld itself into our DNA. The Commonwealth of Virginia, and the *New York Times*, had declared that we were married. So we were.

On the penultimate day of our honeymoon, Michael got a rotten ear infection, so Mr. Gideon took us in his red truck taxi down to the pharmacy in Port Elizabeth, where we got a dropper bottle of Cipro for a few Caribbean dollars. That night, as we drew out the last dinner before returning home, the hotel cats purred and rubbed themselves against our legs. I drank too much wine, and we took a midnight walk on the sand, the waves mimicking the pounding in Michael's head. It was time to go home, to just be married.

The next morning, we boarded the tiny island hopper back to Barbados, and Michael laid his head in my lap as we tipped up into the sky. The cabin wasn't pressurized, and the closer we got to our cruising altitude of five thousand feet, the more miserable he was. He closed his eyes, and I could feel his shoulders twitch, his body relaxing into a fitful sleep.

We picked up some passengers at the airstrip on Canouan, and the pilots turned the plane toward Barbados and home. I watched the Caribbean float by below us, and my mind wandered to what the weather was like back in New York. It was the first week of May; I knew the tulips on Park Avenue would be in full bloom. We would start sleeping with the windows open again, and the horses at Kensington Stables, just behind our building, would neigh us awake in the morning. I needed to place a grocery order, or maybe we should just order Mexican food and deal with groceries later. I wondered if we had any wedding presents waiting for us at the post office, and whether we had coffee at home.

The details of our life swam back into place, hazily and lazily, as the plane floated its way northeast to Bridgetown.

And then I felt a jolt. I am not the world's happiest flier, and the more I've done it over the years, the more nervous I tend to get. I board each flight mourning the fact that my luck has finally run out, which made a turbulent thirteen-hour crossing to Australia particularly miserable. Like many nervous fliers, I pay attention to the engines, and I know conclusively that only I will be able to hear the exact second when they've sputtered their last, just before 250 people and God knows how many suitcases and animals in the hold will be plunged into the darkest depths of the ocean. I use my clenched body to will the engines to keep going, minute after minute, even if it's just a thirty-minute hop from D.C. to New York. When I was younger, I flew free and easy, but not so much now. If I don't pay attention to the engines, then they will stop, and everyone on the plane will die. Of this I remain firmly convinced.

But on that plane five thousand feet over the water, I really did feel a jolt, and then a sudden silence. We were sitting right behind the pilots, who had been chatting amiably over the drone of the props. The jolt snapped them out of their conversation, and they stopped talking and looked at the dashboard, where a red light on the dashboard had started to blink. The first officer whacked at one of the dials with his index finger. The props, it seemed, had stopped spinning, and this plane, carrying the pilots, us, and a lovely Canadian family who had loaned us twenty Caribbean dollars for the exit tax, was about to ditch into the ocean. My stomach dropped right down into the water. This was it; it was not a drill. I was going to die with my husband's head in my lap, and there was nothing I could do about it.

I looked down at Michael's newly tanned face, his noble slope of a nose, his beard that had gone rogue over the week on Bequia. I thought: *I should wake you before we nose-dive. I should kiss you once more. Whither thou goest, I will go, right down to the bottom of the Caribbean.* I looked around at the rest of the passengers, and no one else had noticed what was going on. What was wrong with them? I screamed in my head; how could they not know they were all about to die? I swerved back to the pilots, who were doing things I didn't understand, but all with an air of *holy shit.*

And then just as quickly as the silence had begun, it stopped. The props roared right back into action, and the cabin filled again with their buzz. The pilots calmed their hands, looked at each other, and shrugged. They *shrugged.* I hooked my trembling hands onto the luggage rack above, the only place I could find to put them where I wouldn't disturb Michael. I calculated how long the engines had stopped: Three seconds? Five seconds? Ten hours? Long enough to worry the pilots and me, but a fraction of time otherwise. A blip at the end of a trip, and the beginning of a marriage. I sometimes wonder if those few seconds on that plane actually happened, or are they just a part of a fever dream? But they were absolutely real, and I can still taste the bile that rose in my throat when I saw everything about to break apart, five hundred miles from home.

I found the altimeter on the dashboard and didn't take my eyes off it until we were wheels down full stop in Barbados, where the landing bumps shook Michael out of his sleep. He studied me curiously as we gathered our things. "Are you OK?" he asked, as I rushed into the terminal, away from that plane, unable to say anything. "Fine, I just need to pee," I mumbled. I decided I wouldn't tell him what had happened until we were safely back in Brooklyn, in our messy apartment with the piles of mail, the windowsills filthy with pollution off Ocean Parkway, the life that please, God, I'd keep on living with him. We found our flight to New York, and I drank my way back up the East Coast, my face still blanched, and my hands unwilling to let his go.

SO, WE GOT married. And the rest of it—well, it's just a different ball game. You may be surprised to know, given our baseline combative state, that we landed in a happy marriage, even with all the twists and turns that came before.

But a happy marriage, even just a mostly happy marriage, isn't as interesting as the drama in the early innings. You play on, round the bases, run home, and hope, oddly, that it goes into extra innings. With luck and care, it does, and soon you find that the teams that once faced off to win are now in it together.

It's a funny thing how it happens, though. Assuming you make it back from your honeymoon alive and intact, you spend the first couple of months reliving the wedding, prodding your friends and families for the wedding stories and gossip you missed because you were too busy hugging everyone, cutting the cake, adjusting your dress. Here's one I missed: a dear friend who'd brought her new boyfriend as her plus-one got so drunk that they basically humped each other on the shuttle ride back to Charlottesville. I would not have found this remarkable—get it where and when you can, I say—but for the fact that my work colleagues asked me who that was, and wondered whether they could have waited until the children got off the bus.

Here's another: my dad's sister was so determined to attend this wedding that she made the five-hour drive in her beat-up Toyota Tercel with her seventy-eight-year-old veteran diabetic husband, who could barely breathe on his own, and then left him at the Hampton Inn, preferring to party by herself. She shut down the reception.

Anyway, all this stuff comes out, you write the thank-you notes and marvel at your newly kitted-out kitchen, and then life just kind of goes on. Your mom stops calling as much; there are no more floral emergencies or questions about table settings that need to be answered right then. Your aunts start asking your mom about when you'll have a baby, which she ignores, but quietly wonders. You chum up with your other long-partnered or married friends, preferring in some way the company of those who have been through it, who know what it means to choose the same person day after day, who have faced the meaning of forever and decided that they're OK with that. The people who have committed.

You swim through the first year of marriage not unlike the first year of parenthood; getting to the first anniversary, the first candle on the cake, feels like a feat of untold strength, of besting a tide you didn't expect. I'm not quite sure why. For Michael and me, it marked our sixth full year together. It wasn't like we didn't know each other; I mean, Jesus. But just like the year of our engagement, the first year of our marriage was a challenge unlike any other. We pushed against each other during the day, even as we sought each other out in the night. We got a dog, and I took hours-long walks with her in Prospect Park, all of a sudden in desperate need of the solitude among the throngs. But over the months, even with the push and pull, we learned to navigate each other as husband and wife, as legal or life partners, whatever you want to call it; as friends and lovers for the back of beyond, for Friday night fights and Sunday morning lie-ins, weddings and funerals and all the rest of it.

No one ever knows the interiors of another's marriage, and marital bliss always comes with an asterisk. The bliss that we found lay in the idea of the permanent and the possible. It took almost a year to relax into each other again, but somewhere around March, at the eleven-month mark, we felt ourselves flying. Outside our walls, things were changing: we both took on bigger roles at work, and we learned how to pair the headiness of ambition with the sublime calm of home. I didn't return to the Weddings desk. What I'd seen in New Orleans and on my Neediest Cases assignments pushed me toward a different kind of journalism than the one I'd become so comfortable in. So I moved down to the main news desks permanently. I worked as a research assistant for a national columnist, edited political stories and dispatches from Iraq and Afghanistan, and spent long hours on an overnight desk shift, where I felt unprecedented—and completely false—power as the only employee in the newsroom at three a.m., except for the creepy janitor with bad taste in music. Michael joined the copy desk and unlocked his talent as an editor on the Metro desks. Things just got better and better.

Right before our second anniversary, we bought a weekend cabin in the Catskills. To my mind, this felt like the correct next step as card-carrying members of the creative class. We didn't have the down payment for a half-million-dollar two-bedroom fixer-upper in Windsor Terrace, but we could afford a small mortgage on an escape from the city. We spent nearly every Friday evening speeding up the New York State Thruway to Route 17B, Eleanor the mutt panting from panic in the back seat of our purple Honda. We filled our little place with Craigslist finds and IKEA necessities and immediately spent thousands on the ancient stone chimney that was, to our great dismay, falling off the side of the house. We lolled for hours on the screened-in porch and took Eleanor for long meanders around the lake, watching for snakes and bears. It was heavenly.

And then one cool evening in June, I was changing clothes in the bedroom, and Michael sneaked up on me and gently tweaked one of my breasts, as he was, and is, wont to do. It felt like someone had hit me in the boob with a canoe paddle. "Get off me!" I yelled, grabbing my chest.

"Sorry!" He jumped back in surprise; that wasn't my normal reaction. I wondered what that was all about, and then thought: *Ohh, fucking hell.*

The next evening, I stopped on the way home from the gym and bought a pack of pregnancy tests. I didn't keep them in the house, and this gynecologist had assured me six years before that I'd need help getting pregnant anyway, so I wasn't worried about it. That was perhaps the wrong way to proceed, as anyone who has played Russian roulette may attest. I peed on the First Response stick and put it on the sink, peeled off my spandex to get in the shower, and looked back at the test, which had developed a big fat double magenta line in about five seconds. *Ohhh, fuck me.* Michael got home right as I got out of the shower, and my whole body shook as I walked into the kitchen to tell him the news. "I guess that's what we're doing now," I said, and he sat down on the couch and laughed.

Seven weeks later, I was on my back at a hospital in Borough Park, as a man named Dr. Schwartz scraped dead tissue out of my uterus. I'd started bleeding in the newsroom, and it had intensified when I got home. No heartbeat, no chance, game over. The anesthesiologist, I remember, had just gotten engaged, and in my drugged haze I scoped out her huge emerald-cut diamond and asked her if she'd set the date yet. When we got home, I called in a giant sushi order, Michael made me a triple old-fashioned in a pint glass, and over the next six months, we ate and drank our way out of a heartbreak that surprised and shattered us both. We didn't know what we wanted, but we knew when we'd lost it. So we started the fertility dance: basal body thermometers, early-morning doctor visits, Clomid shots, yoga, acupuncture, horse-pill prenatal vitamins, keeping calm and carrying on. We started to see the regulars at Dr. Stein's office near Columbus Circle, until they disappeared, and their luck might have swung either way. I wanted to know what happened with those couples too.

And then. One winter weekend, I turned to Michael and said, "Wouldn't it be funny if we had a red-haired, blue-eyed girl?" Neither of us has red hair or blue eyes. But ten months later, on the shortest day of the year, a bald, blue-eyed, six-pound sprite landed in our arms, bearing a single scratch on her forehead from forceps and absolutely livid about what had just happened to her. We wrapped her in a block-print scarf and named her after my mother-in-law. Eighteen months later, she finally grew hair, and it is the most beautiful gingery red. We found a new teammate, and she's got a swing that one day is going to make a pitcher shake on the mound.

So life goes on, with or without a wedding, with or without an announcement. Every so often, I do a little digging on my couples. I want to know what happened to them. Did their marriages live long and prosper, or did they flicker out like a candle in the wind? I shared in their joys at the beginning of their marriages, and I am still invested in their stories somehow. A journalist never reveals her sources, but I can tell you a little bit about what happened to some of these people.

As most of us know, Sheryl Sandberg's kind husband, Dave Goldberg, died in Mexico while the couple was on vacation, leaving her and their two children behind. If it's possible to be heartbroken for someone you don't know, I was. When the news broke, I immediately thought back to our phone calls, and how she glowed through the phone when talking about her almost-husband. He did the same. I kept thinking about the warmth and absolute admiration with which he described her, and how her ambition and his generous spirit seemed to have found a home together. Sheryl Sandberg's public persona has taken a beating in the past few years, and my opinion of her professional doings is of little use here. What I know is this: the care and love she showed after his death, for their children, his legacy, and herself, is a road map for strength within grief and the definition of commitment itself. Their partnership, while bolstered by privilege and finances that most of us will never achieve, was one of shared perspective, responsibility to one another, and fluid equality. It was, and is, love.

Scarlett and Rhett live in Brooklyn, of course. They're still married; that sidewalk union somehow cemented a soul match. I imagine they consider the pavement in front of that jewelry store as sacred ground, and I don't blame them one bit.

The Ivy League Marine and His Lovely Wife split about eighteen months after their wedding, which I found out while gossiping with another reporter during the Iowa caucuses. "That got . . . yeah, that got nasty," she whispered, as we waited for Hillary Clinton to speak. Obviously, I Googled. The bride reverted to her maiden name—honestly, there was maybe a 10 percent chance that she'd changed it in the first place—and the Marine moved back to Arizona, where he established himself in local Tea Party politics, remarried, procreated, and got arrested on domestic abuse charges. Nice guy.

The Pretty-Well-Known Asshole and his wife split in a divorce that kept the tabloids busy for months. The Famous Music Producer and the Taste Maker are also no longer together. He's living in Southeast Asia and selling music bundled with fried chicken, and making a mint, while she's raising the kids on this side of the world and enjoying herself immensely. The Junior Heiress lives in Paris with her husband, where he sells boats or something, and she produces research on obscure works of pre-nineteenth-century art. It's all very lovely in the 16th arrondissement. The Feminist and the Professor seemed to have found the truest of love on the last try; they're still alive, married, marching and theorizing and professing. Every so often she writes something that goes viral, and I think she's doing just fine.

The Woman Who Wanted to Save the World and her husband split, to my dismay, and while she's no longer in the White House, she's still working hard to make things right. Her ex lobbies for companies that—well, anyway, I can see why they split. Mitzi and Trey are still together, ensconced in Greenwich, obviously, and show up in dozens of Patrick McMullan photos. They have achieved their destiny, she's produced a Fourth, and has, as documented by Mr. McMullan, found a plastic surgeon and discovered the art of the filler. So it goes.

As for the desk, the hands have changed. One morning as his bus pulled into Port Authority, Ira started feeling a bit woozy and couldn't lift his body up off the seat. He called April at her desk, and her vacation substitute, Janine, picked up. "I can't move," Ira said. Janine rushed across 8th Avenue and wound her way through the Port Authority warren to Ira's bus, where she found him, slumped in his seat, unable to move at all. He'd had a stroke on the way to work, which led to months in the hospital and rehab, and a retirement from the *Times* far earlier than he'd wanted. His deputy, Linda, took over the desk, and the changes that Ira had wanted to make for so long finally started to happen: the society desk became the Weddings desk; the features got more fun and became more engaged with the weddings industry itself; and the announcements, a little at a time, started to reflect more of America as we live now. Abraham and Kenneth have both gone to their reward, and I still miss their fights and Abraham's double-breasted blazers. Tony is the only one left on the desk from my days, and he remains a gift to the *Times*, and to us all.

A year or so after our kid was born, the *Times* decided to offer buyouts. By that point, we'd freaked out and moved upstate permanently, which led to a two-hour commute each way and a marriage that had been cracked open a bit, by the first year of parenthood and by not seeing each other. I worked during the days and left the house in the wee hours before anyone else rose, and Michael worked evenings on the politics desk, which meant we shared a cup of coffee in the cafeteria right before I rushed to make the 5:15 bus to Tuxedo. He got home at midnight and worked until two a.m. It was a misery of our own making, and when the buy-out came around, we saw a way to make it all right. Michael was in the throes of the 2016 presidential election, which was chipping away at his soul; I was working on the Food desk, whose ambitious pace I could not match through my sheer exhaustion, and missing my little girl desperately. We'd been at the *Times*, our home, for a combined thirty years. We had done one big thing. It was time to go.

We landed back in North Carolina, where I joined a communications shop and Michael started teaching journalism at the University of North Carolina. He discovered the thing that lit him up inside, and I found a way to make some money and see my family at the same time. My creative team was made up of former journalists, writers who needed to make more money and have dinner with their kids more than once a week. One of the writers, Robert, a New York expat, became a friend, and every so often, we'd wrap up the week with a nip of Irish whiskey in his office. It was deeply civilized.

Robert reminded me so much of the *Times* people I worked with, and not just because he'd held on to his mild Bronx accent after years in North Carolina. He was sensible but loved a tangent; he was low-key but unabashed and un-ashamed of the things he loved, like old movies, good whis-key, and baseball stats. What started off as discussions over some client demand quickly devolved into dissections of movie dialogue, recollections of life in the city, and a rehash-ing of the finer plot points in *Bull Durham*. I was happy to have a friend in a new place, with shared sensibilities and a firm belief that even though we were here, and happily so, New York would always be the greatest city on earth.

One afternoon, we got into talking about the weirdest jobs we'd ever had. "I once interviewed a Well-Known Ass-hole for his wedding announcement," I said after several sips of Tullamore Dew. Robert laughed; the Pretty-Well-Known Asshole had been a bit player in his political con-sciousness for decades. "When did you write the wedding announcements?" he queried. I told him the date range, and he smiled.

"Would you have been writing them in September 2004?"

"I sure was. Why, did you get married then?"

He opened up a browser window and Googled himself and another name. *Abigail Farrington, Robert O'Brien*, read the link that popped to the top. He clicked through, and Firefox revealed the wedding announcement he shared with his wife, Abbey: *Abigail Louise Farrington and Robert James O'Brien were married yesterday at the Ashokan Inn in New City, N.Y. The Rev. Jessalyn Barksdale, an interfaith minister, officiated.*

I gasped, and then laughed out loud. "Wait. I think I remember Jessalyn Barksdale." Some of these people, I'm telling you, they just stuck in my head, and that minister was one of them. We looked her up, and her website emanated patchouli oil. "She was the only not-very-religious person we could find for that particular date," Robert said, a bit sheepishly. "And she was inexpensive."

"Let's see if she's done any others," I said. "Because if she didn't, I definitely wrote your announcement." We searched around the *Times* site for a bit and found no other evidence of the Rev. Barksdale, who, as far as we could tell, gleaned her income from several sources, including teaching Martha Graham–style dance, doing spiritual counseling, selling homemade sachets, and practicing what she called "Native American ceremonies," which smelled like hot-mess appropriation to me.

"So the first time we met was not when you interviewed me for this job," I said, and grinned. "It was when I interviewed you for your wedding announcement."

"I expect so," Robert said. "And fifteen years later, look at us."

I tipped my head sideways and thought. "It all kind of

worked out, didn't it." I looked at the artwork by his two daughters that peppered his walls and bookshelves.

He nodded. "It did."

We raised our glasses to each other.

"Slainte," Robert said.

IN THE END, most of it all still matters: the vows Michael and I spoke to each other remain the underpinnings of our lives now. But the things that we thought so important are the ones that matter the least. My beautiful lace wedding dress, which I fussed over and dreamed about, hangs limply in a plastic bag in a closet at my parents' house, the hem still ringed with mud. My daughter got it out the other day and wrestled it on, and it pulled at her slender shoulders. We eat now with a set of Wedgwood silver that belonged to my great-grandmother Virginia Burke Burchett; the Repousse, which I still adore, is a pain in the ass to polish. And that engagement ring, over which Michael cried and I fumed, is gathering dust on my bedside table. I changed it out again, for a thick gold band made of tiny family diamonds and sapphires with our kid's name engraved inside. It nestles against my wedding ring, a mismatched familial pair. My whole life and all my loves—the family that made me, and the family we made together—I wear every day on a single finger.

As for that *Times* wedding announcement, it didn't get us much. A few old friends saw it and reached out to us, and it was a quick thrill to see it in the paper the morning after. Gawker included us and our picture in their Monday morning roundup, and I was roundly criticized in the comments for not knowing how to take a proper engagement photo, which filled me with total glee. But I couldn't tell you whether we have a copy of our wedding announcement. It isn't the first thing that comes up when you Google either of us anymore. I'm not sure I can even find our marriage license. What we do have, after sixteen years, is far more enticing, and infinitely more valuable, than soy ink on paper—even if it's the Paper of Record.

© ÁNGEL FRANCO

ACKNOWLEDGMENTS

THIS IS A book about love and commitment, and the personal mergers that bind, support, and care for us. It would not have come into being without the following people, and I owe every one of them a debt of thanks.

To the team at G. P. Putnam's Sons, who ushered this book into existence with care, candor, and unmatched talent. My extraordinary editor, Michelle Howry, knew what this book could be long before I did. Thank you for your peerless editorial eye, patience, and a sensibility that complements my own. Yuki Hirose and Laura Rosenblum protected me from myself and from running afoul of brides, grooms, and the law. Janice Kurzius and Amy Schneider asked the right questions to keep my thoughts honest and my sentences clean and clear. Sandra Chiu and Anthony

Ramondo designed a cover that captured this book's spirit and heart, and Katy Riegel made its interior pages beautiful. Ashley Di Dio kept everything on the rails with kindness. Also, to my champions Sally Kim and Ivan Held: thank you.

To Gillian MacKenzie and the team at MacKenzie Wolf, the best bunch of agents and advocates a woman could ask for. A thousand thanks to Gillian for her counsel and enthusiasm, right from our first rollicking conversation; to Renée Jarvis, for fielding my many questions with good cheer; and to Kirsten Wolf, for keeping it legal for me and mine. And to Josie Freedman at ICM, for representing me well in other interesting matters.

To the employees and institution of the *New York Times*, who taught me everything I know about journalism, and a lot of what I know about everything else. I owe nearly everything good in my life to that place, and the honor will always be mine. In particular, I'm grateful to have worked with Robert Woletz, Vincent M. Mallozzi, June Cuddy, LeAnn Wilcox, and Katherine Gooch-Breault. I am indebted to Susan Edgerley, Lon Teter, Lori Moore Baldino, Pasquale Baldino, Simone Oliver, and Finn Cohen, for helping me remember and capture what was, and remains, crazy and glorious about every day at the Paper of Record. My newsroom is one that exists mostly in memory now, and the giants there stand tall still: Jill Abramson, Robert Pear, Johnny Apple, Rick Berke, Greg Brock, Erika Sommer,

Steven McElroy, Alexandra Pelletier Paul, David Firestone, and Ángel Franco. I am chuffed to know and adore Sam Sifton, Emily Weinstein, and Sara Bonisteel. On a frigid night in Iowa, Carl Hulse encouraged my husband to think of me as more than just a coworker, and while that might have been a breach of human resources etiquette, thank goodness he did. Jennifer 8. Lee was the first person who told me I should write this book, and it only took fifteen years; I'm glad she kept pushing on. Margaux Laskey Garapolo slogged in the wedding trenches with me and was generous enough to share her memories, and I am so grateful for nearly two decades of mutual adoration, through work, wedding planning, cake cutting, child wrangling, and everything else. And I wouldn't know how to slow down a story and tell it right, and neither would I be married, without the grace and friendship of Dan Barry.

To my friends who allowed me to slip parts of them and their memories into this book: Sarah Jane and Joe Crompton, Laura Araman, Stacey Miehe and Erik Kever Ryle, Anna Ogier-Bloomer and Delano Dunn, Rachel and Matthew Holtzclaw, Jim Doughty, Rebecca Catalanello and Steve (not Steven Lee) Myers, Kinda Serafi and Mike Wilson, Jonathan B. Cox, Maggie Dickson, Carlos Fernandez, Sefton Ipock, Nancy Kelly Kistler, and Deblina and Joe Danborn. In particular, I owe Amy and Josh McKinley a debt of love and thanks, for showing me early on that young love can be true love, across hemispheres, in the face of loss and chaos and jet lag.

To Cate Lineberry, Eleanor Spicer Rice, and Cat Warren, whose love and encouragement made this book possible. I am grateful to these brilliant women for their creative thinking, their boundless enthusiasm, and this book's title.

To Ginny Sciabbarrasi, for quick and early reads, encouragement, pragmatic optimism, and twenty-two years of friendship and a conversation that never stops for breath.

To Gail Riggs Anderson, Jinny Riggs Gentry, and Alice Riggs Youst, for never hesitating to tell me what's what. To Peggy and Andy Lucchi, for treating me as their own from the start. And to Susan B. Doty, for understanding and flowers.

To Mark Doty and Nancy Riggs Doty, who for more than forty years have shown me what commitment is. As I learned, no one should take anyone else's marriage as a model for their own—but I know how to love because of them. And to Steven Doty and Marcy Ogden, for their deeply practical buttressing during the longest days.

To my daughter, Flynn, for trying to leave me alone while I worked; for the endless, insistent hugs when you didn't quite succeed; for your fire and dearest of hearts.

To my husband, Michael. You and I know what this world can do. So this is all for you.

BIBLIOGRAPHY

"The Knot 2019 Real Weddings Study," The Knot, accessed May 2020, https://www.wedinsights.com/report/the-knot-real-weddings.

Baker, Katie. "Matrimonial Moneyball." *Grantland*, December 12, 2012, accessed May 2020, https://grantland.com/features/matrimonial -moneyball.

Baldrige, Letitia. *The Amy Vanderbilt Complete Book of Etiquette: A Guide to Contemporary Living*. New York: Doubleday, 1978.

Beasley, Maurine H., and Sheila J. Gibbons. *Taking Their Place: A Documentary History of Women and Journalism*. Washington, D.C.: The American University Press, 1993.

Blumberg, Paul M., and P. W. Paul. "Continuities and Discontinuities in Upper-Class Marriages." *Journal of Marriage and the Family* 37, no. 1 (February 1975): 63–77.

Brady, Lois Smith. *Love Lessons: Twelve Real-Life Love Stories*. New York: Simon & Schuster, 1999.

———. "Vows: Deborah Hull and Nathaniel Koren." *The New York Times*, August 22, 2004, accessed May 2020, https://www.nytimes.com/2004/08/22/style/weddings-celebrations-vows-deborah-hull-and -nathaniel-koren.html.

Brooks, David. *Bobos in Paradise: The New Upper Class and How They Got There*. New York: Simon & Schuster, 2001.

———. "New Class Nuptials." *The City Journal*, Summer 1997, accessed March 2020, https://www.city-journal.org/html/new-class-nuptials -11825.html.

Centers for Disease Control/National Center for Health Statistics, National Vital Statistics System. "Provisional Number of Marriages and Marriage Rate: United States, 2000–2018," accessed June 2020, https://www.cdc.gov/nchs/data/dvs/national-marriage-divorce-rates -00-18.pdf.

Chambers, Deborah, Linda Steiner, and Carole Fleming. *Women and Journalism*. New York: Routledge, 2004.

Colwin, Laurie. "The Lone Pilgrim." *The New Yorker*, April 12, 1976, accessed June 2020, https://archives.newyorker.com/newyorker/ 1976-04-12/flipbook.

Cook v. Advertiser Company, 323 F. Supp. 1212 (M.D. Ala. 1971), accessed May 2020, https://law.justia.com/cases/federal/district-courts/ FSupp/323/1212/1572580.

Coontz, Stephanie. *Marriage, A History: How Love Conquered Marriage*. New York: Penguin Books, 2005.

Cott, Nancy F. *Public Vows: A History of Marriage and the Nation*. Cambridge, MA: Harvard University Press, 2002.

Dunlap, David. "When the *Times* (Finally) Recognized Gay Unions." *The New York Times*, February 9, 2017, accessed June 2020, https://www .nytimes.com/2017/02/09/fashion/weddings/gay-unions-new-york -times.html.

Engstrom, Erika. *The Bride Factory: Mass Media Portrayals of Women and Weddings*. New York: Peter Lang Publishing, 2012.

Garber, Megan. "The Wedding Data: What Marriage Notices Say About Social Change." *The Atlantic*, September 6, 2013, accessed April 2020, https://www.theatlantic.com/technology/archive/2013/09/the -wedding-data-what-marriage-notices-say-about-social-change/279411.

Hannah-Jones, Nikole. "When Ida B. Wells Married, It Was a Page One Story." *The New York Times*, January 23, 2017, accessed July 2020, https://www.nytimes.com/interactive/projects/cp/weddings/165 -years-of-wedding-announcements/ida-wells-wedding.

Hatch, David L., and Mary A. Hatch. "Criteria of Social Status as Derived from Wedding Announcements in *The New York Times*." *American Sociological Review* 12, no. 4 (August 1947): 396–403.

Hoyt, Clark. "Letters: Wedding Announcements." *The New York Times,* July 25, 2009, accessed June 2020, https://publiceditor.blogs.nytimes .com/2009/07/25/letters-wedding-announcements.

———. "Love and Marriage, *New York Times* Style." *The New York Times,* July 12, 2009, accessed June 2020, https://www.nytimes.com/2009/ 07/12/opinion/12pubed.html.

Mead, Rebecca. "Gay Old Times." *The New Yorker,* September 2, 2002, accessed May 2020, https://www.newyorker.com/magazine/2002/ 09/02/gay-old-times.

Montgomery, Maureen E. *Displaying Women: Spectacles of Leisure in Edith Wharton's New York.* New York: Routledge, 1998.

Noah, Timothy. "Abolish the *New York Times* Wedding Pages!" *Slate,* August 29, 2002, https://slate.com/news-and-politics/2002/08/abolish -the-new-york-times-wedding-pages.html.

Otne, Cele C., and Elizabeth Pleck. *Cinderella Dreams: The Allure of the Lavish Wedding.* Berkeley: University of California Press, 2003.

Paul, Pamela. *The Starter Marriage and the Future of Matrimony.* New York: Villard, 2002.

Ray, Dr. J. H. Randolph. *My Little Church Around the Corner.* New York: Simon & Schuster, 1957.

Robinson, Nathan J. "Can the *New York Times* Wedding Section Be Justified?" *Current Affairs,* July 30, 2016, accessed June 2020, https:// www.currentaffairs.org/2016/07/can-the-new-york-times-weddings -section-be-justified.

Schwartz, Maryln. *A Southern Belle Primer, or Why Princess Margaret Will Never Be a Kappa Kappa Gamma.* New York: Broadway Books, 1991, 2001.

Seremet, Pat. "Gloria Steinem's Husband, David Bales, Dies." *The Hartford Courant,* January 3, 2004, accessed May 2020, https://www .courant.com/news/connecticut/hc-xpm-2004-01-03-0401030630 -story.html.

Sexton, Anne. *The Complete Poems.* New York: Mariner Books/Houghton Mifflin, 1999: 15.

Steverman, Ben. "Divorce Destroys the Finances of Americans Over 50, Studies Show," *Bloomberg,* July 19, 2019, https://www.bloomberg.com/

news/articles/2019-07-19/divorce-destroys-finances-of-americans-over-50-studies-show.

Stocking, Ben. "Cotillion Class First Rejects, Then Invites Black Girl." *The News & Observer* (February 1994): 3A.

Voss, Kimberly Wilmot. "Redefining Women's News: A Case Study of Three Women's Page Editors and Their Framing of the Women's Movement" (PhD diss., University of Maryland, 2004), 55.

WeddingWire, "Newlywed Report 2020," accessed May 2020, https://go.weddingwire.com/newlywed-report.

Wharton, Edith. *The Age of Innocence*. New York: Barnes & Noble Classics Series, 2004.

Yalom, Marilyn. *A History of the Wife*. New York: HarperCollins, 2001.